Framing American Politics

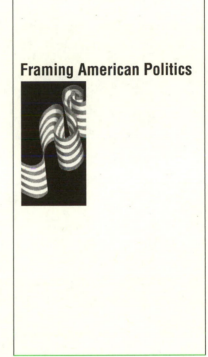

Framing American Politics

Edited by

Karen Callaghan and Frauke Schnell

With a Foreword by Robert M. Entman

University of Pittsburgh Press

Published by the University of Pittsburgh Press, Pittsburgh, PA 15260

Copyright © 2005, University of Pittsburgh Press

Manufactured in the United States of America

Printed on acid-free paper

10 9 8 7 6 5 4 3 2 1

LIBRARY OF CONGRESS CATALOGING-IN-PUBLICATION DATA

Framing American politics / edited by Karen Callaghan and Frauke Schnell ; with a fore-word by Robert M. Entman.

    p. cm.

Includes bibliographical references and index.

ISBN 0-8229-5864-3 (pbk. : alk. paper)

    1. Communication in politics—United States.   2. Press and politics—United States. 3. Mass media—Political aspects—United States.   I. Callaghan, Karen (Karen J.) II. Schnell, Frauke.

    JA85.2.U6F73 2005

    320.973'01'4—dc22

                    2004019673

Contents

Foreword

Considering the centrality of framing to the process of political communication and the exertion of political power, it is a bit surprising that it has taken until 2005 to publish a book like *Framing American Politics*. This volume clearly illustrates the contributions that the concept of framing makes to empirical and normative understanding of politics and public opinion in the United States. By illuminating undertheorized and insufficiently studied paths of influence among elites, media, and mass publics, this book makes significant strides in developing theory on just how American democracy works.

As Karen Callaghan and Frauke Schnell write in the introductory chapter, the framing perspective is necessary to finally dispatching the notion of minimal media consequences that long dominated political science. Despite the essentially unanimous belief of those in the actual trenches of political warfare that managing the news—that is, framing the political messages transmitted by the media—is essential to winning elections and governing, the minimal consequences orthodoxy survived for decades. The persistent disconnect between political reality on the one hand and political science on the other was self-reinforcing. Research in political communication remained marginalized and underdeveloped. With virtually no theory guiding inquiry, scattered findings suggestive of media influence remained just that, rather than being integrated into even a tentative research paradigm. The continued traces of the minimal consequences assumption can be seen in the glancing attention granted communication processes and media in some of the most important recent scholarship on American democracy (e.g., Dahl 1989; Erikson, MacKuen, and Stimson 2002). But as this volume demonstrates, framing theory holds the promise of finally providing an integrative structure that will place political communication at the center of political science as it has long been at the center of political practice.

Some of the many important points brought out here include the following:

• Framing—in my own terms, "selecting and highlighting some facets of events or issues, and making connections among them so as to promote a particular interpretation, evaluation, and/or solution" (Entman 2004, 5)—is inescapable. To report the news is to frame. When putting together their texts, journalists *must* make decisions that influence people's perceptions of the political choices they face. By definition, that gives the media power.

• The news media themselves make important independent contributions to politically influential frames. They are not entirely passive channels that merely reflect the play of power, but players themselves.

• Major events like the September 11, 2001, terrorist attacks can reshape political agendas and public thinking, and one essential way to understand these changes is through exploring how frames of the event interact with pre-existing public attitudes.

• Although news frames demonstrably and significantly affect the public's views in such areas as racial policy, gun control, terrorism, and criminal justice, those sentiments also reflect larger ideological themes and moods and real-world conditions. Frames in the news always interact with schemas inside people's minds.

• The provision or withholding of context when asking political questions, whether in polls or in the news, has large consequences for outcomes. How a question is framed in political discourse helps to determine how people will connect the matter to their existing schemas, their internal networks of political thoughts and emotions. Strip an issue of context, and the public may react one way; provide another context (i.e., frame it differently), and they might react another way. Slight alterations in question wording can make for decisively different responses to surveys, and similarly, slight alterations in news frames can change public perceptions of a matter. This lends considerable importance to decisions on framing that are often made by journalists and by pollsters on the fly, without careful consideration of their political potential. This has unsettling implications for democracy.

• The ability of candidates for office to influence news frames varies widely, and here too the repercussions for democracy are troubling. Sometimes frames are so deeply ingrained or institutionalized that they are for all intents and purposes unassailable (even if they should be assailed). Some candidates, specifically in the case reported here, incumbent U.S. senators, enjoy an enormous, systematic advantage over challengers in shaping newspapers' framing of their campaigns. (If there were much coverage of the U.S. House or state legislative elections, this finding would presumably hold there as well.) Even having more money does not necessarily help much to counteract the incumbents' edge, at least when it comes to news coverage.

This brief listing naturally cannot do justice to the depth and breadth of the insights on display in this book. With *Framing American Politics* as a guide, scholars and students will be well positioned not merely to put the minimal consequences paradigm to rest but to begin formulating a new paradigm that provides a more thorough, empirically accurate, and normatively revealing framework for research on democracy in America.

Robert M. Entman, professor of communication and political science at North Carolina State University and author of *Projections of Power: Framing News, Public Opinion, and U.S. Foreign Policy*

Preface

Over fifty years ago, Bernard Berelson and Paul Lazarsfeld wrote about the significance of issue frames in American politics, first in *The Analysis of Communication Content* (1948) and then in *Voting: A Study of Opinion Formation in a Presidential Campaign* (1954). Persuasively they argued that the "theme" (i.e., "frame") is "one of the most useful units of content analysis, particularly for the study of the effect of communications upon public opinion, because it takes into account the form in which political issues and attitudes are discussed" (Berelson 1971, 139).

Today, scholars from several social science disciplines, including political science, communications, psychology, sociology, and linguistics, have become increasingly interested in the notion of frames, the role they play in structuring political issue debates, and their influence on public opinion. Framing refers to the way in which political elites, such as the news media, politicians, interest groups, and other political players, define the political space and erect the boundaries within which a public policy issue will be considered. Most issues of American politics are multifaceted and complex, thus making them subject to alternative interpretations. For example, what is gun control policy? Is it a debate about constitutional freedoms and the abuse of government power? Or are gun laws simply "feel-good" laws that do little to prevent crime and violence in society? What about the possibility of guns being acquired by terrorists? Similarly, what is affirmative action? Does it provide "remedial action," or does it perpetuate reverse discrimination? And what values frame public policy issues? Does public discourse on social welfare center on egalitarian or individualistic concerns about the welfare state? Finally, is the "war on terrorism" a defense of freedom and liberty, values deeply ingrained in American society, or a government plan to intrude upon privacy and other cherished constitutional rights? The chapters in this volume aspire to answer questions like these.

This is the right moment for this book. Framing, as we use the term here, has produced a coherent collection of ideas. Yet they are not entirely well established; plenty of ideas still need to be discussed and debated. New theoretical directions are waiting to be discovered. Up until now, however, the cumulative value of framing for American politics has not been understood thoroughly.

This collection presents key research that cumulatively expands the concept of framing. We are pleased that several outstanding scholars in the framing literature, along with some relative newcomers, have agreed to share their theoretical insights, to communicate their research findings, and to speculate about new directions and integrative approaches to framing theory. Contributors were asked to present literature in their areas of expertise that would highlight a key aspect of framing theory. Their essays (commissioned for this volume) highlight the most significant framing debates in U.S. politics. These include policy issues such as urban crime, race, affirmative action, the economy, gun control, and the "war on terrorism," as well as an examination of the dynamics of framing in political campaigns and electoral contests. Several chapters focus on media framing of public policy disputes. As Harold Lasswell (1941) aptly pointed out, "democracy depends on talk." Since the news media are the major vehicle for public discourse and "the site on which various groups, institutions, and ideologies struggle over the definition of reality" (Gurevitch and Levy 1985, 19), it is important to explore the role that journalists and editors play in framing the issue debates of American politics.

Of course, personal choice and space limitations have influenced our treatment of framing theory. We have chosen to stay within the domain of American politics, with emphasis on social policy framing. Models of issue framing in other contexts such as foreign affairs or economic policy are idiosyncratic and thus beyond the scope of this volume.

We have also chosen not to emphasize framing as defined in the behavioral decision literature or in discourse models of communication. The inclusion of these theoretical insights, although important, would have produced a volume larger in size than we judged expedient.

Furthermore, the chapters in this volume focus primarily on elite models of framing; there is less attention to the role that citizens play in driving the frames that elites adopt. This is consistent with the dominant approach to the study of public opinion research.

Our collection is also guided by our belief that the comprehensive story on framing involves a dynamic interplay between the *micro-* and *macro*levels of politics in American society. *Micro* approaches focus on *framing effects*—that is, how frames influence public attitudes and opinions. At the *macro*level, we are interested in the *origins* and *processes* of issue framing, for example, how political players and institutions (the media, interest groups, political candidates, Congress, the president) attempt to define themselves strategically and frame political issues for public debate. The contributors to this volume show how these two aspects of framing—the ability of elites to generate frames that influence the meaning of political issues and ultimately change mass opinion—relate in a cohesive way.

We have also endeavored to make methodological pluralism a defining feature of this volume; the contributors employ a diverse array of approaches and methodologies to explore the complexities of framing, substantiate their claims, and inform their conclusions. Some scholars use content analyses to identify and describe how political elites frame issues for the media and the public. These studies analyze political communications (e.g., news texts, press releases, party platforms, the published debates of deliberative bodies like Congress, and other major political pronouncements) for dominant frames. From these data, the contributors test scientific hypotheses about the origins and development of issue framing in American politics and the impact of frames on citizens.

Experimentation is the methodological tool of choice for researchers interested in analyzing the impact of frames at the microlevel. Framing experiments provide the researcher with absolute control over the structure of the issue frames and certainty of an individual's exposure to them. One can also carefully manipulate certain subject factors and randomly assign individuals to different issue-framing conditions. With proper controls, any significant variation in subjects' responses can be attributed to the frame, thus enhancing internal validity. However, due to the nonrepresentative nature of the sample, a purely experimental approach to the study of framing carries a liability: the inability to generalize findings to larger settings. Furthermore, experiments are often undertaken in artificial settings that have no exact counterparts outside of the laboratory. Therefore, several contributors to this volume have included framing experiments with realistic stimulus materials in state or national opinion surveys to produce an even stronger methodology, one that maximizes external validity while maintaining high levels of internal validity. These include "question-wording" experiments that mimic the dialogue surrounding controversial political issues and studies that employ real newspaper articles about relevant political issues as the stimulus materials. These approaches are innovative for what they can tell us about framing and real-world political debates.

Despite the wide range of authors, the diversity of approaches, and the variety of topics that are being investigated, the essays in this volume converge on the same important questions: Who decides how public policy issues are packaged or "framed"? Who sets the boundaries of the debate? Furthermore, do frames influence how citizens understand policy issues and thus affect public opinion? If so, how widely? Finally, what significance do frames have for democratic politics? Do they hinder or enhance political participation and understanding?

When framing is placed in the broader context of American democracy, several concerns emerge. Democratic concerns focus on the political impact of cognitive-processing biases and persuasion effects, the capricious shifts frames cause in citizen choices, the neglect of some frames in favor of others, the problem of control, and the strategic manipulation of frames by self-interested groups and individuals. The chapters in this book address these concerns. They do not constitute a manifesto on issue framing and American democracy. None of the authors claims that frames are always good for American democracy. Nor do they suggest that frames are inherently bad. Instead, the authors argue for a complex view of framing. Much healthy debate emerges as the authors consider the prospects and perils of framing for American democracy.

To the institutions that have provided support for our research on framing and the development of this volume, we are greatly indebted. They include the University of Massachusetts at Boston; West Chester University; the American Political Science Association; and the Joan Shorenstein Center on the Press, Politics, and Public Policy at the John F. Kennedy School of Government, Harvard University. We also thank our contributors, who have been unfailingly gracious in responding to our editorial comments. We are especially grateful to Paul Freedman and Bob Boynton for their helpful advice. In addition, we thank editors Niels Aaboe and Nathan MacBrien at the University of Pittsburgh Press for their guidance. We also owe a special debt of gratitude to our families for their unending support. Finally, we thank our friend and colleague Nayda Terkildsen for her assistance with this project.

Framing American Politics

Introduction
Framing Political Issues in American Politics

Karen Callaghan and Frauke Schnell

In 1937 the Institute for Propaganda Analysis, a government-funded research center for social scientists and journalists, examined the use of persuasive messages and urged Americans to scrutinize and weigh the arguments the media presented to them. Demagogues such as Adolf Hitler and Joseph Goebbels in Germany, Benito Mussolini in Italy, and Huey Long and Father Charles Coughlin in the United States had recently gained national recognition and political power by cleverly using the media to manipulate the beliefs and behaviors of citizens.[1] Their political success paralleled the increase in radio ownership, thus evoking fears about the creation of a mass audience of millions of easily swayed, captive, and gullible listeners across the United States (see Oskampf 1977, 41). These concerns triggered a major change in the orientation of social science research. Scholars, worried about the media's potential negative effects on society, were now very interested in media effects research. With limited evidence available, their initial attempts to document media influence failed to unearth powerful persuasion effects, and they concluded—perhaps with a sigh of relief—that the media simply reinforced the political choices people had already made.[2] Interpersonal communication was the only factor considered to influence citizens' attitudes and opinions.[3] These findings heralded what Joseph Klapper (1960) called the "minimal effects" paradigm of media research.

Six decades of media research have clarified matters considerably. In the last few decades especially, media effects research has undergone a dramatic paradigm shift, changing from Klapper's "minimal effects" paradigm and the denial of substantial media influence to the recognition that, to use Walter Lippmann's (1922) term, the media select and arrange the "pictures in our heads." Improvements in the precision, reliability, and scope of research design and methods allowed researchers to uncover a wide range of media effects. Scholarly interest in political attitudes and advances in cognitive theory, especially human information processing, have informed the debate by identifying the cognitive effects of media influence.

Today, scholars in a variety of disciplines, including political science, communications, and psychology, have dispelled Klapper's rather narrow view of media power.[4] In particular, political scientist Larry Bartels calls the minimal effects paradigm "one of the most noticeable embarrassments of modern social science" (1993; quoted in Kinder 1998, 189). Studies now show that, in the context of reflecting social and political reality, the media influence citizens in two ways. First, by deciding which issues to cover, the media set the public agenda, which in turn influences the importance citizens ascribe to reported issues (see Iyengar and Kinder 1987; MacKuen 1981; McCombs 1981). Second, by elevating certain issues over others, or "priming," the media influence citizens' evaluations of political actors and alter the criteria by which political players are judged (see Krosnick and Brannon 1993; Krosnick and Kinder 1990; Iyengar and Kinder 1987; Iyengar et al. 1984).[5] However, agenda-setting and priming are far from the media's only powers. Framing research represents a relatively new domain of media effects, and it has changed the way scholars think about public policy issues and political discourse. Although the study of framing dates back to the 1940s, thus preceding empirical research on priming and agenda-setting, its focus was on the content analysis of news frames. It wasn't until the 1980s that empirical work on "framing effects" emerged. From this research, it became clear that even subtle differences in the way an issue is framed can have a decisive influence on public opinion; thus, framing effects have been called "one of the most stunning social science discoveries of the last quarter century" (Druckman 2003, 1).

Conceptual Framework

Rochefort and Cobb (1994b, 9) argue that "if policy making is a struggle over alternative realities, then language is the medium that reflects, advances, and interprets these alternatives." Commonly, all political players use language to give influential cues about how an issue is to be interpreted. This process by which all political players, including the media, use linguistic cues to define and give meaning to issues and connect them to a larger political environment has come to be known as framing. Essentially, frames set the boundaries of public policy debates.

An example is the "War on Terrorism" frame that emerged after the September 11 attack and that continues to dominate U.S. news coverage of political affairs. This frame allowed elites to alter public debate on a variety of domestic policy issues (e.g., airport security, immigration, electronic surveillance, military tribunals, and gun control); suggest other remedies for terrorism (e.g., bombing Afghanistan, invading Iraq); and justify U.S. foreign policy decisions on moral grounds. In press releases, televised speeches, and other formats, President George W. Bush consistently used the phrase "war on terrorism" to frame U.S. military action abroad. As a series of public opinion polls confirmed, the "War on Terrorism" theme resonated strongly with the American people and will continue to do so for a long time.

However, as Donald Kinder and Thomas Nelson point out in chapter 4, frames lead a "double life." They exist not only as structures embedded in elite discourse but also as cognitive structures that citizens use to make sense of politics. This volume focuses primarily on "frames in communication"—that is, the thematic aspects of an issue emphasized in elite discourse (such as when a politician emphasizes terrorist concerns during a campaign) and the impact these frames have on public attitudes and opinions. It pays less attention to "frames in thought," or the social-cognitive structure of framing (i.e., how frames interact with a perceiver's social knowledge and prior experiences to influence his or her understanding of the campaign).[6]

Our conceptualization of a frame also differs from the experimental demonstrations of "equivalency" framing by Amos Tversky, Daniel Kahneman, and others in the behavioral decision literature.[7] Given the prominence of this research, it should be distinguished explicitly. From this perspective, a framing effect occurs when slight alterations in the linguistic formulation of statistically identical choices (e.g., a policy option framed in terms of "gains" versus "losses") produce divergent responses, even though the denotive meanings of the wordings are the same. For example, laboratory subjects will support a policy proposal when it is said to produce 90 percent employment but oppose the same proposal when it results in 10 percent unemployment. Essentially, the first wording casts the employment issue in a positive light, causing individuals to have more positive preferences. The chapters in this volume conceptualize frames more broadly as thematic or stylistic structures of political issue discourse.

Frames in Historical Context

The framing of issues in American politics is at least as old as public debate about the democratic form of governance. One of the first major framing debates in U.S. history emerged in 1787 in the battle over ratifying the U.S. Constitution. Delegates to the Constitutional Convention in Philadelphia presented competing "frames of representation." The "Federalist" frame argued persuasively that an independent representative model of government was necessary to guard against excessive democracy. The "Antifederalist" frame focused on the "Threat to Liberty" and the "Danger of Consolidation," asserting that close constituent control of government was necessary for democratic responsiveness (Riker et al. 1996) This framing debate played out in pamphlets, public speeches, papers, and letters to the editor, the most infamous being the *Federalist Papers,* the collection of essays written under the pen name Publius by Alexander Hamilton, James Madison, and John Jay.

Although framing was a politically significant concept over two hundred years ago, the empirical study of frames began about fifty years ago. As a focus of systematic analysis, it originated in content analysis. Scholars realized that interesting questions about politics could be answered with a quantitative analysis of political communications (e.g., newspapers, news magazines, speeches, radio broadcasts). Content analysis opened the door to the systematic analysis of political news into thematic slants, often ideological (e.g., liberal or conservative, pro- or antigovernment).

For instance, Harold Lasswell, Daniel Lerner, and I. De Sola Pool (1952) analyzed trends in media coverage of the international political system between 1890 and 1950. Using the editorial pages of prestigious European newspapers, they identified two distinct ideological themes emphasized in the political discourse on European politics: "Nationalism" and the "Proletarian Doctrine." The evolution of these frames in the news correlated highly with the emergence of international social revolution, thus suggesting that framing research was a useful tool for understanding the dynamics of real-world politics.

Framing studies were also conducted in the nonpolitical context during this period. In 1942, for example, Thomas Hamilton showed how various themes related to individual responsibility shaped the Sunday-morning sermons of Protestant ministers. Although these earlier studies did not use the term *frame* explicitly, they characterized the process as one in which communication content is systematically assigned to specific categories or "themes."[8]

Since then, a great deal of research—both theoretical and empirical—has been devoted to issue framing. Today, framing is an important research paradigm;[9] its vocabulary has thus become more precise. Contemporary framing studies distinguish conceptually between *issue-specific* frames, *thematic* and *episodic* frames, and *generic* frames. Research on issue-specific frames examines the impact alternative descriptions of a policy issue have on political attitudes and preferences. Examples include the "War on Terrorism" frame mentioned earlier or the social policy frames several chapters in this volume address.

Any frame can be presented in a *thematic* or *episodic* fashion. *Thematic* frames place political issues or events in a context, while *episodic* or "event-oriented" frames focus on a specific event or person. For instance, television news coverage of the terrorist attacks on 9/11 often focused on the perpetrators and victims, their lifestyles, family situations, and upbringings. Thematic frames, though less common, focused on underlying motives and the broader structural reasons for the attack—that is, what groups were involved, what political ideology drove them to commit this act, what type of government sponsored the terrorism, and what type of relationship they had with the U.S. government in the past. By the same token, news frames about issues like crime are often depicted episodically; they emphasize specific murder stories and focus on the race and ethnicity of the perpetrators. Different frames can alter people's judgments about who is responsible for the crime (see Gilliam and Iyengar, chap. 7).

A *generic* frame is an even broader concept. The term usually refers to a narrative device journalists use to convey political information. For example, a political campaign is often described in terms of a horse race or the political strategy of the contestants, rather than the salient issues of the campaign (e.g., Hallin 1992; Patterson 1980, 1993; Robinson and Sheehan 1983; Delli Carpini, chap. 2; Fridkin and Kenney, chap. 3). Generic frames can also act as broader frames for specific policy issues. For example, in his contribution to this collection, Paul M. Kellstedt shows how the news media used egalitarian and individualistic "values" frames to convey racial issue information, thus influencing the ideological slant of Americans' racial policy preferences.

No matter which framing definition is used, the studies converge. Framing research in the American political domain has focused on two key areas: how frames emerge and how frames influence public opinion. In the next section, we explore how interest groups, the media, and key political figures compete to frame issues for public consumption (macrolevel forces).

The Framing Contest in American Politics

In *The Semi-Sovereign People: A Realist's View of Democracy in America*, political scientist E. E. Schattschneider (1960) noted that the central analytic question in public policy formation is who has the power to define policy alternatives. Schattschneider wrote, "we shall never understand politics unless we know what the struggles are about" (vi)—that is, "who can get into the fight and who is excluded" (10). Yet disentangling the influence of any one set of players and their messages, let alone the impact of all key agents, may be akin to solving the riddle of the Sphinx. In a democratic society, frames can be generated by a variety of policy actors who are "free" (politically speaking) to seek to change or protect the status quo by configuring issues to their advantage. Among the central participants are elected officials, political parties, interest groups, the media, and citizens. While other actors are involved in this process, such as the Supreme Court, policy experts, bureaucrats, and political consultants, they are not consistently effective and visible. Thus the contributors to this volume focus on the former group of actors because only they can exert influence over both the electoral and the policy arenas—the most important for issue frames.

On one point there is a consensus: political elites do not have carte blanche to mold or shape issues completely to their liking. Although each player tries to persuade other elites and the mass public to adopt his or her issue frames, in a true pluralistic fashion, the competition among groups, as well as their relative strength and resources, restricts the ability of one side to dominate the framing process. On most issues, highly vocal and well-organized promoters appear on both sides of a debate; therefore, one group's frame will almost certainly be "countered" by another, in true Hegelian fashion.[10] Thus, no theme emerges without a *countertheme*—whenever one is evoked, the other is always present in latent form, ready to be activated with the proper cue (Gamson 1992, 135).[11]

Counterthemes play a politically significant role in American politics: they elicit distinct predispositions, attitudes, or beliefs and result in opposing positions on the issues. For example, proponents of legalized abortion package the abortion debate as a question of women's rights and individual freedom, while their opponents appeal to moral principles and "the rights of the unborn." Loggers in the Pacific Northwest depict the cutting of the giant redwoods as sound economic policy that ensures their professional livelihood, while their opponents frame the issue as a problem of environmental preservation and the "protection of endangered species." Supporters of gun control argue that terrorists are aided by lax gun laws, while their opponents assert that law-abiding Americans can fight terrorism by learning to use guns safely and responsibly "for purposes of national defense." Tobacco lobbyists frame tobacco legislation as a "grab for new taxes" ("Washington's at it again"); anti-tobacco groups focus on smoking as a "health problem" or emphasize "tobacco wealth" and the cozy financial relationship between tobacco executives and legislators. In the world of frames, each group tries to expose the flaw in an opponent's argument.[12]

Institutional-level constraints also make it difficult to frame the policy debate and persuade other elites. Within Congress, for example, issue frames are tightly controlled by party leaders and committees, making it hard for elected officials and interest groups to determine the form of the issue debate (e.g., Aldrich and Rhode 1996; Cox and McCubbins 1993; Shepsle 1979). Even the president is constrained in dealing with an often reluctant Congress, particularly during periods of divided government (Kernell 1993). Thus, one player's control over a public policy debate appears to be quite difficult to maintain because framing is a process of checks and balances.

By the same token, not all issues are debated in a pluralistic fashion. Some groups enjoy "issue niches" free of competition. For example, research suggests that agricultural interest groups like the Farm Credit Council, the Food Research and Action Council, and the National Peanut Growers Group minimized organized challenges to their issue frames because they committed resources and had perceived expertise behind their claims. They also provided many services to policy makers (e.g., Browne et al. 1992; Gray and Lowery 1996). In foreign policy framing, the government also enjoys an issue niche that is relatively free of competition. The media and other elites often take framing cues from government officials. During a crisis situation, especially, these cues often come directly from the White House.[13]

Thus, in framing issues for American politics, contrary to pluralist theories of democracy, the frames of dominant players may be more powerful and crowd out other players' frames.

Putting Frames on the Public Agenda

Most political agents make direct attempts to capture attention and mold the political interests of the citizenry. However, policy frames do not automatically shift from elites to the public agenda. Certain forces must be in place. Following, we identify some of these moderating forces, particularly those that are relevant to this book. These factors include an election outcome that favors a certain elite, positive media attention, a policy entrepreneur's decision to expand a conflict and "go public," or exogenous "shocks" from a politically significant "focusing" event.

Political players may use election results to reframe public policy issues (e.g., the Republicans' "Contract with America") or may push for public hearings (e.g., anti-smoking forces). In the 1994 election, for example, House Republican candidates pledged to support the party's goals and proposals in their Contract with America.[14] Every single Republican incumbent for Congress and governor won, and Republicans won in most state legislatures. What did this victory mean? Republicans could now go public with their major policy initiatives and frame and reframe issues in ways that fit their needs. For example, instead of framing the issue of Medicare reform as "Cuts in Elderly Entitlements"—a rights-based claim—the Republicans used words like *save, protect,* and *preserve* to describe their scaled-back version of health benefits for the aged. Spinning off existing social welfare frames, the Republican leadership emphasized its attempts to "Protect Elderly Rights to Health Care."[15] During the 1996 election the Republicans used this unique framing opportunity to gain a great degree of political leverage.

However, elite framing strategies are limited by the level of public information about the issue and the "public mood." As Teena Gabrielson points out in chapter 3, when an issue is not highly salient to the public or when the public mood is at odds with an elected official's ideology, elected officials and other political elites do well to use an "insider strategy" and try to achieve their desired ends through the quieter compromises of consensual politics (Baumgartner and Jones 1993). On the other hand, "going public" is the appropriate strategy if the public opinion climate supports such a move.[16]

September 11 provides a case in point. Americans strongly supported decisive action against the Taliban government and the Al Qaida terrorist attackers. Polls indicated that 92 percent of respondents favored direct military action in Afghanistan (Gallup Poll, October 11, 2001). Moreover, 77 percent of respondents favored such action even if it meant a protracted war (Opinion Dynamics Poll, October 17, 2001). Thus, President Bush had an incentive to pursue the framing and reframing of U.S. involvement in Afghanistan for his own benefit since the environmental constraints that typically limit the framing strategies of elected officials were absent.

The ability of elites to frame an issue for the public via the media is also influenced by a political actor's status, credibility, and organizational resources. Some political actors (e.g., the president, prominent policy entrepreneurs, incumbents, and powerful interest groups) can take advantage of an institutionalized network of media relationships that facilitate the communication of issue frames. Among the political players, the president is the most capable of commanding the attention of the national media. In addition to regularly scheduled televised addresses, speeches, and press conferences, the president's daily activities receive media attention on an ongoing basis (Kernell 1993; Hess 1984; Grossman and Kumar 1981). Clearly, such access is an invaluable asset for a president seeking to exert leverage over a policy issue.

The president's ability to frame issues and events is even more pronounced during times of war or international crises because the president is able to exert tight control over the flow of information and other elites do not immediately weigh into the conflict (Brody 1991). Ronald Reagan (the "Great Communicator") often conveyed policy frames to the media that were not particularly popular in Washington. During the Nicaraguan conflict, for example, news reports consistently adopted two prominent Reagan themes to frame the foreign policy debate: the "Saving the Freedom Fighters" theme, which argued in favor of supporting the Nicaraguan contras, or "freedom fighters," against the communist Sandinistas, or "military thugs," who had formed a totalitarian government; and the "Exported Revolution" theme, which argued that U.S. involvement in Nicaragua was necessary to prevent communism from spreading throughout Central America (see Sahr 1993). Reagan enhanced the media appeal of his framing strategy with televised appearances displaying maps of Mexico and Central America that showed flowing lines that slowly turned red and bled all the way up toward the U.S. border. The visuals were stunning.

When reporters see policy players as experts and credible on a given issue, they are less likely to question those issue frames or counter them. Of course, no political actor can match the president's access to the mass media; however, some actors can frame issue debates because of their strong credibility on specific issues. Policy entrepreneurs, such as Senator Edward Kennedy on health care policy, Senator Henry Hyde on abortion, or Senator Charles Schumer on gun control, serve as de facto media sources: each has developed a solid policy reputation, can convey newsworthy quotes, and is seen as able to exert significant influence over the policy debate (Carmines and Kuklinski 1990). Skillful media manipulators like these often see their dominant themes on the nightly news.

In electoral contexts, some candidates are particularly advantaged in framing issues for the media.[17] For example, in presidential nomination campaigns, particularly early in the process, front runners and other successful candidates receive large amounts of positive media coverage (Bartels 1988; Aldrich 1980). Politically seasoned incumbents are also generally more effective than challengers at convincing the press to adopt their preferred themes, with some qualifications (see Fridkin and Kenney, chap. 2). This media attention gives these candidates a valuable opportunity to set the theme of the campaign (e.g., "this campaign is about jobs for the American people") and present themselves in a positive light (e.g., "and I will not rest until every man or woman who wants a job has one").[18]

A similar dynamic describes interest groups' access to the mass media. Specialized interests need the recognition and attention of the mass media in order to acquire legitimacy and visibility, as well as to communicate their issue frames to the public. Media definitions of newsworthiness are heavily influenced by a group's organizational resources. For example, Thrall's (1997) analysis of media coverage of interest groups shows that only large (i.e., over one hundred thousand members) and wealthy groups (i.e., with a budget exceeding ten million dollars) are able to receive significant media attention and thus function as quasi-official spokespersons for larger groups (e.g., the National Association for the Advancement of Colored People represents the political goals of African Americans; the National Organization for Women embodies the goals of the women's movement). On the other hand, the frames of interest groups that lack the resources of well-established organizations are likely to be overlooked by reporters and editors (Goldenberg 1975) unless they involve conflicts or dramas that meet the imperatives of the press or television.

Finally, exogenous shocks from "focusing" events can direct media—and therefore public—attention to particular issue frames (e.g., Kingdon 1984; Baumgartner and Jones 1993). For example, the 1999 mass shooting at Columbine High School in Littleton, Colorado, focused public attention on the problem of school violence and gave proponents of gun control the opportunity to frame weapons-safety proposals (e.g., trigger locks and other child-protection features) as "Sane and Sensible Legislation" that would "stem the tide of violence in this country" (Callaghan and Schnell 2001a). Similarly, the nuclear accidents at Three Mile Island in 1979 and at Chernobyl in 1986 gave the antinuclear movement the opportunity to replace the once-dominant "Progress through Technology" theme with others reflecting more skepticism about nuclear power, such as "Public Accountability" (Gamson 1992; Gamson and Modigliani 1989).

Furthermore, the 1996 ValuJet crash in the Florida Everglades gave air-safety proponents an opportunity to frame improved-standards proposals, especially new cargo regulations. Interest in this framing debate was brief, however. Before September 11, Americans were relatively unconcerned about reports of lax security and foot-dragging by the Federal Aviation Administration, the agency in charge of securing the airports. No plane had been hijacked since 1991. Apparently, no one worried much about outdated training programs and screening machines or poor monitoring of sensitive areas. After the September 11 hijackings of four commercial airplanes, political elites from both parties used the "war on terrorism" to reframe a variety of aviation-security issues (e.g., background checks of airport workers, certification standards for screeners, federal oversight of airports).

The framing influence of 9/11 is not limited to airport-security issues, however. In chapter 5, we show how quickly the events of 9/11 were brought into the center of the gun control debate and how this change in frames struck a raw nerve in Americans already afraid of terrorism. Similarly, Teena Gabrielson demonstrates how 9/11 opened up framing opportunities on several domestic policy issues (e.g., oil drilling in Alaska, the missile defense program, homeland security) for congressional candidates in the 2001 elections. These politicians effectively used the war on terrorism to highlight some aspect of the democratic process and make their opponents appear less credible.

Thus, the framing of issues in American politics is often limited to an elite level when participants in the process restrict the scope of the conflict. However, focusing events can trigger media attention, making policy players more likely to "go public" to expand the conflict over a variety of issues and issue definitions.

Still, the policy frames citizens ultimately read about in the news are not the result of the simple aggregation of political actors' activities (e.g., the staging of events, press releases, media interviews) or the offshoots of focusing events; rather, they stem from a complex interaction between the media and other political players, who in turn are largely dependent on the media's decisions about what frames constitute news. One of the most prevalent and prolific lines of inquiry in the framing literature looks at the role that the media play in framing issue debates for American politics.

The Media's Role in the Framing Process

In order to activate broad levels of support, political players rely on the media to convey issue information to the general public.[19] Direct forms of communication accessible to policy makers include newsletters, expert testimony, and official correspondence. However, these methods, while effective for elite communication to highly motivated or strongly ideological citizens, are less likely to produce mass awareness or political mobilization. Thus, most political players compete for media attention. As a result, journalists get to pick and choose from the frames offered by political elites. This practice gives the media tremendous power to control the framing debates in American politics.

Just what role do the media play in the framing process? How far do their powers extend? Clearly, strategic political actors try to control the shape and tone of issue debates because they seek outcomes favorable to their political interests, but are the media different? Do they passively transmit multiple issue frames and a plurality of views or consciously select the themes of a few key players? Or are they more active players who generate their own frames? Can we place the media alongside other strategic actors, all attempting to redefine and alter public policy debates? What is the reality?

Surely the claim that the media alone drive the framing debates in American politics is vacuous. Few scholars would endorse this view. But they equivocate on just how much the media create their own unique frames and insert them into the public debate. Some studies provide striking evidence of a politically independent media. Examples are the print media's framing on health care reform (Jamieson and Cappella 1998); gun control (Callaghan and Schnell 2001a); and the women's movement and related issues like abortion (Terkildsen and Schnell 1997; Terkildsen, Schnell, and Ling 1998). For instance, we found that among the gun control frames transmitted by the broadcast news media, some were created by the media and some came from other elites (i.e., interest groups, members of Congress). Furthermore, although elites adopted a range of gun control frames, the media disproportionately pushed one theme that we call "Crime and the Culture of Violence." This theme was the most dramatic, especially when it included a racial subtext (i.e., black

Americans as perpetrators of crime or as victims). The media also presented their own issue frames (e.g., the "Political Contest" theme), ignoring the frames of other players, especially the gun lobby.

Thus, within the context of social policy issues and election campaigns, there seems to be a certain degree of media intervention.[20] That is, journalists, in framing issues for public consumption, impose boundaries, structures, and forms. Independently, they can contribute to the public policy debate.[21] Apparently, Schattschneider has not left us in a quandary after all. With careful analyses, we can disentangle media frames from other elite frames to see who controls public policy debates. Unlike that of the Sphinx, this is a riddle that we can solve.

Two chapters in this volume explore the media's role in the framing process. In chapter 2, Michael X. Delli Carpini presents a provocative analysis of the media's unintentional framing of political information. Despite journalistic norms suggesting that news reporting should be done in a neutral manner, Delli Carpini argues that the process of information gathering causes journalists to frame information for elites and citizens. This process inevitably produces frames that emphasize candidate strategy and political conflict rather than the substantive issues that candidates wish to address.

In chapter 3, Kim Fridkin and Patrick Kenney analyze the process by which information filters from political candidates to citizens via the media. Although the authors do not explicitly address the role that journalists play in shaping political-campaign news, their results are suggestive. For example, Fridkin and Kenney find that journalists pay close attention to negatively framed commercials, quite possibly because these types of ads provide drama and conflict, which sell newspapers. Furthermore, the authors find that the political-endorsement decisions of newspapers significantly alter the tone of their campaign coverage—that is, papers that endorse incumbents tend to frame the candidate's platform in a more positive manner than papers that endorse challengers. Thus when editors and journalists stake out a political position, it narrows their framing choices.

In a democracy, multiple voices and multiple viewpoints are required for informed political debate; thus, it is crucial to explore how the issue frames in American politics emerge, are debated, and are eventually resolved by democratic processes. Yet understanding how issue debates are formed represents only the first piece of the puzzle. The next and equally important part is linking issue framing to public opinion. In the end, framing matters insofar as it influences public opinion.

Framing Effects and Political Judgments

When President Bush addressed the nation in the first days after September 11, he framed the possibility of a military reprisal against Afghanistan in terms of "Infinite Justice" for "our fellow citizens killed or wounded in the terrorist attacks." Perhaps on advice from his aides about the potential negative impact of this frame on the Muslim community, Bush refocused his speeches to stress "Enduring Freedom."[22] This theme reminded Americans that democracy is precious and that an attack on the Al Qaida network was necessary to "preserve our way of life." Bush's frame was compelling: it coincided with a strong show of public support for the use of military force. Furthermore, fully 71 percent of Americans surveyed said they "completely believe[d]" that the purpose of the war in Afghanistan was to "defend freedom and democracy."

Did citizens internalize the language of the White House debate? To what extent was public support for military action due to citizens' exposure to the frame? Poll data do not allow us to make such inferences because the causal link between the "frame" and "public opinion" is not established. To show that frames actually influence public policy attitudes, we need experimentation. In an experiment, we can control the information environment and determine whether alternative ways of framing a public policy issue influence how an individual responds to that issue.

The Psychology of Framing Effects

How do frames work? What is it about frames that makes them so effective? First, frames can alter policy attitudes by changing what citizens think about an issue and their net levels of policy support. For example, if a citizen is unaware that lax gun laws have allowed terrorists and other foreign agents to purchase guns easily, then media coverage linking the "war on terrorism" to the gun control debate might change her beliefs about the issue and shift her preferences toward stricter gun control legislation. This shift can be so large that it leads her to switch support from one side of the issue to another (Feldman and Zaller 1992; Nelson, Clawson, and Oxley 1997). In this case, attitude change occurs via a change in the *content* of beliefs about the political issue being evaluated (the "beliefs-content" model).

In addition to influencing policy attitudes, frames can affect perceptions about who is responsible for policy outcomes (Moskowitz 1998), as well as who is to blame for social problems and how they should be treated by society (see Iyengar 1991; Iyengar and Kinder 1987). In chapter 6, for example, Franklin D. Gilliam Jr. and Shanto Iyengar demonstrate the link between media framing of the crime issue and society's attitude toward race and violence.

Their work shows that media framing shapes the public's understanding of crime and violence and may account for the general shift toward a more punitive and retributive orientation in public debate over the issue.

The process by which frames bring certain values and other beliefs to mind is called "priming." Priming as conceptualized by social psychologists refers to the activation and enhanced accessibility of concepts and considerations in memory (Kinder and Sanders 1996; Zaller 1992; Iyengar and Kinder 1987; but see note 5). For many citizens, frames subtly and often unconsciously direct which beliefs or information are primed or "cued" (i.e., made accessible psychologically) for subsequent evaluations. Although there is a variety of considerations that citizens could reasonably access when thinking about a particular policy issue, the primed considerations will have relatively more influence on citizens' policy attitudes and opinions. For instance, framing the abortion debate in terms of women's rights, individual freedom versus morality, or fetal rights (or using catchphrases like "partial-birth abortion" versus "third-trimester procedures" to reframe the broader issue debate) can activate differing values (e.g., moral conservatism, religious traditionalism), which in turn produce varying levels of policy support (Freedman 2003a; Terkildsen and Schnell 1997). In a similar vein, shifts in the reference points used to evaluate affirmative action (e.g., portraying the policy as an "unfair advantage" versus "reverse discrimination") produce judgments that are based on a unique set of values.[23] Frames thus encourage citizens to draw heavily on the principles and concerns the frame emphasizes.

Frames also change opinions by influencing the importance citizens attach to issue-relevant beliefs (the "beliefs-importance" model; see Nelson and Oxley 1999; Nelson, Clawson, and Oxley 1997). For example, Nelson and Oxley exposed subjects to a news article about hotel development in south Florida that used either an "Environmental" frame, in which "the rights of the people to preserve wetlands areas" were emphasized, or an "Economic Impact" frame, which highlighted the fact that "thousands of jobs would result from the development." As expected, subjects in each condition said that their beliefs about each theme were significantly important as they considered the issue. Thus, belief *importance* is an intervening mechanism between the frame and citizen response; it is a conscious process, distinct from priming.

Frames also play a central role in shaping how citizens interpret political events. In-depth interviews and other forms of narrative in which subjects are given ample opportunity to speak or write freely about political issues reveal that the frames citizens choose to describe issues and events (e.g., a political campaign) often match the frames used by the media (e.g., Rhee 1997; Gamson 1992). In general, citizens learn to associate a particular frame of reference with a position on an issue (the "learning model").

Do frames also heighten emotional response? In chapter 5, we report an experimental study that investigates citizens' emotional response to terrorism frames related to gun control. We find that with traditional frames (e.g., gun control as a "Constitutional Rights" issue), emotional response to the frames is not particularly significant. But when media frames on gun control are linked to the war on terrorism, anxiety is activated, making the frame more evocative.

Understanding media framing effects is important. We live in a mediated world. That is, we learn about most events from the media, not from direct experience. Because the media alone describe and interpret the events of public life that few citizens experience daily, they play a key role in shaping policy support by presenting or framing issues differently. Furthermore, citizens, whether politically sophisticated or not, depend on the media for their point of view. Opinion leaders and other influentials also depend on the news media to sift through competing issue frames to evaluate policy issues.[24] Moreover, media frames are ubiquitous. As Michael X. Delli Carpini notes, "on any issue of import, it is impossible to talk about an 'unframed' media portrayal." Finally, on most issues, the vast majority of citizens have no strong personal stake or cognitive ballast; thus media frames are a particularly potent way to orchestrate public opinion.

Three chapters in this volume analyze media framing as the key independent variable: chapter 5 (by Karen Callaghan and Frauke Schnell), chapter 6 (by Franklin D. Gilliam Jr. and Shanto Iyengar), and chapter 7 (by Paul M. Kellstedt). This research contributes to the framing literature by exploring novel dependent variables, framing effects in different political contexts, the micro- and macrolevel aspects of framing, and dynamic processes.

Taken in total with agenda-setting effects, priming, earlier-documented framing effects, and some of the results presented here, we suggest that media power reaches beyond "minimal effects." Thus, Bernard Cohen's (1963) classic observation that "the true power of the media lies not only in telling citizens what to think, but in telling them what to think about" needs amending. The true power of the media lies in telling the public what issues to think about, as well as how to think about those issues; in turn this "directive" ultimately suggests what their policy positions should be. We suspect that even further media powers are awaiting documentation. However, we acknowledge that these speculations are controversial, and, as will soon be clear, not all the authors in this volume endorse them.

Organization of the Book

The book is divided into four sections: an introduction, a closer look at the origins of issue frames, an examination of the impact of frames on citizens' attitudes and opinion, and a conclusion. In chapter 1, the first of three chapters focusing on the macrolevel aspects of framing, Michael X. Delli Carpini takes up the contemporary debate about "public journalism" as a mechanism to understand the role played by journalists in the framing process. Examples drawn from journalists' self-examinations show how the norms and practices of contemporary journalism affect the news-gathering process and the framing of policy debates and election campaigns. Delli Carpini argues that traditional journalists cover public affairs as a struggle between competing elites over scarce resources, thus framing politics as a strategic game defined by winners and losers. Delli Carpini's findings also turn the causal arrow of framing effects back toward the media, with citizens' frames influencing media frames. Public journalism thus includes the notion of "listening" to citizens.

Delli Carpini's observations that conventional journalism tends to portray politics as a game of winners and losers are affirmed in chapter 2, by Kim Fridkin and Patrick J. Kenney. These authors examine the emergence of frames in the electoral arena. They focus on the ability of Senate candidates to successfully frame media coverage of their campaigns. Using a content analysis of candidates' campaign commercials and local media coverage, they find that incumbents have a modest influence on media frames, while challengers have a weak to modest influence. Furthermore, reporters and editors devote space to certain frames more as a response to a close election than to the specific nature of candidates' messages. Thus, in order to insert their desired frames into the media's coverage of a campaign, candidates must understand the news media's criteria and tailor their messages accordingly.

In chapter 3, Teena Gabrielson significantly advances our understanding of the framing process by discussing the dynamics of agenda-setting, focusing on the ability of elites to frame issues for other elites and the factors affecting the movement between the elite and public agendas. An extended discussion of the 2002 congressional elections illustrates the opportunities and obstacles that emerged as politicians sought to frame issues for electoral gain in the post–9/11 political climate.

Moving to an examination of the microlevel aspects of framing, Donald R. Kinder and Thomas E. Nelson, in chapter 4, show how framing provides context and meaning to otherwise confusing and even opaque political issues, encouraging citizens to express opinions when they might have hesitated to do so. Kinder and Nelson argue that framing provides the material that enables citizens to express "real" opinions, although they remind us that this material is not necessarily evenhanded. Thus, when elites fail to provide citizens with helpful frames that might assist their understanding of political issues and events, "public opinion deteriorates" and opinions are constructed "on the fly." The authors explore the implications of their findings with respect to American democracy. They conclude that although framing does not completely resolve the problem of democratic representation, it does mitigate a common complaint about public opinion (and public opinion research): unresponsive citizens.

As we argue earlier, traumatic national events give political players a unique "window of opportunity" to alter the framing debates on a variety of policy issues. In chapter 5, we document how the terrorist attacks on September 11 and the subsequent "war on terrorism" introduced new terrorism frames on gun control and influenced public opinion, thus linking micro- and macrostudies of framing. The sudden change in frames after 9/11 struck a raw nerve in Americans already afraid of terrorism. When gun control frames are linked to the war on terrorism, they evoke significant emotional and evaluative responses, mobilize issue activism, and have important agenda-setting effects. Thus, political context plays a significant role in moderating framing processes and framing effects in American politics.

In chapter 6, Franklin D. Gilliam Jr. and Shanto Iyengar present experimental work on the media's role in framing public perceptions on crime and punishment. Specifically, the authors test the proposition that media portrayals of non-white and gang-related violent crime result in heightened concern about crime and increased support for punitive measures toward the perpetrators. Gilliam and Iyengar argue that our society has not widely supported punitive criminal justice policies because we see juvenile offenders as less dangerous.

In chapter 7, Paul M. Kellstedt proposes a theory of racial policy framing that explains the ebb and flow of Americans' racial policy preferences over time. To test his theory, the author compares mass-level opinion on race policy issues with national media coverage of these issues. Kellstedt finds that changes in media emphasis on egalitarian and individualism principles lead to mass-level opinion differences. Specifically, public opinion on race conforms to the media's "values" frames, which center on egalitarian principles. However, Kellstedt reminds us that while news frames may be influential in shaping mass-level attitudes toward race policy, the aggregate shift in opinion is small. Further, policy preferences are influenced by other factors, not just media framing.

PART I

The Origins and Development of Frames

1
News from Somewhere
Journalistic Frames and the Debate over "Public Journalism"

Michael X. Delli Carpini

Our reporters do not cover stories from their point of view.
They are presenting them from nobody's point of view.

Richard S. Salant, former president of CBS News

[Journalists] make judgments all the time. . . . I don't think the kind
of bias journalists are usually accused of—ideological bias, personal
animus—is generally worrisome. Far more subtle and more dangerous are the conventions of journalism: the ways in which journalists
go about dividing the world, framing public life for us, picturing the
world of politics. There are values and assumptions hidden in those
decisions that are extremely important to name and debate, and I
think, at this point, to change.

Jay Rosen, former director of the Project on Public Life and the Press

In July of 1993 a handful of journalism and philanthropy trade
publications reported that the Knight and Kettering Foundations,
the American Press Institute, and New York University were col-
laborating on a project called "Public Life and the Press." The
project was described as an "initiative to explore and develop ways
for journalists to help strengthen citizenship, improve public debate and revive public life."[1] At an inaugural meeting of interested
journalists at the American Press Institute in November of 1993,
Jay Rosen, a professor of journalism at New York University and
director of the project, described the purpose of the gathering as
not to debate *whether* newspapers should take a more active role in
communities but rather to discuss *how* to do so effectively. Key to
this endeavor would be finding ways to enable the community to
interact with the newspaper, to reground news coverage so that it
was based on what matters to citizens, to spark public discussion
and action, and to restructure newsroom cultures in ways that
were less hierarchical and more connected to the community.[2]

By the end of 1997, when the Project on Public Life and the

Press officially ended, experiments in "public" or "civic" journalism had been tried by hundreds of newspapers (and many radio and television stations) around the country, with a number of papers rethinking their entire philosophy of news gathering and reporting.[3] It had also sparked a major controversy within the journalistic profession, generating hundreds of columns, editorials, and stories both in favor of and, more often, in opposition to this fledgling movement.

My purpose in discussing public journalism and the controversy surrounding it is not to assess the movement itself (though I confess to being sympathetic to its goals and supportive of many of its practices). Rather it is to use it as a way to better understand the role played by journalists in the framing process. Members of the press seldom publicly discuss the premises and practices of their profession as openly, in as much detail, or with as much fervor as was the case in the four-year debate over public journalism. Since much of this debate centered—often explicitly—on what academics would call the framing process, it provides a rare and valuable window through which to view the way journalists see themselves in this process. In turn, this self-examination and the insights it provides serve as a useful platform from which to more fully explore how media frames are constructed.[4]

Journalism and Framing

"At the most general level," writes Shanto Iyengar (1991, 11), "the concept of framing refers to subtle alterations in the statement or presentation of judgement and choice problems." A large body of social scientific and cognitive research suggests that such alterations in the way information is presented (e.g., emphasizing certain facts over others, the choice of descriptive adjectives and adverbs, the amount and type of context provided, or the sounds and images included) can "prime" recipients of the information in ways that affect both the issues they attend to (agenda-setting) and the construction of their specific opinions about these issues.[5]

Framing is a particularly useful concept in the study of media, politics, and public opinion. Doris Graber (2002, 173) defines a media frame as "reporting the news from a particular perspective so that some aspects of the situation come into close focus and others fade into the background." As the major source of information on public officials, candidates for office, political events, and policy debates, the mass media are uniquely positioned to frame the way citizens come to political judgments. In addition, newspapers, magazines, talk shows, television and radio news, and the like all serve as important, even central forums in which political issues are publicly discussed. As such, the media are more than the *providers* of information to be used in political debate; they are the *places* where much of this debate occurs.

This point is not lost on political elites. Increasingly, battles over the "hearts and minds" of citizens involve attempts to shape the way in which choices are presented and discussed in the media. Indeed, the now common technique of "spin control," practiced by interest groups, candidates for office, and public officials, is little more than the practical-politics version of framing. The growing importance of media campaign consultants, the increasing use of media strategies by organized interests, the blending of media and policy strategies by policy makers, the growth of an institutionalized communications bureaucracy in government, and even the increasing use of media strategies by foreign governments seeking to influence U.S. policy all signal the important role played by the media in framing the way political choices are presented and thus resolved.[6]

But the media are neither passive providers of information framed by other political actors nor simply the stages on which these battles over spin control are performed. Rather, they are active, albeit unique, players in the ongoing drama over the representation of public affairs. I say unique because unlike other players in this process, whose agendas are intentionally, if not always explicitly, designed to frame issues in ways that are favorable to their particular interests, journalists and reporters operate under norms and procedures intended to resist both their own and others' biases and to lead to the presentation of information and debates in an objective, fair, and balanced manner. Columnists, editorialists, and news analysts are more explicitly opinionated and so play roles that come closer to those of more avowedly political actors. But even in these cases the roles are not identical, since with few exceptions, the former still speak as members of the journalistic profession and thus are at least somewhat constrained (and privileged) by this vantage point. Members of the journalistic profession are also in a unique position because they serve as gatekeepers, playing the central role in determining both the form and the content of what is seen, heard, and read in the media.

My argument is that while the norms and practices of contemporary journalism deeply affect the specific way members of the press frame political issues, they do not remove them from the framing process. Indeed, I would argue that on any issue of import, it is impossible to talk about an "unframed" media portrayal. Journalistic norms provide guidance regarding specific decisions that must be made by members of the media. But these decisions—what story to cover, what sources to interview, what quotes to include, what descriptive language to include, what order to present information in, what photo or video to use, what the headline will be, and so forth—remain "subtle alterations in the statement or presentation of judgement and choice problems" and so are, by definition, forms of framing.

The observation that journalists frame the way information is presented to the public is not new.[7] Truly objective, fair, or balanced presentations are viewed as goals rather than as accurate descriptions of most actual media portrayals. The hypothesized reasons why the media fall short of these goals run from intentional bias, to manipulation by sources, to unconscious belief systems, to inherent limitations in the news-gathering process. While all of these explanations have merit, what I am suggesting is that the norms of contemporary journalism *are themselves journalistic frames* and, like all frames, *necessarily* produce alterations in the presentation of choice problems.

More specifically, I argue that media frames emerge from the interplay of facts; the framing of these facts by competing, authoritative, and/or self-interested sources; and the framing of both the facts and the elite frames by journalists. In turn, the frames used by journalists are determined by: (1) the normative assumptions of contemporary journalism; (2) the practical constraints on the news-making process; (3) the institutional practices of journalism that emerge from the combination of normative assumptions and practical constraints; and (4) the way in which these assumptions, constraints, and practices are internalized as professional norms by journalists.

The Normative, Practical, Institutional, and Professional Roots of Journalistic Frames

As Walter Lippmann (1922, 223) observed: "Every newspaper when it reaches the reader is the result of a whole series of selections as to what items shall be printed, in what position they shall be printed, how much space each shall occupy, what emphasis each shall have. There are no objective standards here. There are conventions." Conventions can be powerful, subtle, and often unrecognized influences on the choices made by journalists. The conventions (or norms and practices) of contemporary journalism, while constantly evolving in response to social, technological, and economic changes, remain at heart deeply rooted in normative assumptions about the purpose of the press, assumptions that can be traced back over two hundred years.

The Normative Assumptions of Contemporary Journalism

The central goals of the press have remained relatively unchanged throughout most of U.S. history. Siebert, Peterson, and Schramm (1974, 74) summarize these goals as: (1) servicing the political system by providing information, discussion, and debate on public affairs; (2) enlightening the public so as to make it capable of self-government; (3) safeguarding the rights of the individual by serving as a watchdog against government; (4) servicing the economic system, primarily by bringing together the buyers and sellers of goods and services through the medium of advertising; (5) providing entertainment; and (6) maintaining the press's financial self-sufficiency so as to be free from the pressures of special interests.

Though these goals have remained stable, the presumptions regarding how best the press may achieve them have not. Throughout the eighteenth and nineteenth centuries the chief mechanism was the market. Given a relatively unfettered opportunity for privately owned presses to develop, and few limits on what they published, it was assumed that an economic free market would produce a parallel marketplace of ideas. This open exchange of ideas would create a "self-righting process" (Milton 1951) in which "a livelier impression of the truth [would be] produced by its collision with error" (Mill 1975, 16). In essence, the civic good described by Siebert and his colleagues would be a by-product of the sixth goal.

While actual practice often fell short of its idealized goals (Emery and Emery 1988), the "libertarian" theory of the press (Siebert, Peterson, and Schramm 1974) dominated until the twentieth century, when economic and technological changes forced a rethinking of how best to preserve the goals of a free and democratically useful mass media. Growing centralization of ownership and decreasing competition in the printed press, coupled with the rise of an inherently centralized and expensive electronic media, led to increasing criticisms of press practices. These criticisms included the beliefs that owners were using the press to propagate their own views and/or those of the business class more generally, that the press was resistant to social change, that it emphasized the sensational over the substantive, that it was unjustly invading the privacy of individuals, and that it was endangering public morals (Siebert, Peterson, and Schramm 1974, 78–79).

Such criticisms had long been aimed at individual stories or publications. However, the growing centralization of ownership and information created an environment in which one could no longer assume a marketplace of ideas or a self-righting process. As a result, one could also no longer assume that the truth would emerge as a by-product of competition among self-interested but diverse publications. The solution to this problem was found in the development of a new theory of the press, a theory that emerged slowly but that was codified in the 1920s and early 1930s by, among others, the Federal Radio and Federal Communications Commissions and by professional associations such as the American Society of Newspaper Editors, the National Association of Broadcasters, and the Newspapers Guild (Emery and Emery 1988). At the heart of this emerging theory was the growing consensus that journalism was a profession that required a more self-conscious awareness of its social responsibility and a clearer set of professional practices that would be aimed at meeting this social responsibility.

The elements of this "social responsibility" theory of the press (Siebert, Peterson, and Schramm 1974, 87) were most clearly summarized in a 1947 report issued by the privately funded Commission on Freedom of the Press. First, the press should provide "a truthful, comprehensive, and intelligent account of the day's events in a context which gives them meaning." Within this requirement were the expectations that the press would be accurate and objective, would distinguish fact from opinion, and would provide balance by presenting competing points of view. While providing competing views, however, the press was also expected to "provide the truth about the fact" by weighing the reliability of various sources and putting facts into some kind of context. Second, the press should serve "as a forum for the exchange of comment and criticism," thus assuring some diversity of opinion. Third, the press should present "a representative picture of the constituent groups in society." Fourth, the press was responsible for "the presentation and clarification of the goals and values of society." And finally, the press should provide "full access to the day's intelligence" (88–91).

Taken as a whole, these requirements represent an attempt to preserve the *ends* of the libertarian theory of the press through different *means*. If the press separated fact from opinion; provided competing facts, opinions, and critiques; fairly represented different groups; presented and clarified societal values; and provided a full range of critical information *in the same publication or broadcast*, competition among numerous and separately owned media voices was no longer vital. But in exchange, media professionals were required to take this new social responsibility seriously and were subject to formal and informal monitoring and regulation by the public, the profession, and, when necessary, the government.

There are several tensions within both the general goals of the press and the specific theories designed to achieve these goals. Regarding the former, the greatest tensions are between the civic goals (providing information, discussion, and debate; enlightening the public; and serving as a watchdog of government) on the one hand and the goals of entertainment and economic self-sufficiency on the other. Put simply, being entertaining and economically successful often can come at the expense of being informative, enlightening, and vigilant (Postman 1985; Bagdikian 1992). This potential problem is exacerbated under the social responsibility theory, since in the world of media conglomerates, the economic stakes are greater and the civic impact of the choices made by these media giants more far-reaching.

In addition to this tension among the civic, entertainment, and economic goals of the press, there are also tensions within the specific tenets of the social responsibility theory. Under this theory the same media outlet is expected to be a neutral information provider, a facilitator of debate and discussion, an expert that determines the truthfulness and utility of different facts or opinions, and a watchdog that guards against government corruption and moral decay. Any one of these responsibilities would be difficult, if not impossible, but their combination creates competing identities that can be drawn on (and ultimately internalized) selectively and thus can affect the way in which information is framed.

The libertarian and social responsibility theories of the press provide the underpinnings for much of the current structure and practice of journalism. But to fully understand the impact of normative concerns on structure and practice, it is necessary to also consider the 1920s debate between Walter Lippmann and John Dewey on the nature of "the public." For Lippmann (1925), the modern public was a "phantom," an artificially constructed collection of individuals who were generally uninformed about and disconnected from politics; who lacked the time, skills, and interest to take a direct role in their own governance; and who were easily swayed by seemingly persuasive arguments of the moment. The contemporary media, from this perspective, could easily become a propaganda tool used to manipulate and misrepresent the public in ways that could threaten the stability and order of society. To avoid this, the press must serve as a vigilant watchdog, guarding against demagogues. The goal of the press was not to provide information that would allow citizens to come to their own conclusions on the substantive issues of the day but to create an environment in which they could choose among competing elites who would be responsible for the real work of democracy and policy making. Since the substance of politics and policy would be determined by experts, the substance of journalism should focus on this expert class. At best, the press could signal citizens when certain elites, experts, or ideas posed a threat to the democratic process.

Dewey (1954), too, saw problems with the modern public but drew different conclusions from these observations. While he acknowledged the existence and importance of experts, Dewey believed that citizens were capable of engaging experts and their ideas and contributing to public deliberation. The nature and quality of public deliberation were not preordained but depended upon the opportunities presented to citizens by the public sphere. Given these opportunities, Dewey had faith that the public could play a more active, direct, and rational role in its own governance. These opportunities would come from many places, such as the education system and other public institutions. One key institution was the press. The press's responsibility was to provide the kind of information that not only could be used by citizens to understand the issues of the day but that would also provide the context within which to use that information and the skills necessary to do so. In addition, the public required a public sphere that would allow them to openly deliberate about civic issues. Here again the press was critical, as it could serve as a public space for such deliberation. In short, where Lippmann saw citizens necessarily as passive consumers of the news, and saw the press as the place for an exchange of facts, opinions, and ideas among elites and experts (including journalists and columnists), Dewey saw citizens as potentially active participants in this exchange and saw the press as a fundamental part of the social fabric and the place where experts would inform, educate, and engage the public in issues of the day.

Elements of Lippmann and Dewey can be found in the tenets of both the libertarian theory of the press and its reincarnation in the social responsibility theory. However, the specific ways in which these theories are put into practice vary significantly depending on whether Lippmann's or Dewey's views prevail. As has been noted by several students of the press (Carey 1988, 1989; Rosen 1999), by and large Lippmann's view has come to dominate the journalistic profession. At the same time, internal tensions within the social responsibility theory, and the continued if muted impact of both the libertarian theory and Dewey's views, can make for a complicated, inconsistent, and sometimes schizophrenic self-definition within the press. These tensions have been partially resolved (or, more accurately, suppressed) through the development of particular frames. But these frames, while arguably consistent with many of the normative goals of journalism, necessarily privilege certain of these goals over others and so remain open to criticism and, on occasion, evaluation. This can be clearly seen in both the way in which the social responsibility theory of the press has become institutionalized by mainstream journalism and in the critique of this institutionalization by public journalists.

Practical Constraints on the Framing Process

The normative guidelines discussed above must be applied in a world with numerous practical constraints.[8] These constraints have been well documented (Epstein 1973; Gans 1980; Manoff and Schudson 1986; Jamieson and Campbell 1992) and include the limits imposed by time, space, expertise, technology, and cost. Time is a constraint in several ways. News is defined as information about *recent* events, usually defined as what has happened since the last publication or broadcast. There are also time constraints (deadlines) for producing a story, established by the news cycle of the particular medium in question. Time is also a relative constraint, in the sense that releasing information before your competitor (the scoop) is valued. And, for electronic media, time is a constraint in that it limits the number and length of stories and thus what can be included as news.

Space is a constraint in several ways as well. It limits the number and length of stories in print media much as time does in the electronic media. Placement of stories within a given space (the page number, the position on the page, the section of the paper or magazine, etc.) signals their import and affects their likelihood of being read. Geographic space can shape the ease with which information can be accessed and thus affects both the likelihood and the way that certain parts of the nation (e.g., urban versus rural, Northeast versus Midwest) or regions of the world (e.g., South America or Africa versus Europe or the Middle East) will be covered. Expertise, or lack thereof, can greatly affect news coverage. A journalist's familiarity with a particular culture or subculture; mastery of a foreign language; knowledge of relevant historical, scientific, or political information; and so forth all influence the way an event or topic is researched, perceived, and thus presented to the public.

Finally, technology and economics set the broader parameters within which the news-gathering process operates. Technological advances can change the impact of time, space, and expertise (Abramson, Arterton, and Orren 1988), as can differential calculations regarding acceptable costs. In addition, and as noted above, economic considerations can shape broader notions of newsworthiness in ways that can conflict with the civic goals of a free press.

The Institutional Practices of Journalism and Their Impact on Framing

The combination of normative expectations and practical constraints problematizes the process of news gathering. To prevent these difficulties from becoming overwhelming, professional journalism has developed routines and practices designed to rationalize the process so as to manufacture a news product in an efficient, timely, and consistent way. These practices include the routinization of the release of news; the structuring of newspapers, magazines, and news broadcasts into identifiable sections or segments; the creation of specific beats for surveillance of the political and social world; the cultivation of reliable, authoritative sources of information; and so forth. They also include the standardization of definitions of newsworthiness so that it becomes easier to sort through the incredible number of possible events and issues one might choose to cover.

What is important about these practices for my purposes is that they represent ways for the profession to institutionalize the normative underpinnings of journalism while taking the practical constraints of news gathering into consideration. At the same time, however, these practices should be viewed as choices—each is one of several equally rational ways in which the news *might* be constructed (Romano 1986). In turn, these choices affect the way in which other actors in the negotiation over deciding what is news (public officials, interest groups, the public, etc.) interact with the media. In short, institutionalized practices become important, perhaps even central, rules that determine how news is framed.

The Internalization of Institutional Practices: Journalistic Norms

The normative goals, practical constraints, and resulting institutional practices are seldom open to critical rethinking but instead become internalized in journalistic norms. This internalization of norms produces schemas, or "cognitive structure[s] that represent organized knowledge about a given concept or type of stimulus. A schema contains both the attributes of the concept and the relationships among the attributes" (Fiske and Taylor 1984, 140). Schemas serve as filters through which journalists see the world, make professional judgments about it, and thus present it to the rest of us. Further, since schemas include "the relationships among the attributes" of the concept or stimulus in question, they can naturalize what could under other circumstances be problematic (or at least contestable) relationships among the particular ways in which normative goals and practical constraints are combined into institutional practices. Included in these schemas are, of course, attitudes, beliefs, ideologies, and so forth that are the result of personal experience and the socializing effects associated with class, gender, ethnicity, and the like. But of central interest here are those that result from the internalization of professional practices.

To illustrate this, consider the journalistic schema of "politics as a strategic game" identified by, among others, Thomas Patterson. According to Patterson (1993, 57–58): "The dominant schema for the reporter is structured around the notion that politics is a strategic game. When journalists encounter new information during an election, they tend to interpret it within a schematic framework according to which candidates compete for advantage. The candidates play the game well or poorly. . . . The core principle of the press's game schema is that candidates are strategic actors whose every move is significant. . . . The reporter's first instinct is to look to the game." Patterson goes on to illustrate, first, how the game schema shapes the specific ways the media report on elections; second, how this schema differs from the schema used by most citizens; and third, how this combination unintentionally results in reporting that ill serves the democratic process of selecting representatives.

Though he does not use this terminology, Patterson is describing the cognitive processes associated with journalistic framing. What is less clear in his and other analyses that describe how journalists cover politics is *why* particular schemas develop. What I am suggesting is that these schemas result from the internalization of institutional practices based on the interplay of normative concerns and practical constraints.[9] Consider the specific, unexamined attributes that make up the game schema. Least controversial, but most easily missed, is the notion that campaigns and elections *are* news. This is clearly tied to the libertarian theory's mandate that the press inform and enlighten the public so as to make it capable of self-government. Second, by providing relatively equal coverage of the major candidates for any particular office, journalists arguably satisfy the social responsibility theory's requisite that the press perform its civic responsibility in a balanced way. The expectation that the press should provide discussion, debate, and diversity of opinion, found in both the libertarian and the social responsibility theories, is also satisfied by giving coverage to the major candidates for office.

At the same time, however, journalists are also expected to be watchdogs of government, to provide forums for comment and criticism, and to provide "the truth behind the fact" by assessing the reliability of sources and putting facts in a context. It is as a result of these expectations, I would argue, that the "game schema" takes on its more controversial characteristics. The goal of the campaign, and thus the overarching context in which stories are written, becomes winning the election. In this context, the truth behind the fact is defined as the strategic reasons for candidate statements and behavior. Criticisms are also situated within this context—evaluations about the reliability of sources are based on the implicit assumption that winning is the underlying motivation for all behavior. In its watchdog role, the press assesses the behavior of candidates with a cynical eye, assuming that platforms, policy statements, promises, and so forth are primarily attempts to win support and thus likely to be self-serving and misleading. Points of disagreement between candidates are evaluated in a similar light. Finally, the near exclusive focus on elites—candidates, campaign consultants, pollsters, and so forth—is the institutionalization and internalization of Lippmann's view of the proper role of journalism.

The emphases on winning and losing, strategy, elites, and so forth also satisfy the economic incentives of the media, since the inherent drama this schema contains is presumed to attract readers and viewers. That this drama can also be entertaining serves yet another goal of the media. And it helps simplify news reporting, given the practical constraints of time, space, and expertise. This simplification is assisted by the candidates and their surrogates. Candidates, interest groups, even "neutral" experts adjust their behavior to fit journalistic schemas, thus hoping not only to be covered but to be covered in ways that advantage their own agendas. Defining news about campaigns as a strategic game leads interested parties to become more strategic. In turn, this confirms the essentially strategic nature of campaigns for journalists, thus also confirming the legitimacy of their worldview. Behavior that runs counter to this schema is either ignored or viewed as ineffective or manipulative strategy. The result is what Entman (1989) describes as a dysfunctional interaction that ultimately frustrates journalists, elites, and the public alike, which Cappella and Jamieson (1997) call the "spiral of cynicism."

In short, the game schema allows journalists to do their job in a way that is arguably consistent with their goals and constraints and to do so without having to constantly revisit these goals and constraints. However, this frame is only one of many that could serve this purpose, with alternative frames producing different emphases and so different reporting. Thus, the choice of the strategic-game frame alters the way in which choices are presented to the public by filtering what is or is not deemed newsworthy and, ultimately, by affecting the actual conduct of campaigns. Further, the centralization of the media and the professionalization of journalistic practices mean that, once developed and internalized, a limited set of frames comes to dominate reporting. This increases their likely impact while also naturalizing them, thus making less visible the fact that they are choices—choices that can have costs as well as benefits associated with them. Ironically, the result of this process can be a failure to meet the very civic responsibilities upon which these frames are at least partially based.

What the Public Journalism Debate Tells Us about Journalistic Framing

The game schema, and its resulting frame, is only one of several employed by the press. What is common across these frames, however, is that they are the internalization of some combination of normative assumptions, practical constraints, and institutionalized practices. This internalization is often so complete as to be invisible to members of the press, with the distinction between the general goals of journalism and the specific ways in which these goals are applied blurred beyond recognition. The first few decades of the twentieth century, when the social responsibility theory of the press emerged, was one of the few periods when journalists openly discussed the relationship between the theory and the practice of their craft. The current debate over public journalism is another.

"By its own admission public journalism is about experimentation, and so is resistant to simple definitions. . . . Nobody, not even me, knows exactly what it is," says Davis "Buzz" Merritt, former editor of the *Wichita Eagle* and one of the principal founders of the public journalism movement.[10] At root, both chronologically and philosophically, it is a critique of mainstream press practices. This critique can be traced to several dissatisfactions with the state of both journalism and public life. In the late 1980s journalists and academics alike noted the growing alienation of citizens from politics, as indicated by low voter turnout, as well as by surveys that indicated a general mistrust of and disinterest in politics and politicians. At the same time, citizens seemed increasingly disengaged from and dissatisfied with the media, with polls indicating a low opinion of the press and a willingness to blame the media for much of their frustration with politics. Declining readership of newspapers and viewership of the news provided more tangible evidence for this disconnect among the press, politics, and the public.

These trends coincided with a growing frustration among many journalists and editors that their coverage of important issues had become misguided and superficial. This was especially evident in the 1988 presidential campaign, during which a consensus emerged among journalists, academics, and the public that coverage had overemphasized personality, strategy, and the horse race over substantive policy issues. There was also concern over the excessively negative and image-oriented nature of the campaign. While much of the blame was laid at the feet of the candidates, members of the press were forced to admit they had lost control over their coverage and had been too easily manipulated into covering the campaign in reaction to the strategies of the campaign organizations themselves. At the same time, candidates complained that the media were unwilling to cover them unless their messages were simplified and sensationalized. While campaign coverage was an especially evident example of this problem, it extended far beyond this. Similar concerns were raised regarding coverage of government more generally, of national and local policy issues, and of public officials.

These self-assessments cut to the heart of both the civic and the economic underpinnings of the press, thus forcing a reassessment of journalistic practices. While numerous editorials and columns lamented this state of affairs, what distinguished the public journalism critique was the extent to which it linked together declining civic involvement; declining public trust in and use of the news media; the declining quality of news coverage of government, policy, and politics; and the resulting frustration among members of the press. Further, public journalists much more aggressively located the source of this spiral of cynicism within the press itself. In part this critique was a continuation of criticisms that have existed since the nation's founding. In part it was a continuation of more recent debates emerging from economic and technological changes beginning in the latter part of the twentieth century and complicated by the development of new information sources. And in part it was a departure from traditional views of the proper role of the press. In each case, however, it involved opening up for discussion the press's role in the framing process. In particular, public journalism exposes and challenges a number of the frames employed by traditional journalism.

Journalists and editors who would become identified with the public journalism movement did more than critique the traditional practices of the press—they acted on their critique. Beginning somewhat idiosyncratically in the late 1980s and early 1990s, and then developing more formally after the creation of the Project on Public Life and the Press in 1993, they experimented with alternative forms of news coverage. While these experiments varied in form and content, they were all motivated by an understanding of the central role played by the press in the framing process. For public journalists there is no pretense that the press is simply a mirror on the world: "Journalism is not now and has never been value-neutral, all protestations to the contrary. . . . The fact, *to which we are blind* but that is obvious to the public, is that we exercise our own values when we choose to, and use the convenient claim of value neutrality when citizens want us to expand our reportorial efforts beyond the traditional targets of investigative reporting. . . . It comes across to citizens as either judgmental arrogance or a lack of civic concern, creating yet another disconnect between us and the people we are trying to reach and inform" (Merritt 1995, 11–12; emphasis added).

This acknowledgment forces public journalists to confront the underlying assumptions of mainstream schemas, asking directly, "From whose perspective should the news be framed?" The answer, for public journalists, is from the perspective of citizens: "The real purpose of objectivity," according to one newspaper article summarizing the views of Jay Rosen, "is to frame problems in ways that enable society to talk about them."[11] More specifically, this entails: (1) giving citizens a greater role in setting the agenda; (2) covering particular issues and events in a way that is meaningful and useful to citizens; (3) giving the public a greater, more visible voice in the ongoing conversation about public affairs; and (4) seeing the press as a member of the community in which it operates, responsible not only for identifying problems but also for helping find solutions to these problems.

Public journalism, as both a theory and a practice, became a news story in its own right, generating a substantial debate among its supporters, its critics, and those who were curious but ambivalent. At the heart of the debate over public journalism is the issue of how best to perform the civic role expected of the press, given the constraints journalists face. What is important to underscore is that in this debate, both mainstream and public journalists accept the responsibility of informing the public; providing debate and diversity of opinion; uncovering the truth behind the fact; being objective, accurate, and balanced; and so forth. The disagreement lies in how best to do this. All four of the operating principles of public journalism mentioned above can be tied to the normative assumptions guiding the mainstream press, but all four challenge the particular ways in which the mainstream press has come to codify these principles within their traditional frames. This challenge, and the response to it by mainstream journalists, provides useful insights into both the variety of frames employed by mainstream journalists and the logic underlying these frames.

Who Sets the Agenda? Elite versus Citizen Frames

One of the major dilemmas faced by journalists is determining what to cover, given the overwhelming number of issues and events that might legitimately be considered newsworthy. This agenda-setting function is fundamental to the framing process, as the decision to cover or not cover an issue or event (or how much to cover it) affects the information citizens have available in making judgments. If, for example, the press covers the president's stand on health care, but not his stand on abortion, the latter is less likely to come into play in citizens' assessments of the president.

Public journalism openly acknowledges this dilemma, rejecting the notion that story selection is simply an objective or technical process: "Public journalism may be more honest than 'false objectivity,' pretending to be neutral, when even choosing subject matter requires personal judgements."[12] Given the inherent constraints on covering everything of potential import, public journalists argue that citizens themselves, rather than (or in addition to) elites, should set the agenda. This philosophy can be clearly seen in a number of public journalism "experiments." For example, numerous print and several electronic news organizations covered the 1992 and 1996 campaigns by allowing citizens to play a major role in setting the agenda. Public opinion surveys and focus groups, along with more informal outreaches to the public, were used to determine what issues were most important to citizens. These issues were then used to frame media coverage of the campaigns, with candidates expected—and sometimes required—to address these issues throughout the campaign. Jennie Buckner, editor of the *Charlotte Observer* in North Carolina, described this approach as follows: "From the *Virginia Pilot* of Norfolk, Va., to the *Seattle Times* of Washington, news organizations across the country made citizens, and their concerns, a key part of election coverage. We listened to voters. Then we took voters' concerns to the candidates, asking them where they stood on the people's issues" (1997, 65).

This notion of listening to citizens is not limited to campaigns. Public journalism employs this practice in all aspects of its coverage of the social and political world. Indeed, "journalists-as-listeners" becomes a defining characteristic of the journalist, a new schema that helps members of the press reframe issues: "Maybe—*what we are* is listeners—the key here is listening. *It's a different perspective* of what we are used to doing."[13] The goal, according to Walter Isaacson, managing editor of *Time Magazine,* is for journalists to "be a little more sensitive and if we are lucky a little smarter about what interests Americans—about what they feel is news and what they feel is important" (quoted in Germillion 1997, 25).

Key to this approach is the belief that citizens should more regularly serve as authoritative sources in determining what is newsworthy. According to the Pew Center for Civic Journalism, civic or public journalism is "an effort by print and broadcast journalists . . . to listen to how citizens *frame* their problems . . . and then to use that information to enrich their newspaper or broadcast report" (Gartner 1997, 70; emphasis added). Also important is the belief that journalists have traditionally ignored the public's agenda and depended instead on the views of experts and elites: "Where, in the past, candidates were allowed to dictate their political platforms to a reporter scribbling in his notepad," says Edward D. Miller, the former editor of the *Morning Call* of Allentown, Pennsylvania, "now they're being forced to respond to more citizen-identified issues."[14]

The attempt to reframe the news from citizens' own perspectives is especially illustrative for what it reveals about the frames used by traditional journalists. This becomes clear in considering criticisms leveled against the "citizen frame." Typical of these reactions were those of Michael Gartner, former president of NBC News and current editor of the *Daily Tribune* in Ames, Iowa. Reacting to a public journalism experiment in coverage of the 1996 U.S. Senate race between Jesse Helms and Harvey Gantt in North Carolina, Gartner argued that efforts to understand and incorporate the public's agenda, while well-meaning and broadly consistent with the goals of traditional journalism, ultimately "cede editorial judgement to pollsters or, worse, to readers and viewers in focus groups who have no particular knowledge of a state, of politics or of politicians. . . . What *isn't* being covered? What *isn't* being said? The 'community involvement' takes up time and resources of newsrooms. What would reporters and editors be doing if they weren't involved in this 'civic' effort? What rocks would get turned over? What issues would be explored that didn't turn up in polling data?" (1997, 73). Gartner also raised concerns that the voices of candidates themselves are lost in this process: "You had to read through more than a foot of copy on the Helms-Gantt views on education before you found Gantt [being quoted]. You had to go 19 paragraphs into a budget story before you found a quote from either gubernatorial candidate" (1997, 72).

The reaction of mainstream journalists is illustrative of both the frames they employ and the connection of these frames to institutional practices, practical constraints, and normative assumptions. From this perspective journalists are professionals who are ultimately responsible for deciding what information is most valuable for citizens. They do this in an environment of limited time, space, and resources. Elites (in this case candidates for office, but the point can be extended to other elites) are both the subject of the news and the authoritative sources who set the agenda. It is the journalist's responsibility to both report on the actions and statements of elites and to question or challenge those actions and statements (to serve as a watchdog, provide context, and find the truth behind the fact). This admittedly involves choices, but these choices are best made through the exchange between elites and journalists. The goal of this process is to inform the public, but the public should and can play only a marginal role in this process. The public's role begins *after* the journalist's ends. "After all," writes one *New York Times* critic of public journalism, "the big issues are no secret, and if journalism schools have not been producing professionals who can sort out substance from sensation without polls and panels, that's a good subject [for future discussion]."[15]

While mainstream journalists view public journalism as ceding too much of its own power to citizens, they also argue, somewhat paradoxically, that it gives too much power to journalists. According to one critique of public journalism's coverage of the 1996 Helms-Gantt Senate race:

The fraud was the notion that a self-selected group of reporters and editors somehow could or should determine the fit subjects for debate in an election. The journalists, of course, pointed to their polls to claim that it was the voters who had defined the issues, but that claim falls apart at the slightest examination. First of all, the universe of choices for those polled was limited to a list of issues that the consortium [of North Carolina newspapers and radio and television stations] had already selected. And those polled in July identified not four issues on which it was "very important" for them to know how the candidates would act but eight. . . . In fact, the issue of Families and Values was considered "very important" by seventy-nine percent of those polled, one point more than Taxes and Spending. But the consortium selected Taxes and Spending over Families and Values as one of the four big issues to put before the voters in the Gantt-Helms race. This was an extraordinary decision.[16]

This criticism is instructive for both what is said and what is presumed. The criticism—that journalists are powerful gatekeepers who in attempting to frame news from citizens' perspectives inevitably make choices that can distort that perspective—is a valid one. What is missed, however, is the realization that while one can always dispute particular choices, this is as true for the choices made by mainstream journalists as it is for those made by public journalists. The difference is in the choice of frame: elite or citizen. Here we see how deeply embedded the norms of mainstream journalism are, so much so that the choices found in traditional practices can become invisible—even as they are being debated. While the decision made by the consortium could legitimately be questioned, it was *not* "an extraordinary decision." It is the kind of decision that journalists of all stripes are constantly making by the very nature of their job.

What Constitutes "Usable" Information? Strategic versus Issue, and Conflict versus Consensus Frames

The disagreement between mainstream and public journalists goes beyond the question of *what* issues and events to cover. It also involves differences regarding *how* to cover these issues and events. Two specific and related concerns consistently emerge from the public journalism critique of mainstream issue framing: the emphasis of strategy over policy and the emphasis of conflict over consensus. Both of these frames follow "naturally" from the elite frame used by mainstream journalists.

For public journalists, the news is too dominated by the "strategic-game" frame discussed earlier. By emphasizing strategy over substance, and winning and losing over issues, politics "becomes something to watch, like a sporting event, instead of something [citizens] can join."[17] According to Davis Merritt, more appropriate coverage of public affairs would "focus on how well each party was addressing the nation's problems . . . rather than on how each party was addressing tactical problems as defined by politicians and journalists."[18]

Changing the way public affairs are covered requires changing the worldview—the schema—of journalists, a point that is not lost on public journalists: "Campaign reporters need to change *the basic premise* of coverage from an emphasis on who's winning and how the other candidates hope to catch up, to an emphasis on what problems citizens want the government to address and how the candidates propose to address those issues."[19] In describing a public journalism effort in Charlotte, North Carolina, Jennie Buckner acknowledges how deeply ingrained mainstream frames are: "We focused less on the inside stuff of strategy. Some of us *even tried to kick the political junkies' toughest addiction* and placed less emphasis on weekly horse-race polls" (1997, 65; emphasis added). Or, as Tom Fiedler, the *Miami Herald*'s political editor put it, "We had to question our own culture."[20]

Again, the response to this criticism of the strategic-game frame by mainstream journalists is illustrative. While rare, direct defenses of horse-race journalism could be found in these responses. One such defense is provided by David Hawpe, editor of the *Courier-Journal:* "The civic journalists and 'good government' types want to push passions out of a system that is designed to accommodate base passions. In this country we get to reconcile our base passions on the campaign trail, instead of in street warfare. That's what Jefferson and Madison had in mind. When we do stories about the tactics and strategy of politics, we are describing how passions and interests have engaged each other in a campaign. Among other things, in the much-vilified 'horserace' polls, we show how each candidate's choices are moving the electorate—how voters, the ultimate decision-makers, are reacting to the contest of passions, interests, ideas, values, and personalities."[21] Others defended the strategic-game frame less directly, by suggesting that this frame has substantive concerns contained within it—for example, several critics of public journalism noted that the issue of campaign finance reform, an issue that is generally quite low on the public's radar screen, emerged from coverage of the strategic game.[22]

More common were acknowledgments of the weaknesses of the strategic-game frame, a point that further demonstrates that, once open for discussion, journalistic practices are measured by *all* journalists against the normative assumptions discussed earlier. Indeed, Howard Kurtz, a *Washington Post* reporter and media critic, admits both the shortcomings of the strategic-game frame and how deeply ingrained it is in journalistic norms: "The biggest critics of press coverage of campaigns are in the press themselves. . . . It's interesting that we rarely act on that hammering and self-flagellation. . . . We have an awfully hard time weaning ourselves from the same sort of coverage we're used to" (quoted in Buckner 1997, 65).

Even in acknowledging the limitations of this frame, supporters of mainstream journalism nonetheless found fault with public journalists' solution to this problem. "It is true," wrote William E. Jackson Jr., an unsuccessful candidate for the House of Representatives, "that campaign coverage has often been reduced to horse-race analysis, but this cure is worse than the disease."[23] The specific concerns raised by critics of public journalism centered on several issues. First, as discussed above, by allowing the public to determine what issues are central to them, many important issues may be ignored or downplayed: "If journalists had polled Americans about the issues that were facing the nation in 1950, the scourge of Appalachian poverty would not have been on that list. Only when the dissident voices of inspired journalists spoke to the issue did mountain poverty begin to move onto the national agenda."[24] Or as Jackson put it, "I quickly discovered that it didn't matter what a House candidate did or said. Even debates received minimal attention. . . . The major newspapers decided to concentrate on issues that did well in their surveys. . . . What about other issues like the economy and the environment? What about race?"[25] Here again we see the tension between the elite and citizen frames, with supporters of traditional journalism—à la Lippmann—opting for the former even if it means an overemphasis on strategy.

Second, and revealing of the ongoing interplay of the civic, economic, and entertainment functions of the press, emphasizing issues over the horse race was accused of producing "boring" coverage: "You would expect [a Gantt-Helms] rematch to be pretty hot stuff—the candidates slinging mud and raw meat, the press egging them on, the happily appalled public thronging to witness the ugliness of it all. Instead, there are the scenes of last week—the candidates muted, the press disengaged, the public looking elsewhere for its entertainment."[26] Michael Gartner concurs, arguing that public journalism stories "tend to read like a civics textbook" (1997, 72).

Finally, several critics noted that certain candidates were able to use public journalism to their strategic advantage. For example, a *Washington Post* op-ed noted that a newspaper engaged in public journalism perpetuated the "fiction that Helms was running on other issues by printing blank spaces for Helms's positions—although he has a 24-year public record on the issues being debated."[27] Similarly, the campaign manager for Harvey Gantt argued that public journalism "encouraged precisely the sort of race the do-gooders wished to avoid—a repeat of the Gantt-Helms race of 1990, which was dominated by harshly negative television commercials. By not declaring 'race relations' and 'values' official issues . . . the consortium has discouraged the candidates from openly discussing issues like affirmative action. The result: a muted Helms and a careful Gantt on display, with both campaigns blanketing television with demagogue attack ads."[28]

Here, again, we see the interplay of the normative and practical concerns that make up mainstream journalism's worldview. Yes, say mainstream journalists, campaign coverage tends to overemphasize strategic issues, though this kind of coverage serves some useful democratic functions. Further, breaking out of this frame is difficult for journalists, given how deeply embedded it is as a way of viewing politics and the costs involved in reframing the newsgathering process. And even if journalists could wean themselves from traditional practices, the cure is worse than the disease. Not only would it fail to better achieve the normative goals of an informed public, but it would limit and distort public debate, since the public is ill prepared to make judgments on newsworthiness and because candidates are either disadvantaged by citizen frames or quickly learn to use them to their strategic advantage. Beyond this, public journalism produces boring, dry coverage that will fail to hold readers' and viewers' attention, sending them to seek their entertainment elsewhere. In the end, the strategic-game frame, while admittedly flawed, serves its normative, practical, and institutional purposes well enough. It provides an efficient, familiar routine that allows journalists to cover public affairs in an arguably balanced, informative way. It also allows the press to serve its watchdog function in a way that requires professional judgments but that keeps journalists from appearing biased, since issues of strategy are less ideologically loaded than are those of policy. And it provides drama, thus fulfilling the press's entertainment (and economic) functions.

A second and related concern raised by public journalists regarding how issues are covered is the excessive emphasis on conflict over consensus: "Conflict is the highest coin in the journalistic realm."[29] Mainstream journalism is viewed as overly concerned with "rancorous debate, point-counterpoint, and mean-spirited partisanship."[30] This emphasis on conflict, like the other frames discussed, is part and parcel of a journalist's worldview: "A generation of journalists," writes Jon Shure, have been "taught to make their mark through cynical questioning and confrontational tactics."[31] Inherent to an emphasis on conflict is excessive attention to the negative aspects of public affairs: "Excessive negative coverage of government, for example, can breed cynicism that makes people unwilling to serve or even vote. The news-is-conflict model can overemphasize differences."[32]

The roots of the conflict frame can be traced in part to the watchdog function of the press: "In the modern era, *watchdog* has become synonymous with *adversary or opponent*" (Steffans 1993, 3). But again, it is the interaction of this normative goal with other goals, as well as with specific practices, that determines how specific frames are constructed. As Cole Campbell, former executive editor of the *Norfolk Virginian-Pilot,* notes: "Conventional journalism too often emphasizes conflict and polarization rather than search for common ground. It exalts experts and public opinion over citizens and public judgement."[33] In the mainstream interpretation of the watchdog role, "journalists tend to think of themselves as the heroic antagonists to government power."[34] The conflict frame is also tied to the journalistic commitment to objectivity, a commitment that public journalists view as often becoming a frame in and of itself: "Many critics now worry about a *politically neutral bias* that shapes news coverage by declaring that all public officials, indeed all people in the news, are suspect. In this version of journalism, all politicians are manipulative, all business people are venal, and all proposals have ulterior motives."[35]

The solution, from the public journalism perspective, is to reframe news so as to accentuate areas of consensus and shared values: "Is it any wonder most Americans don't find their values and voices represented in the current process? The fact is, many of us on many issues are somewhere in the middle, but that messy, uncertain middle doesn't show up in polarized diatribes couched in extremes."[36] This approach does not mean ignoring genuine differences of opinion but rather suggests showing these differences in a way that makes them understandable. Ellen Hume describes one example of this approach, involving coverage of growing racial tensions because of the closing of a local park that was used by black youths: "Editors learned of police concerns that a race riot was brewing. . . . Many local news organizations would see this as a great story, full of controversy and drama. However, instead of inflaming the situation by deliberately seeking the most incendiary quotes from polarized sides, the newspaper tried something different. . . . Reporters sought thoughtful suggestions from all sides, including people in area neighborhoods, the [black] youths whose behavior was under question, and the white families. . . . These diverse views were presented with respect and authority" (1995, 9). Needless to say, this "consensus" frame raises red flags among mainstream journalists. In part this reaction is based on the belief that people have good reason to be cynical. Reacting to the argument that journalists are the cause of the public's alienation from politics, Paul Greenberg, editorial page editor of the *Arkansas Democrat-Gazette,* responds: "Unlike, say, the presidential campaign just drearily concluded? Or the scare tactics that dominated it? Or the loaded statistics that candidates at all levels threw around, or the wild accusations they made? The reason people are cynical about politicians—skeptical might be a more accurate term—is that they have reason to be."[37] From this perspective, journalists report conflict and bad news because the world is full of conflict and bad news. At worst, journalists are guilty of being "pathological truthtellers," to use Maureen Dowd's phrase.[38] According to Jack Fuller, publisher of the *Chicago Tribune,* "A newspaper that fails to reflect its community deeply will not succeed. But a newspaper that does not challenge its community's values and preconceptions will lose respect."[39]

What is telling in these exchanges is how they reveal the complexities of the normative underpinnings of journalism, the need to simplify these complexities into manageable standard operating procedures, and the internalization of these practices in journalists' worldviews. For public journalists, citizens are capable of knowing their own interests: "There is a certain wisdom that resides within a community . . . that may never come from experts or reporters or official sources or any other people journalists routinely talk to."[40] Further, unlike journalists, citizens are presumed to be more interested in substantive issues than strategic games. And while citizens may have conflicting opinions (both across different issues and across different groups), ultimately these opinions reflect core values and goals that are identifiable and shared. The journalist's job is to frame issues in a way that gives voice to these public concerns, provides information that will assist citizens in better understanding the issues that matter to them, and clarifies where elites and their fellow citizens stand on these issues. Given this goal, traditional beats and standard operating procedures need to be restructured away from centers of elite power, opening up new channels of communication between citizens and the press. While the press should still interact with elites, journalists should come to this exchange as representatives of the public. "If you are a reporter," says Lisa Austin, former research director of the Project on Public Life and the Press, "your whole culture and reward system is tied to the experts on the issues. . . . We're trying to help reporters and editors be the translator between experts and the public" (quoted in D. Brown 1994, 11).

For mainstream journalists, the public interest is best determined through competing elites, since elites are best positioned to know the issues. This competition often reflects deep-seated differences in values, so journalism is about presenting these competing views in as stark a manner as possible. Since the clash of competing values inevitably involves winners and losers, mainstream journalists are "naturally" led to an emphasis on strategy and conflict. At the same time, however, elites are presumed to be less than forthright in their words and actions, so journalists, in their watchdog function, must deconstruct the "real" motives behind these words and actions. The journalist's job is to represent elites to the public, but to do so from a position that is removed from both.

Who Speaks for the Public? Information versus Conversation Frames

As noted earlier, the press is presumed to both provide information about public affairs and be a place where public affairs are deliberated. But who participates in this public deliberation? Not surprisingly, public journalists argue that citizens themselves should be at the heart of this civic conversation. Letting citizens help determine the press's agenda, and then providing information that is relevant to this agenda, begins to bring the public more centrally into the news-gathering process. Public journalists take this a logical step further, however, by not only listening to citizens but also allowing them to more regularly speak for themselves. Cole Campbell describes this as marrying two traditional journalistic practices, investigative reporting and storytelling, with a third, new one: "We came to call the model the three-legged stool: All three legs are needed to keep superior journalism upright. . . . The third [leg]—the new one—is a conversational model. . . . This approach looks at readers as actors—

people who have a stake in the news, who want to see the possibilities behind often-troubling developments, who want to participate in solving shared problems."[41]

Publishing readers' comments is traditionally done in the "Letters to the Editor" section of papers or through listeners' and viewers' comments in the electronic press. In this new approach, however, "journalists . . . should regard readers—and non-readers—as a 'public capable of action.' . . . This process . . . should be achieved not only on the editorial pages but throughout the newspaper."[42] For example, in covering a 1995 congressional debate over funding for the arts, Dennis Royalty, the Arts and Entertainment editor for the *Indianapolis Star,* incorporated the views of congresspersons, artists, and local citizens. Royalty explained this approach to his readers as follows:

A good newspaper should stimulate thought and discussion of important issues. On the editorial pages, or in signed opinion columns, it is appropriate for a writer to take a stand. But not in news coverage. For that reason, we've done our best to cover this story like we would other news stories, as objectively as possible. We've reported how tax dollars for the arts are distributed, and we've written about what federal cuts to the arts and public broadcasting mean in terms of program cuts. But we've also made the decision in this case to go a step further. We're using what is labeled in our business as "public journalism." We decided to make the reader a more active partner in discussing an important issue.[43]

Public journalism articles are often peppered with direct quotes from citizens, sometimes intermixed with views of elites and experts, sometimes in separate articles or columns. In each case, journalists and editors explain this approach—to their own readers and to critics of public journalism—in terms of a new way to approach the traditional goals of journalism: "As I think of it, the traditional conduct of public affairs has meant an apathetic or alienated public versus an isolated elite of public officials, with an aloof professional press more or less lecturing, or preaching, to both of them. The new model has the public and its leadership continuously interacting—talking and listening—with the latter ultimately reflecting the will of the former. Our role as news media (literally 'channels of communications' in the dictionary) is to inform and facilitate discussion. . . . [Public journalism] assumes that some of the best truth, and wisdom, can come from the people, if only they can be brought, or allowed, into the public debate."[44]

Mainstream journalists acknowledge the importance of giving the public a voice but see this voice as generally limited to either the editorial page or to public opinion polls. This view emerges from the elite frame discussed above: "In a gesture to the 'public journalism' movement, which is getting tiresome even as it launches itself, *CNN* kept jumping to its 'heartland' focus group, than whom there have been few more ill-informed bunches, for reaction to convention rhetoric."[45] If the public is viewed as generally ill informed and only modestly interested in public affairs, then how can citizens serve as authoritative sources? The journalist's role is to provide "news and information that will help citizens understand issues,"[46] not to bring them directly into the debate: "Public journalism, as opposed to the real kind, blurs a lot of essential and useful distinctions between news and opinion, and between people and the press."[47] Max Frankel defends this "information frame" in his review of James Fallows's book *Breaking the News:* "By allowing a choice only between *entertain and engage,* Fallows leaves no room for the customary journalistic ambition to *inform and instruct. . . .* The [latter] aims to depict and explain, the [former] to win over—a difference worth preserving."[48]

What Is the Press's Relationship to the Community? Outsider versus Member and Problem-Identification versus Problem-Solving Frames

Perhaps the most controversial aspect of public journalism is its "belief that newspapers and communities succeed or fail together" and thus that the press is part of the community that it covers.[49] This view is succinctly captured in the closing lines of a *Dayton Daily News* editorial on teen violence: "None of *us* has the luxury to sit this one out. The solution must come from *us* all. *We're community.*"[50] While editorials and columns urging citizens to act are not new, public journalism goes a giant step further by not only identifying the press as part of the community but also seeing the press as responsible for facilitating public action. As such, the press has a stake (both economic and civic) in not only identifying problems but helping to solve them. According to Jonathan Krim, an assistant managing editor at the *San Jose Mercury News,* public journalism is "experimenting with a non-traditional role for the media, one that goes beyond simply putting out information to the community. . . . In this role, we also facilitate public discussion and help people get involved in addressing the issues that face them. As a community institution, we think we're uniquely qualified to play such a role in a non-partisan way."[51] From this perspective, traditional journalism "illuminates the problems, [but] ignores the solutions."[52] Public journalism, on the other hand, "encourages journalists to recognize the impact of their work on public life and to adopt as a general concern whether public life goes well. It is . . . concerned with whether communities solve problems, and whether citizens 'get involved.'"[53]

Helping to solve problems and facilitate public action means more than simply listening to the public and giving it a greater voice in the press, though this is part of it. It means changing journalistic practices. In part this involves changes in the way individual stories are written, so that once a problem is identified, potential solutions are also offered: "options for action that are presented in the paper [are] recalibrated around how various options affect what is valuable both pro and con—there would always be more than two options—and each option would have both some attractive and unattractive things about it."[54] It also means sticking with an issue beyond its traditional journalistic life cycle. For very specific problems this means continuing to cover an issue until a solution is reached. For more structural or complex problems (e.g., crime or race relations) it means rethinking standard operating procedures so that the issue becomes a regular part of coverage and doesn't simply reappear in the press when a particularly dramatic event occurs: "In one sense, we are breaking out of the traditional format . . . like putting in new kinds of pages in our paper, new kinds of information pages."[55]

Finally, it means taking an active role in *creating* public debate and action when none exists. Many experiments in public journalism have involved the media in not only covering a story but setting up public forums; bringing community leaders, public officials, and citizens together in face-to-face meetings; and the like. The following call to action is typical of this approach:

> Beginning on January 23, along with the Maine Council of Churches, [the *Maine Sunday Telegram*] will sponsor a program of "Reader Roundtables" over four successive weeks. We hope to gather small groups of readers in informal settings to exchange experiences and ideas on the issue of education in Maine: What should public education accomplish, and what needs to change? . . . *The Telegram* will publish background information and viewpoints to support the roundtables. We also will stay abreast of the discussions and report the opinions of people who participate. . . . Reader Roundtables is an attempt to use the good offices of our newspaper . . . to create public spaces to encourage discussion of an important public endeavor, education, and to help revive the lost art of public discourse. We hope you will join in the conversation.[56]

Similar efforts on a wide range of local and national issues have been made by newspapers and by radio and television stations around the country, often with different media outlets working in cooperation with each other.

Neither the libertarian nor the social responsibility theory *directly* calls on the press to play the role of community leader or problem solver, though it could be argued that the full range of civic responsibilities articulated in those theories implies these roles—much like the Supreme Court found the right to privacy in the penumbras emanating from more directly stated civil liberties. Certainly they are consistent with John Dewey's vision of public life and the press. At the same time, they highlight the tension between the notion of the press as a facilitator of public debate, on one hand, and the notion of the press as an objective presenter of information, on the other. For public journalists, this tension is resolved by seeing themselves as facilitators of the democratic process rather than as partisans for any particular substantive interest or outcome. As such, public journalists distinguish themselves from both the libertarian press, which was avowedly ideological, and the traditional interpretation of a socially responsible press, which is studiously uncommitted.

But traditional journalists see great problems with this approach, again revealing their own worldviews in the process. Some of these critiques draw on practical concerns: "It is more costly and time-consuming to keep close connections with readers."[57] "Newsrooms have limited resources and . . . devoting large amounts of attention and money to big ticket public journalism activities could shortchange (or further shortchange) basic news gathering."[58] Others go further, arguing that public journalism itself is simply a ploy to attract new readers and viewers: "It's sometimes difficult to tell the difference between public journalism, which may be motivated by noble aims, and marketing schemes intended to pander to readers."[59] However, most concerns focus on the fear that becoming problem solvers and actively mobilizing public debate violate the central tenets of journalism—objectivity and neutrality. In turn, this defense of traditional journalism reveals its own "journalist-as-outsider" and "journalist-as–problem identifier" frames: "No matter how strongly I feel about something that's going on out there, my job is not to try to influence the outcome. I just don't want to cross that line, no matter how well-meaning the reasoning may be for crossing it."[60] Or: "We grew up in an age when detachment was the byword for a good reporter. . . . Many journalists feel that our role is to cover and report the news, not set the agenda. . . . Put simply, [public journalists] like to see members of the press remove their self-imposed, artificial constraints and become an active player in this world around us. It's going to take a lot of digesting to embrace this feel-good, service oriented journalism role. The fear is that in the process we might lose some of the fairness and objectivity that we worked so hard to achieve for so many years."[61] Summarizing the views of different journalists, one article provided the following opinions: "'We must stay out of the community power structure if the newspaper is to sustain credibility,' [one journalist] responded. Another more pointed opinion: 'I'm a journalist, damn it, and journalists don't get involved. . . .' [Yet another journalist wrote:] 'It's easy to get accused of boosterism. We don't want to fall into that trap. . . .' 'We don't have to lead the parade to report on the parade,' [said another]" (Albers 1994, 28). And according to an editor of the *Philadelphia Inquirer*, "Traditional rules about the distance and impartiality of reporters from their subjects are a key source of our strength. . . . It is crazy to break those rules, and there is no reason to break these rules."[62]

The ultimate fear is that by attempting to facilitate public discussion and problem solving, journalists unwittingly will become mouthpieces for *particu-*

lar points of view. This can mean pandering to those in government: "In public journalism, the newspaper becomes part of the administration creating propaganda, and no voice remains for those opposing public policy" (Witters 1994, 5). It can mean pandering to the business community: "Readers may think it worthwhile that the *Wilmington News Journal* teamed up with a Chamber of Commerce sponsored think tank to hold a summit on the state's economic problems. But how would you assess the paper's coverage of the chamber and the businesses it represents?"[63] It can mean pandering to liberal elites in the media and journalism schools: "National surveys have indicated a ratio of more than three liberal journalists for every conservative. And among students at Columbia's J-school, prep school to many Big Media elitists, liberals outnumber conservatives 8 to 1. . . . Suppose Public Journalism becomes the New Paradigm? With the objective of settling the outcome, there would be every reason for readers to suspect a deliberate tilt to the left."[64] It can even mean pandering to the foundations that have sponsored many of the experiments in public journalism: "Many critics such as William Woo, former editor of the *St. Louis Post-Dispatch,* believe the press risks its independence and credibility by aligning itself and becoming financially beholden to foundations with a very ideological view of America, a very definite view of the road America should take."[65]

Reframing Journalism

The debate over public journalism reveals several different frames used by traditional journalists: the elite, strategic-game, conflict, information, outsider, and problem-identification frames. While each of these frames has a somewhat different emphasis, one could argue that, taken together, they reflect a single "metaframe." This frame is built upon six underlying but connected beliefs. First, public affairs is about the struggle between competing elites over the allocation of scarce resources. Second, this competition is based on fundamental differences in values and ideologies that necessarily involve winners and losers. Third, what political actors say and do is motivated by a desire to win—often at any cost—but this motivation is hidden. Fourth, citizens are uninformed, disinterested in public affairs, and fickle in their views. Fifth, the role of the journalist is to inform the public about the ongoing struggles between competing elites, revealing the underlying strategies and pointing out who is winning and who is losing, both among elites and within the public. And sixth, the credibility of journalistic reporting depends upon maintaining objectivity, with objectivity defined as the neutral presentation of facts coupled with a balanced portrayal of "both" sides of an issue, told from the perspective of an uninvolved, uncommitted, but somewhat skeptical—even cynical—outsider.

It is important to note that these beliefs are all defensible: much of politics *is* about the allocation of scarce resources by political elites; differences in opinion *are* often rooted in irreconcilable values; political actors are partially motivated by winning and *do* behave strategically; citizens *are* often disinterested, uninformed, and inconsistent; it *is* important for citizens to be kept abreast of the struggles occurring among political decision makers and how their actions affect who gets what; and it *is* necessary for journalists to remain removed enough from the fray so as to report on public affairs in a way that does not privilege some views over others. It is also true that these beliefs, and the frames they produce, allow the press to perform its civic responsibility (inform the public, provide a range of viewpoints, and serve as a watchdog), while still being entertaining and profitable—and to do so in a way that addresses the numerous practical constraints that complicate and constrain the news-gathering process.

This being said, it is also true that framing is by definition a subtle alteration in how choices are presented, and so the domination of any one frame (or set of related frames) necessarily means the subordination of others and thus the influencing of how elites and the public think and act. The frames recommended by public journalists—citizen, issue, consensus, conversation, member, and problem-solving—could also be combined into a metaframe. This frame, too, is based on six related beliefs. First, public affairs is about the formation and expression of the public will and the allocation of public resources (by government and citizens) in a way that is consistent with this public will. Second, this process, while often involving competing opinions and real trade-offs, is based on fundamental values that are often shared and, if not shared, can be understood and respected. Thus, decisions can be reached by consensus rather than by compromise or through clear-cut winners and losers. Third, what political actors say and do depends in part on what journalists and citizens say and do. Given the opportunity and the incentive, political actors are able and willing to address issues in a way that is more substantive, less conflictual, and more clearly tied to the public's agenda. Fourth, citizens, given the opportunity, are capable of reasoned, informed, and fair-minded deliberation about public affairs. Fifth, the role of the journalist is to understand, cultivate, and express the public's voice and to facilitate and illuminate public conversations about timely issues among citizens and elites. And sixth, the credibility of journalistic reporting depends upon the press acting as a member of the community, albeit a member with a special responsibility to help encourage civic life and to facilitate problem solving without advocating particular solutions.

As with the beliefs underlying mainstream frames, these six beliefs are also defensible: politics *is* about responding to the public will; many problems *can* be resolved through consensus; political actors *are* willing and able to address public concerns seriously, civilly, and substantively; citizens *are* capable of reasoned, informed deliberation; journalists *should* understand, facilitate, and express citizens' concerns; and the press *is* a unique member of the community with a responsibility to help maintain its civic, social, and economic vitality. Like mainstream beliefs and their resulting frames, public journalists' beliefs and frames allow the press to perform its civic responsibility (inform the public, provide a range of viewpoints, and serve as a watchdog). There is some debate over whether the press can achieve this while still being entertaining and profitable, and the rethinking of journalistic routines and standard operating procedures required by public journalism has consciously complicated the way in which practical constraints should best be addressed. Still, there is little reason to think that public journalism cannot combine its normative emphases with a style and routines that can be at least as entertaining, profitable, and manageable as those of traditional reporting.

The juxtaposition of these two metaframes makes clear that: (1) the norms of mainstream journalism shape the way in which news is presented and do so from a particular perspective; (2) there are alternative ways to frame the news that are consistent with the overarching goals of journalism; and (3) *any single* approach to news gathering and reporting necessarily involves choices that inevitably affect how issues are framed for the public. These points are dramatized by examining the way in which the debate over public journalism was framed in the mainstream press.

Tellingly, this framing occasionally took on characteristics of public journalism. For example, one could find elements of public journalism's "consensus" frame, with mainstream journalists acknowledging that they inevitably make choices, that these choices have shortcomings, and that the goals of public journalism are worthwhile and consistent with the underlying purpose of journalism writ large. In addition, mainstream journalists sometimes directly involved citizens in the debate, addressing readers directly in their columns, quoting the views of citizens regarding the debate, and so on. At times these efforts were clearly aimed at finding common ground and treating views with which they disagreed with respect and fairness. For example, one *New York Times* article was simply an interview with Jay Rosen, allowing him to state his views extensively and without editorial comment.[66] At other times, however, this "agreement" was framed in ways clearly designed to discount public journalism. For example, it was often the case that critics of this movement would expropriate certain elements of public journalism, arguing that it really "isn't anything new" and that "some of it sounds like what the better papers have been doing for years."[67]

Despite examples of public journalism frames, more traditional frames clearly dominated the pages of the mainstream press. For example, traditional journalists often drew on the "conflict" and "problem-identification" frames, writing stories that highlighted areas of disagreement and particularly controversial public journalism experiments and using quotes from both sides that dramatized this conflict—what Jay Rosen (1999) has described as "doing journalism to public journalism." These frames can be seen in the titles of many of these articles and columns: "Public Journalism: Seeing through the Gimmicks"; "Does National Public Radio Feel Pressure When Foundation Donors Specify Topics?"; "Public Journalism Pushes Elitist Agenda"; "Gannettization of the News: Boosterism Runs Rampant"; "Pitfalls of Public Journalism"; "Public Journalism: Bad News"; "We Regret to Report That Civic Journalism Is a Bad Idea."[68]

Mainstream framing of public journalism can also be seen in the way some critics defined public journalism: "A philosophy that holds that newspapers not only have a duty to report and comment on events but to actively shape them."[69] "The idea of [public journalism] is that journalists and civic officials are to become partners. . . . Then the partners put their heads together to decide what news would be in the best interest of the peasantry to report."[70] "The guiding principle of 'civic journalism' is that the public, through polls and 'focus groups' usually financed by the foundations, should play an important role in setting the news and editorial agendas of the press."[71] "Public journalism is what newspapers that have forgotten their readers are latching onto to win them back."[72] "There are many definitions of public journalism, but it boils down to having the press push a political agenda."[73] "The idea is to employ focus groups and let readers say what to read, sort of like going to a dentist who will let you decide which tooth to pull or which root needs a new canal."[74] "Public journalism . . . seeks to make liberal bias in reporting Standard Operating Procedure."[75] "An attempt to increase the power of a journalistic upper class to dictate what are and are not fit subjects for public debate."[76] "Wherein stories are written and segments aired promoting what is deemed by the media to be for the public good."[77] "Where reader committees decide what goes into the paper and advocacy replaces objectivity."[78]

Mainstream journalists and columnists also framed the debate by their choice of descriptive language. Most common was describing the movement and its principal advocates in religious terms. Public journalism "is a kind of new age cult or rather, an old fashioned religion . . . which spawns a hierarchy equivalent to archbishops and bishops among editors and in the ranks, preachers, evangelists, elders, and deacons."[79] It "seeks to convert the media from dispensers of salacious gossip into something more Good Samaritan–like."[80]

"Salvation, the theory goes, lies in public journalism."[81] One article, entitled "The Gospel of Public Journalism," used the religious theme throughout, describing Rosen and Merritt as "preachers," calling the movement "the hottest new secular religion in the news business," and describing supporters as "believers" and opponents as "agnostics" who are harder to "convert."[82] Rosen has also been frequently described as "the guru" of public journalism and as a "crusader."

It was also common to describe public journalism (and thus to frame the debate) in condescending terms. Public journalism was frequently described as "a fad," "a hot new trend," "a gimmick," "a largely discredited, yet 'hot' movement." The debate was further framed by distinguishing journalists-practitioners from academics-outsiders. Public journalism is "a mostly academic-favored movement."[83] It is the brainchild of "foundations" and "elite universities."[84] "Now, along come these professors—and editors who need to be, so they won't be messing up any actual newsrooms—advising us to tear down every safeguard that has been laboriously built up over the years."[85] Many of these attacks were aimed specifically at Rosen: "Rosen is a heavy hitter in the world of academic journalism, a made-man in the world of foundation money. . . . But while passionate about journalism, he seems quite uninterested in news."[86] In one ultimately positive column on public journalism, Rosen is described as "the inkless professor, this ivory-towered intellectual who dares suggest that political journalists rethink their relationship with their readers."[87]

What would a close reader of the public journalism debate as framed in the mainstream press come away with? Clearly these stories include a wealth of facts and opinions, allowing a reader to get a general sense of the issue and enabling him or her to come to some judgment on the strengths and weaknesses of this new approach. But taken as whole, these articles, columns, and editorials hew closely to the frames of mainstream journalism explored in this chapter, leading to subtle (and sometimes not so subtle) alterations in the way in which the "choice" between mainstream and public journalism is presented. The conclusion reached by our reader, I would argue, would not be unlike those that emerge from reading other mainstream articles and columns devoted to public affairs: that there is a problem brewing; that the issue involves a conflict among competing elites; that while many public journalists may be well-intentioned, editors, owners, academics, foundations, and political actors are mainly motivated by strategic desires to sell more papers or shape the political agenda to their benefit; that there will be clear winners and losers in this debate; that the outcome of this conflict will affect citizens, but this outcome is outside of citizens' control. If the coverage deviated consistently from the

tenets of mainstream journalism, it was in its willingness to advocate for a solution—to return to the tenets of mainstream journalism.

Of course a reader who only read *public* journalists' account of the debate
would be just as influenced by the way in which this account was framed. My
point is not to suggest that either public or mainstream journalists have got it
right—each side raises legitimate concerns about the potential shortcomings of
the other's practices. Rather it is to suggest that the professionalization of journalism in the first half of this century, while producing a number of important
reforms and behavioral guidelines, does not and cannot lead to a single set of
standard operating procedures that assure reaching the normative goals to
which the press aspires. Journalism is by definition framing, in that it necessarily involves decisions that produce subtle alterations in the statement or presentation of judgment and choice problems. In *explicitly* acknowledging this
(and in forcing mainstream journalists to examine their own frames) public
journalists make the question of how best to frame the news, given the competing normative, practical, and institutional constraints under which the press
operates, a frame of its own. In essence, public journalists have reframed the
journalistic process, making fundamental questions—"What issues should we
be covering?" "From whose perspective(s) should a story be written?" "What
are the underlying areas of agreement and disagreement?" "Is the information
we are providing useful to citizens?" "How might we facilitate public deliberation and problem solving?"—part of their normal routines. By regularly re-
visiting these issues, public journalists complicate their craft but do so in ways
that keep the incontrovertible fact that they are constantly framing the news in
the foreground. This may be the single most important contribution of public
journalism and its greatest challenge to traditional journalists.[88]

2
Campaign Frames
Can Candidates Influence Media Coverage?

Kim L. Fridkin and Patrick J. Kenney

In 1992, the nation was in the midst of a recession. Candidates for the presidency, the House of Representatives, and the U.S. Senate were talking about the economy. In addition, media coverage of the economy had spilled off the business pages and onto the front pages. Without question, in the fall of 1992, the principal agenda item for candidates and the media was the ailing economy.

However, different candidates discussed the economy in different ways. Challengers were interested in blaming incumbents for the economic woes. They suggested, for example, that a failure to balance the budget had put in motion an inevitable economic slide, that high taxes choked investment and spending, that invasive government regulation was stifling the creative energies of industry, and that not enough money was being put toward education to stimulate research and development in order to keep the nation on par with its worldwide competitors.

Incumbents found it difficult to shy away from discussing the economy. However, they were interested in pushing the discussion in a different direction. They contended, for example, that although the recession was relatively long, it was not deep; that it was a worldwide recession and the U.S. economy was starting to lead other nations out of the economic doldrums; that the nationwide economy was healthy—there were simply "pockets" where the economy was weak—for example, California; that interest rates were as low as they had been in twenty-five years; and that the number of "quality" jobs was growing. In addition, incumbents attempted to focus the discussion on policies that they had enacted while in office that created jobs, retrained displaced workers, and extended unemployment benefits.

All of these discussions were efforts by candidates to "frame" the economic story to reflect favorably on their own candidacies. As Kinder and Sanders (1990, 74) explain, frames are "devices embedded in political discourse, invented and employed by political elites, often with an eye on advancing their own interests or ideologies, and intended to make favorable interpretations prevail." In this chapter, the "political elites" we are interested in examining are candidates for the U.S. Senate. The "devices" that they use to shape "political discourse" are the frames "embedded" in their campaign messages. Candidates hope to make "favorable interpretations prevail," ultimately on potential voters but initially on the media.

How issues are framed is important because frames affect how people define, discuss, interpret, and come to understand a topic (Kinder and Sanders 1996; Gamson 1992; Gamson and Modigliani 1987, 1989; Tversky and Kahneman 1981; Iyengar 1991). Most scholars agree that there is a direct connection between how an issue is framed and the nature of public opinion. Frames affect the salience of an issue, how an issue is evaluated, and often serve to crystallize support for or opposition to an issue.

Thus, elites struggle to "win the framing debate." For example, during the 1960s, some political leaders framed the burning of predominantly black neighborhoods as the only means to end the poverty brought on by two centuries of racial discrimination, while other leaders called the rioting a destructive act of malice without virtue. Similarly, the nightly reports of Americans killed in Vietnam were often couched by the Johnson and Nixon administrations as the only way to stop the spread of communism, whereas antiwar protesters described the conflict as a wasteful sacrifice of American youth in an unjust war.

Thirty years later, the battle over the framing of the race issue rages on (Kinder and Sanders 1996), but Vietnam has been replaced with other daunting issues, each controversial, all emotional and open to unique frames by groups with differing viewpoints and agendas. Examples include issues such as abortion, AIDS, terrorism, and the death penalty. A common thread across issues and time, however, is that elites need to enlist the help of the news media in order to win the framing debate.

Candidates seeking office during political campaigns attempt to frame issues in order to generate favorable impressions with voters. However, for candidates to effectively influence public opinion, they must influence how the news media frame issues. Most Americans receive the vast majority of their campaign information from the mass media (Graber 1993), and citizens believe the news media's messages are more trustworthy than the messages disseminated by campaigns (Joslyn 1984). Inevitably, then, candidates try to convince the news media to adopt their preferred frames. As Kinder and Sanders (1996, 163) explain, when the press report the frames endorsed by elites, they "necessarily . . . privilege some definitions at the expense of others."

An example of a privileged frame can be found in the 1992 senatorial campaign in New Hampshire. The two rivals struggled to frame the discussion of the economy in ways that complimented their own candidacy. Governor Judd Gregg was running for the U.S. Senate against businessman John Rauh. During Gregg's four years as governor, the unemployment rate in New Hampshire had tripled and the state had lost seventy thousand jobs (Congressional Quarterly 1992, 3,348). Rauh framed the economic story as a failure of Gregg's governorship, blaming the governor for the state's economic woes. Gregg, on the other hand, framed the story as one where a hard-working and earnest governor had taken numerous steps to improve the failing economy.

In the largest-circulating paper in the state, the *Union Leader,* Gregg won the framing contest. Not a single article published during the senatorial campaign held the governor responsible for the struggling economy. In contrast, Gregg's efforts to assist ailing industries and balance the state's budget were displayed prominently in the Manchester paper. For example, on October 2, a headline stressed Gregg's ability to manage the state's budget even in tough economic times: "Gregg, State Officials Agree NH Has Surplus." Again on October 4: "Fact: State Revenues Exceeding Forecast." The *Union Leader* also applauded Gregg's efforts at generating jobs in an article on October 28, proclaiming, "A $25 million bond for the state's Business Finance Agency to aid businesses statewide and a $500,000 agreement clearing the way for new jobs in Keene were approved yesterday by Gov. Judd Gregg and the Executive Council." And, finally, a headline on November 1 indicated an improving economy: "October State Revenues Expected to Top Estimates."

The *Union Leader,* in covering the Senate race, echoed Gregg's chosen frame, while ignoring the alternative frame trumpeted by Rauh. How often does the news media respond to candidates' frames? Which types of candidates are most successful in framing news coverage? Does the ability to effectively frame coverage vary by topic? In this chapter, we seek to answer these questions. We explore the connection between the candidates' frames and the news media's coverage since the frame embraced by the news media is likely to influence voters' understanding of the issue as well as their evaluations of the competing candidates.

Can Candidates Frame News Coverage?

To understand whether candidates can successfully frame the media coverage of their campaigns, it is necessary to review how media organizations report the news. Current theories explaining the operational norms of news organizations and knowledge about the professional habits guiding the behavior of reporters and editors suggest that the actions and rhetoric of candidates often influence news coverage of campaigns.

When a political campaign is deemed newsworthy, editors assign reporters to cover the campaign. Once reporters are on the campaign trail, they rely primarily on routine sources to gather news about the political contestants (Bennett 1996; Clarke and Evans 1983; Cook 1996; Sigal 1973). For example, press releases distributed by campaigns, political advertisements aired on television and radio, news conferences, and speeches are likely to influence the frequency and content of news coverage. Local reporters often shun more enterprising efforts like initiating interviews with the candidates, engaging in library research to explore candidates' backgrounds, or conducting investigative reports (Clarke and Evans 1983). Given journalists' preference for routine sources of news, the behavior of the candidates can have a significant influence on the nature of campaign coverage. In particular, journalists may react to the candidates' actions by adopting their frames when writing stories about the campaign.

Although candidates' behavior on the campaign trail can influence press patterns, it is important to draw distinctions between how the media cover incumbents compared to challengers. The standard expectation is that the professional norms of news making, as well as organizational routines, lead newspapers to pay more attention to the messages disseminated by incumbents, compared to challengers (Clarke and Evans 1983). The underlying reason for the incumbency advantage is simply availability of information. For instance, because incumbents have more resources than challengers, they will have an easier time producing news. The perquisites of the office of U.S. senator (e.g., the availability of broadcast recording studios, an office staff capable of routinely writing and distributing press releases) make it easier for incumbents to publicize their desired message.

In addition, traditional standards of news production require authoritative figures as sources. To be sure, senators are clearly more authoritative than challengers (Cook 1989). Furthermore, reporters may be likely to represent senators' messages more faithfully as a way of maintaining their relationship with these important official sources. Graber (1997, 103) explains that "politicians and other powerful elites flood the media with self-serving materials that are often hard to resist. Intensive, frequent contacts and the desire to keep associations cordial may lead to cozy relationships, which make critical detachment unlikely. The ability to woo reporters and elicit favorable media coverage is the mark of the astute politician. Reporters can rarely resist the blandishment of politicians for fear of alienating powerful and important news sources." Given reporters' dependence on senators as sources of news, they may mirror the senators' choice of frames when covering their reelection campaigns.

Even though the hypothesis that incumbents have an easier time shaping the frames embedded in media coverage has intuitive appeal, we have demonstrated in an earlier study that challengers are sometimes *more* successful than incumbents at setting the news media's agenda in U.S. Senate races (Kahn and Kenney 1999; chap. 6, this volume). Specifically, when challengers discuss certain topics in their campaigns, the news media respond by covering these topics in more detail. Incumbents, in contrast, are less effective in shaping the content of their coverage. Press coverage of incumbents does not depend upon the senators' choices of campaign messages.

Challengers are able to shape the news media's agenda because they are not well-known political figures. Many challengers have never held public office and therefore do not have records that can be scrutinized by the press (Clarke and Evans 1983). Even challengers with elective experience do not enjoy the same level of prominence as sitting senators. Since reporters are likely to be unfamiliar with the challengers' records and accomplishments, they turn to the candidates directly for campaign information.

Reporters' dependence on challengers for information, at least in terms of agenda-setting, increases the correspondence between the challengers' choice of themes and the content of reporters' stories. A similar phenomenon may occur for the framing of the candidates' coverage. For example, if a challenger decides to frame discussion of the economy by talking about the politics of the budget deficit, reporters may mirror this emphasis. The challenger's view on the budget deficit will be clearly articulated in the candidate's speeches and political commercials. Journalists will not need to conduct extensive research to identify the challenger's positions. However, if a reporter decides to frame economic coverage in an alternative way—say, by emphasizing unemployment—the reporter may need to expend considerable effort to identify the challenger's views on unemployment.

In the end, then, we have reasons to expect that both incumbents and challengers will be able to frame campaign coverage. These reasons are derived from the norms and practical considerations driving how reporters and editors do their job. Faced with deadlines and dynamic story lines, reporters covering U.S. Senate campaigns turn to accessible and reliable sources for stories concerning candidates' policy discussions. In the case of incumbents, information is readily produced by a well-organized propaganda machine and given directly to reporters and editors. As for challengers, in many cases, information is only available from the candidate's campaign. Reporters hungry for stories, then, turn directly to the challengers for information on policy matters.

Establishing a Research Design

To see whether candidates are able to frame news coverage of their campaigns, we developed a research design where we examined the messages presented by the candidates and the messages produced by the news media. By analyzing both the content of the candidates' communications and the news media's coverage of the candidates' campaigns, we can determine whether candidates are successful at framing campaign coverage. We examine candidates running for the U.S. Senate between 1988 and 1992.[1]

Senate elections present an optimal setting for the study of framing in campaigns because they provide impressive variance in campaign messages, alternative frames, campaign spending, competitiveness, and media coverage (Franklin 1991; Westlye 1991). Unlike House races, which are usually low-key affairs with minimal campaign coverage, and presidential races, which are often hard-fought contests saturated with extensive coverage, campaigns for the U.S. Senate vary considerably in the content and amount of media coverage.

Measuring the Frames Advanced by Candidates

To measure the content of candidates' messages, we conducted a content analysis of their political advertisements.[2] We examined televised political advertisements since these commercials are a central component of U.S. Senate campaigns. Herrnson (1995) reports that over 90 percent of Senate campaigns employed television advertising in 1992. Ansolabehere, Behr, and Iyengar (1993) explain that television advertising represents the biggest single expenditure by Senate candidates, with campaigns allocating more than one-third of their budgets for political advertising.

We relied on the Political Commercial Archive at the University of Oklahoma to obtain our sample of political commercials. The archive has the largest collection of U.S. Senate advertisements publicly available for the 1988–92 Senate races. The archive has 1,380 commercials for 161 of the 194 candidates. There are two reasons why the archive does not have ads for some candidates: either the archive was unable to acquire ads from a candidate's campaign or from other sources (e.g., local television stations, private collectors) or the candidate did not produce ads because of lack of resources. For example, there were no ads in the archive for Maria M. Hustace during her 1988 campaign against Senator "Spark" Matsunaga of Hawaii. However, it is unlikely that Hustace ran ads since she was grossly underfunded during her campaign. According to the *Congressional Quarterly*, while Matsunaga had over $600,000 on hand in October of 1988, Hustace had only $865 on hand and was $10,000 in debt.

The number of advertisements available for the candidates varied widely since some candidates produced considerably more ads than other candidates. For example, the archive had more than thirty ads aired by Republican Conrad Burns during his competitive bid against Montana senator John Melcher in 1988. In contrast, for the same year, the archive had only one ad for unknown candidate Jasper "Jack" Wyman of Maine. Since we wanted to maximize the number of candidates represented in our political-advertisement sample, we stratified the sample by candidate and randomly selected four advertisements (if available) for each of the candidates running for the U.S. Senate in 1988, 1990, and 1992.

Our sample includes 594 ads for 161 candidates, representing 84 percent of the candidates in the population. We obtained 266 advertisements for 70 of the 80 incumbents seeking reelection and 209 advertisements for 58 of the 80 challengers. We sampled 119 advertisements for 33 of the 34 candidates seeking to fill open seats. The sample included 364 ads from GOP candidates and 230 from Democratic candidates. Finally, of the 594 ads, 33 percent aired in 1988, 32 percent appeared in 1990, and 35 percent aired in 1992.[3]

In our content analysis, we looked at several different aspects of the tone and tenor of the candidates' commercials. First, we examined how often the candidates presented their positions on issues in their advertisements. Second, we looked at how often the candidates claimed credit for positive policy outcomes in their commercials. Third, we looked at the candidates' preferred framing of economic issues. For example, when candidates talk about the economy in their advertisements, do they discuss the budget, taxes, and jobs, or do they prefer to talk in general terms about the economy?[4] Fourth, we examined how often candidates used negative frames in their campaign commercials. In particular, we looked at the number of times candidates criticized their opponents' positions on issues, we investigated the number of times candidates pointed out weaknesses in their opponents' personal characteristics, and we examined the number of times candidates blamed their opponents for unpopular policy outcomes.

Measuring the News Media's Coverage of the Campaign

To examine the connection between how candidates frame their messages and the news media's treatment of campaigns, we conducted a content analysis of the largest-circulating newspaper in each state holding a senatorial election. More potential voters read these newspapers than smaller papers. In addition, small newspapers across the state routinely rely on wire services to "pick up" news stories about local campaigns that have been published by the larger daily papers. Therefore, people around the state read similar stories about the ongoing campaign. For example, in Minnesota, nearly identical stories about a campaign would typically appear in newspapers in the Twin Cities, Duluth, St. Cloud, Rochester, and Moorehead.[5]

Newspapers, instead of television news, were chosen to represent news coverage for substantive and practical reasons. Among the substantive reasons, studies demonstrate that newspapers allocate more resources and more space to their coverage of statewide campaigns, compared with television, thereby producing more comprehensive coverage (Leary 1977). Westlye (1991, 45) finds that, compared with local broadcast news, "newspapers present an amount of information that more closely approximates what campaigns are issuing." In addition, while people rely heavily on television news to keep informed about national politics, they depend on local newspapers for coverage of senatorial and gubernatorial campaigns (Mayer 1993). Similarly, statewide campaign officials consider newspapers more effective than local television news for communicating with potential voters (Graber 1993). People also learn more about statewide campaigns from newspapers than from local news broadcasts (Clarke and Fredin 1978).

Practical considerations also influenced our decision to examine newspapers. Newspapers are routinely saved on microfilm, making them easily accessible for analysis. Tapes of local television news, in contrast, are seldom available after a campaign, making a systematic examination of television news more difficult.

News coverage was examined from October 1 through election day. We examined all articles that mentioned either candidate in the first section, the state section, or the editorial section of the newspaper. We did not restrict our analysis to campaign-related stories since citizens often acquire information about candidates in stories that are not directly related to the ongoing campaign (e.g., stories detailing a senator's work on legislation relevant to the state). In total, 6,925 articles were coded: 2,105 articles for races conducted in 1988; 2,400 articles for the 1990 campaigns; and 2,420 articles for elections contested in 1992.

In conducting the content analysis of media coverage, we were careful to match the content analysis of the newspapers with the content analysis of the candidates' commercials whenever possible. Specifically, we examined the amount of paragraphs devoted to issues in the candidates' coverage and the number of times the candidates' issue positions were discussed in the newspaper. We also recorded the number of times the press credited the candidates with favorable policy outcomes. And we sorted out the number of paragraphs dedicated to various economic frames.[6] Finally, we examined the number of press criticisms published about the candidates during the campaign. By comparing the candidates' campaign messages with news treatment of the candidates' messages, we can investigate whether candidates are successful in influencing the news media's framing of the campaign.[7]

The Results

In this chapter, we look at four distinct frames used by candidates during their campaigns. First, we look at whether candidates are more successful at generating policy coverage when they take clear positions on issues. Second, we examine whether candidates encourage more policy coverage when they claim credit for favorable policy outcomes. Third, we look at whether the choice of specific issues—here we focus on economic messages—produces more coverage for the candidates. Finally, we examine whether the candidates' use of negative frames encourages critical coverage of their opponents.

Position-Taking as a Frame

During Senate campaigns, candidates often focus on issues. In a recent survey of Senate campaign managers, 73 percent mentioned issues as a main theme of their campaign and almost half (46 percent) mentioned an issue first, suggesting the centrality of issues (Kahn and Kenney 1999).

When candidates decide to focus on issues, they have a variety of frames at their disposal. One frame requires candidates to provide potential supporters with concrete information about their stands on important policy matters by emphasizing their issue positions. We found that 53 percent of the candidates' advertisements provided some details about their positions on issues. For example, Bruce Herschensohn of California spent a great deal of time articulating his stands on a number of issues during his campaign against Representative Barbara Boxer in 1992. In his political advertisements, Herschensohn told voters he opposed any cuts in the defense budget, favored a flat income tax, supported offshore oil drilling, and opposed massive federal disaster relief. Such a litany of position-taking goes well beyond identifying policy priorities and offers citizens important cues about the candidate's likely behavior if elected to the U.S. Senate.

Candidates may take clear positions on policy when they care a great deal about the particular issue. Candidates are also likely to publicize a specific policy stand when their stated position is a popular one. Irrespective of the motivation, candidates articulate their positions on issues hoping to generate attention for these issues in the news. In this section, we look at whether candidates can produce more coverage of issues when they emphasize a "positional" frame in their campaigns.

Before drawing conclusions about the effect of a positional frame on coverage, we need to consider additional forces that may also affect press reports. First, the closeness of the race may influence the amount of news attention given to the candidates' issue stands since competitive races generate significantly more coverage than noncompetitive contests (Clarke and Evans 1983; Goldenberg and Traugott 1984; Kahn 1991; Kahn and Kenney 1999). In addition, when candidates are campaigning actively by spending a great deal of money, coverage of their messages may increase (Kahn and Kenney 1999), along with specific coverage of their policy positions.[8] Finally, the presence of competing news events may influence patterns of news coverage. In particular, concurrent elections, such as presidential or gubernatorial campaigns, may limit the amount of space available for stories about Senate contestants (Kahn 1991), thereby depressing the number of Senate stories discussing the candidates' positions on issues.

The findings presented in table 2.1 test the connection between candidates' decisions to articulate clear positions on issues and the news media's coverage of issues.[9] The data in table 2.1 suggest that the positional frame influences coverage patterns, but only for incumbents.[10] When we look at the total amount of coverage about issues (i.e., table 2.1), we find that incumbents who stress their positions on issues receive significantly more issue coverage than incumbents who fail to take stands on specific policy proposals.[11] In particular, incumbents who articulate their positions in their advertisements receive, on average, thirty-three more paragraphs discussing their views on issues, compared to other incumbents.

For challengers, the positional frame does not reach statistical significance, as indicated by the insignificant unstandardized coefficient. In fact, the two measures in the model associated with the challengers' activities (i.e., the positional frame and challenger spending) fail to influence the amount of issue coverage. Instead, press attention to the challengers' issue priorities is influenced solely by the closeness of the race and by the presence of concurrent campaigns. While the competitive nature of the contest and concurrent campaigns are also important for incumbent coverage, the incumbent can alter press patterns by adopting the positional frame and by spending more money.

When we look at the relationship between the positional frame and the amount of coverage devoted to the candidates' positions on issues, we find a similar pattern.[12] Incumbents who emphasize their stands on policy in their advertisements receive more attention for their positions. Relying on the unstandardized coefficients in table 2.1 to calculate point estimates, we find that incumbents who employ the positional frame can expect about twenty-four paragraphs devoted to their issue positions, while the remaining incumbents receive, on average, about fifteen paragraphs presenting their stands on policy.[13]

2.1 The impact of candidates' positional frames on news coverage

Amount of coverage devoted to issues[a]

	Incumbent/open winner		Challenger/open loser	
	Unstandardized coefficient (standard error)	Beta	Unstandardized coefficient (standard error)	Beta
Positional frame[b]	32.90 (18.10)**	.16	10.70 (14.60)	.06
Candidate spending[c]	9.20 (4.40)**	.17	−3.10 (3.70)	−.06
Competition[d]	−2.90 (.52)***	−.48	−3.00 (.43)***	−.59
Gubernatorial campaign[e]	−67.80 (18.90)***	−.33	−45.40 (15.50)***	−.26
Presidential campaign[f]	−68.60 (20.40)***	−.32	−32.00 (16.60)	−.17
Constant	164.70 (32.00)***		193.20 (24.70)***	
R^2	.42		.42	
N	96		96	

Amount of coverage devoted to candidates' issue positions[g]

	Incumbent/open winner		Challenger/open loser	
	Unstandardized coefficient (standard error)	Beta	Unstandardized coefficient (standard error)	Beta
Positional frame	8.40 (4.40)**	.17	3.30 (3.80)	.08
Candidate spending	2.00 (1.10)*	.16	−.12 (.97)	−.01
Competition	− .52 (.12)***	−.37	−.68 (.11)***	−.55
Gubernatorial campaign	−15.5 (4.60)***	−.33	−7.90 (4.00)*	−.19
Presidential campaign	−19.80 (4.90)***	−.39	−7.90 (4.30)*	−.18
Constant	164.70 (32.00)***		193.20 (24.70)***	
R^2	.35		.35	
N	96		96	

Note: All *p*-values are two-tailed except in the following cases, where our expectations are clearly directional: positional frame and competition.

    *p < .10,   **p < .05,   ***p < .01

    a. The dependent variable in the first half of the table is the number of paragraphs about issues.
    b. Positional frame is a binary variable where 1 = candidate articulated specific positions on issues, 0 = otherwise.
    c. Candidate spending is logged to base 10.
    d. Competition is an interval measure ranging from 0 to 72.
    e. Gubernatorial campaign is a binary variable where 1 = concurrent gubernatorial campaign, 0 = otherwise.
    f. Presidential campaign is a binary variable where 1 = presidential year, 0 = otherwise.
    g. The dependent variable in the second half of the table is the number of paragraphs about candidates' positions on issues.

For challengers, the positional frame is once again ineffective. When challengers stress their stands on issues, they do not convince the press to devote more space to these positions. In addition, challengers who spend more money campaigning do not command more press coverage for their positions. Instead, the competitive nature of the contest and the presence of a presidential and gubernatorial campaign are more important for explaining the amount of news space devoted to challengers' stands on issues.

Claiming Responsibility as a Frame

Although position-taking is a common strategy among candidates, such a frame does carry some risks. By offering a clear stand on an issue, candidates may alienate potential supporters who do not share the same position. Instead of articulating specific views on policy, candidates often choose a less controversial strategy. Candidates often use a "credit" frame where they contend that they are responsible for a favorable policy outcome. In our sample of ads, candidates used the credit frame 27 percent of the time.

The press may be responsive to this frame because these messages demonstrate how constituents may be affected by candidates' actions. For example, instead of talking in abstract terms about the economy, a candidate may illustrate how a particular economic policy generated thousands of new jobs in the state. Because the frame may increase the public's interest in the campaign, reporters may be willing to echo the candidates' messages in their campaign stories.

We examined the link between the credit frame and news coverage by looking at whether the amount of press attention devoted to the positive consequences of policy initiatives varied with candidates' reliance on this frame. The findings presented in table 2.2 represent the relationship between candidates' claims of credit and the news media's coverage. When incumbents claim credit for an issue (e.g., national test scores are up because of the implementation of my educational reform package), the news media responds by publicly praising the incumbent.[14] This difference, while not dramatic, is statistically significant.[15] For challengers, in contrast, the use of the credit frame does not influence coverage. Regardless of challengers' choice of frames, newspapers spend little time crediting challengers with popular policy outcomes.

In addition to candidates' frames, the presence of competing campaigns and the type of race influence the number of paragraphs praising candidates for favorable policy outcomes. For both incumbents and challengers, concurrent presidential and gubernatorial campaigns reduce the number of paragraphs linking candidates with the positive consequences of specific policies. For example, incumbents can expect to receive, on average, six fewer paragraphs praising the consequences of their legislative efforts when they run for reelection during a presidential year.

Testing the Economic Frame

When candidates run for the U.S. Senate, they often focus their campaign messages on the economy. In fact, in the contested senatorial races between 1988 and 1992, 30 percent of candidates produced advertisements that ad-

2.2 The impact of candidates' credit frames on news coverage

	Incumbent/open winner		Challenger/open loser	
	Unstandardized coefficient (standard error)	Beta	Unstandardized coefficient (standard error)	Beta
Credit frame[a]	1.30 (.80)*	.16	1.30 (1.40)	.09
Candidate spending[b]	.41 (.49)	.08	.27 (.47)	.06
Competition[c]	−.04 (.06)	−.07	−.05 (.05)	−.10
Gubernatorial campaign[d]	−5.00 (2.10)**	−.27	−2.70 (2.00)	−.14
Presidential campaign[e]	−5.80 (2.30)**	−.29	−3.70 (2.10)*	−.19
Open race[f]	5.30 (2.60)**	.22	8.40 (2.40)***	.36
Constant	4.10 (3.40)		2.20 (3.10)	
R^2	.14		.17	
N	96		96	

Note: The dependent variable is the number of paragraphs giving the candidate credit for a favorable policy outcome.
  Note: All *p*-values are two-tailed except in the following cases, where our expectations are clearly directional: credit frame and competition.
  *$p < .10$,   **$p < .05$,   ***$p < .01$
  a. Credit frame is a binary variable where 1 = candidate took credit for a favorable policy outcome, 0 = otherwise.
  b. Candidate spending is logged to base 10.
  c. Competition is an interval measure ranging from 0 to 72.
  d. Gubernatorial campaign is a binary variable where 1 = concurrent gubernatorial campaign, 0 = otherwise.
  e. Presidential campaign is a binary variable where 1 = presidential year, 0 = otherwise.
  f. Open race is a binary variable where 1 = open race, 0 = incumbent race.

dressed the economy. And during the 1992 recession 47 percent of senatorial candidates discussed the economy in their commercials. Candidates adopt certain types of economic frames to entice specific media coverage of the economy.

An examination of candidates' commercials reveals that candidates frame economic messages in several distinct ways. Some discuss the economy in general terms. For example, candidates often assert that the economy is "healthy" or "struggling," whatever the case may be. Candidates using this frame sometimes present overall measures of economic health, such as trends in Gross National Product (GNP) figures. Other candidates frame their economic discussion around jobs and unemployment, depending on recent governmental figures concerning job creation, unemployment rates, and requests for unemployment compensation. This was a typical strategy of many challengers in 1992.[16] Some candidates choose to focus on the budget deficit. Reacting to all-time record federal deficits in the mid-1980s, candidates of both parties stressed that the deficit was too large and that Congress needed to ultimately bring the deficit "back into line" with revenues. Other candidates link lower taxes to a healthy economy. Candidates typically argue that the economy grows when ordinary people have more money to spend and when rich people have more money to invest. Finally, many candidates combine several frames into one economic message. For example, during the recession of 1992, candidates argued that the creation of new jobs would come more quickly if taxes were low and the budget deficit was reduced. In summary, candidates spent millions of dollars framing their economic messages in various ways between 1988 and 1992. And indeed, the media spent a great deal of time writing stories about the economy during these campaigns. We now examine which of these frames were more likely to generate coverage in the media.

The advertising data allow us to determine which frames were employed by the candidates, while the content analyses of newspapers tell us which frames generated the most coverage.[17] In table 2.3 we present candidates' efforts to generate media coverage of the economy with the four different frames.

Turning first to an examination of the incumbent model, only one of the coefficients representing economic frames, that is, jobs, is statistically significant. Substantively, when incumbents frame the economy in terms of jobs, there is an average increase of twelve paragraphs printed by the media about economic matters. These findings suggest that incumbents are not able to easily frame media coverage of the economy, irrespective of how they present economic issues.

In addition, the remaining findings in the incumbent model indicate that as campaigns become more competitive, the press reacts by producing more coverage linking the incumbent to the economy, irrespective of the specific frame. Incumbents are also able to generate more coverage by spending more money. And finally, election-specific forces, such as competing gubernatorial and presidential campaigns, drain coverage away from senatorial elections.

The story changes for challengers. While incumbents seem to generate coverage on jobs, challengers are able to cajole the press to focus on the budget deficit. Beyond this one frame, however, challengers cannot produce more coverage of the economy, not even by spending more money. These findings suggest that challengers are not able to easily generate media coverage by their own actions. They must wait for the press to respond to other forces, such as the competitive nature of the campaign.

Before leaving the analysis of economic frames, we perform one additional test. It is not uncommon for candidates to attempt more than one frame in order to generate coverage.[18] In table 2.4, we examine whether a more detailed package of economic frames influences coverage. Specifically, we explore whether the media's coverage of economic issues increases in proportion to the number of economic frames emphasized by the candidates. In these analyses we find that incumbents are able to influence media coverage of the economy, while challengers are unable to shape coverage. The coefficient suggests that every additional economic frame emphasized by incumbents increases economic coverage by five paragraphs. Thus, incumbents employing all economic frames, compared to incumbents using none of the economic frames, receive about twenty additional paragraphs about the economy. The challenger, on the other hand, is not helped by presenting additional frames. The coefficient is statistically insignificant, and the substantive impact of the coefficient is less powerful.

In summary, incumbents have a modest advantage at generating media coverage on the economy compared to challengers. Incumbents are most successful at capturing the media's attention when they present an overall discussion

2.3 The impact of economic frames on economic news coverage

Economic frames	Incumbent/open winner			Challenger/open loser		
	Unstandardized coefficient (standard error)	*Beta*		*Unstandardized coefficient (standard error)*	*Beta*	
General economic frame[a]	10.00 (8.80)	.11		3.30 (7.70)	.04	
Budget frame[b]	.02 (7.90)	.01		9.90 (6.40)*	.16	
Tax frame[c]	−1.60 (6.70)	−.02		4.00 (5.90)	.07	
Job frame[d]	12.10 (6.50)**	.18		−3.90 (6.00)	−.07	
Candidate spending[e]	2.80 (1.70)*	.16		−1.90 (1.40)	−.13	
Economic climate[f]	11.70 (8.40)*	.12		9.00 (7.80)	.12	
Competition[g]	−.62 (.18)***	−.32		−.64 (.16)***	−.39	
Gubernatorial campaign[h]	−10.80 (6.50)*	−.17		−8.60 (5.70)	−.15	
Presidential campaign[i]	−36.10 (7.00)***	.52		17.10 (6.20)***	.29	
Constant	23.30 (11.30)**			43.70 (9.80)***		
R^2	.36			.30		
N	96			96		

Note: The dependent variable is the number of paragraphs about economic issues.

  Note: All *p*-values are two-tailed except in the following cases, where our expectations are clearly directional: each of the economic frames and competition.

  *p <.10,   **p <.05,   ***p <.01

  a. General economic frame is a binary variable where 1 = candidate emphasizes the general economy in ads, 0 = otherwise.

  b. Budget frame is a binary variable where 1 = candidate emphasizes the budget in ads, 0 = otherwise.

  c. Tax frame is a binary variable where 1 = candidate emphasizes taxes in ads, 0 = otherwise.

  d. Job frame is a binary variable where 1 = candidate emphasizes jobs in ads, 0 = otherwise.

  e. Candidate spending is logged to base 10.

  f. Economic climate is a binary variable where 1 = the economy is important in the state according to the *Congressional Quarterly* February election report, 0 = otherwise.

  g. Competition is an interval measure ranging from 0 to 72.

  h. Gubernatorial campaign is a binary variable where 1 = concurrent gubernatorial campaign, 0 = otherwise.

  i. Presidential campaign is a binary variable where 1 = presidential year, 0 = otherwise.

2.4 The impact of the number of economic frames on economic news coverage

	Incumbent/open winner		Challenger/open loser	
	Unstandardized coefficient (standard error)	Beta	Unstandardized coefficient (standard error)	Beta
Number of economic frames[a]	5.20 (2.60)**	.18	3.90 (2.40)	.16
Candidate spending[b]	2.70 (1.50)*	.16	−1.90 (1.30)	−.14
Competition[c]	−.54 (.17)***	−28	−62 (.16)	−38
Gubernatorial campaign[d]	−11.00 (6.40)*	−.17	−7.60 (5.60)	−.14
Presidential campaign[e]	−34.40 (6.90)***	.49	−16.70 (6.00)***	.28
Constant	22.60 (10.70)**		42.80 (9.60)***	
R^2	.34		.28	
N	96		96	

Note: The dependent variable is the number of paragraphs about economic issues.

Note: All p-values are two-tailed except in the following case, where our expectations are clearly directional: competition.

$*p < .10$, $**p < .05$, $***p < .01$

a. Number of economic frames is an interval measure ranging from 0 to 4, based on the number of economic frames discussed in the candidate's advertisements.

b. Candidate spending is logged to base 10.

c. Competition is an interval measure ranging from 0 to 72.

d. Gubernatorial campaign is a binary variable where 1 = concurrent gubernatorial campaign, 0 = otherwise.

e. Presidential campaign is a binary variable where 1 = presidential year, 0 = otherwise.

of the economy that includes several frames or aspects of the national economy. Both incumbents and challengers are helped little by focusing on simply one frame.

Negative Campaigning and Patterns of News Coverage

In addition to controlling the content of their own press coverage, candidates also seek to frame their opponents' coverage. When trying to alter coverage of their opponents, candidates often adopt "negative" frames. When candidates focus on their opponents' weaknesses, they hope to encourage the press to follow suit by publicizing criticisms.

Candidates going negative can choose between a number of competing frames. Candidates, for example, can attack their opponents on personal grounds. In the 1992 race in Alaska, Democrat Tony Smith criticized Senator Frank Murkowski for accepting honoraria, for taking more than a dozen junkets, and for being named "the greediest Senator" by the *Washington Times* for his enthusiastic support of Senate pay raises. Smith's attacks were aimed at presenting Murkowski as a self-serving incumbent who was more interested in making money than in helping his constituents back home. We find that 22 percent of the candidates running for the U.S. Senate between 1988 and 1992 relied on personality attacks in their political advertisements (Kahn and Kenney 1999).

Relying on personal attacks can be a risky strategy, while criticizing an opponent on policy grounds is often viewed by voters as more legitimate (Basil, Schooler, and Reeves 1991; Garramone 1984; Kahn and Geer 1994). In our sample of advertisements, Senate candidates relied on policy attacks 18 percent of the time. Candidates focusing on issues tend to pursue two strategies. First, they criticize their opponent's positions on issues. For example, Republican Pete Dawkins of New Jersey aired political advertisements showing Frank Lautenberg as voting for a tax increase on seventeen different occasions while serving in the U.S. Senate. These positions, portrayed as hard facts, illustrate Lautenberg's issue positions and indicate the direction public policy may take if he wins.

Second, candidates blame their opponent for unpopular policy outcomes. For example, in the 1990 campaign between U.S. House representative Robert Smith and former U.S. senator John Durkin, Smith tried to blame Durkin for the spending excesses of the federal government. Smith criticized Durkin for supporting massive spending programs, such as the federal bailout of New York City, and explained that his support contributed to the ballooning federal budget.

In this section of the chapter we examine three different types of negative frames: attacks on opponents' issue positions, attacks on opponents' personal traits, and blaming opponents for failed policies. To explore the impact of negative frames on media coverage of candidates, we must control for the rival factors included in all prior analyses in tables 2.1–2.4, with one addition. In the upcoming analyses, we also control for the endorsement decisions of local newspapers. We hypothesize that these decisions may affect the tone of coverage given to the candidates. Candidates who are successful in securing newspaper endorsements are described more favorably in the news, while more critical comments may be published about candidates who fail to receive endorsements (Kahn and Kenney 2002).

The data in table 2.5 suggest that not all negative frames are equally effective at producing critical coverage.[19] Incumbents are only successful in generating negative coverage when they publicize their challengers' positions on unpopular issues and when they criticize their challengers on personal grounds. For example, when incumbents criticize their opponents' stands on issues, they can expect, on average, about eight more critical comments to be published in the paper. Similarly, when incumbents attack their opponents on personal traits, newspapers respond by printing about ten more criticisms of the challengers in the paper. However, incumbents are ineffective when they blame their opponent for unpopular policy outcomes.

2.5 The impact of negative frames on critical coverage of opponent

Incumbent's negative frames	Challenger/open loser	
	Unstandardized coefficient (standard error)	Beta
Negative position frame[a]	7.80 (5.40)*	.14
Negative trait frame[b]	10.00 (4.90)**	.19
Blame frame[c]	−6.70 (5.70)	−.11
Incumbent spending[d]	1.30 (1.10)	.10
Competition[e]	−.68 (.14)***	−.46
Gubernatorial campaign[f]	−11.50 (4.60)**	−.22
Presidential campaign[g]	−3.00 (5.20)	.06
Endorsement[h]	−2.70 (2.80)	−.08
Constant	38.60 (8.20)***	
R²	.44	
N	96	

Challenger's negative frames	Incumbent/open winner	
	Unstandardized coefficient (standard error)	Beta
Negative position frame	−.14 (6.50)	−.01
Negative trait frame	−.37 (6.00)	−.01
Blame frame	9.20 (6.30)*	.13
Challenger spending[d]	2.40 (1.50)	.13
Competition	−.89 (.18)***	−.42
Gubernatorial campaign	−21.50 (6.30)***	−.30
Presidential campaign	−10.40 (7.00)	.14
Endorsement	−12.80 (3.80)***	−.28
Constant	61.80 (11.00)***	
R²	.48	
N	96	

Note: The dependent variable is the number of paragraphs containing criticisms of the candidate.

Note: All p-values are two-tailed except in the following cases, where our expectations are clearly directional: each of the negative frames and competition.

*$p<.10$,   **$p<.05$,   ***$p<.01$

a. Negative position frame is a binary variable where 1 = candidate criticizes the opponent's issue positions in ads, 0 = otherwise.

b. Negative trait frame is a binary variable where 1 = candidate criticizes the opponent's personal traits in ads, 0 = otherwise.

c. Blame frame is a binary variable where 1 = candidate blames the opponent for unfavorable policy consequences, 0 = otherwise.

d. Candidate spending is logged to base 10.

e. Competition is an interval measure ranging from 0 to 72.

f. Gubernatorial campaign is a binary variable where 1 = concurrent gubernatorial campaign, 0 = otherwise.

g. Presidential campaign is a binary variable where 1 = presidential year, 0 = otherwise.

h. Endorsement is an ordinal variable where 1 = incumbent/winner endorsed, 0 = no endorsement, −1 = challenger/loser endorsed.

Challengers, similar to incumbents, are not always influential when trying to generate critical coverage of their opponent. In fact, only one of the three negative frames employed by challengers significantly influences negative coverage of incumbents. In particular, when challengers blame incumbents for unfavorable policy outcomes, the press responds by publishing, on average, nine more critical comments about sitting senators.

Blaming the incumbents for unpopular policy consequences may be effective for challengers for two reasons. First, the frame is newsworthy since many readers may be personally affected by the negative policy (e.g., an increase in taxes). Second, it is reasonable to blame incumbents for policy ills since sitting senators have been in a position to affect policy. In contrast, the "blame" frame may be less believable when articulated by incumbents since challengers are rarely in positions to affect federal policy.

When challengers attack incumbents on personal grounds and when they criticize them on issue positions, they are unable to generate critical coverage. These frames may be less powerful for challengers because incumbents are a "known quantity," and the criticisms leveled by challengers need to compete with information reporters already hold about senators. For example, if a challenger complains that a senator is unresponsive to the needs of state residents, but a reporter knows the senator has been instrumental in delivering several large federal projects to the state, the reporter may be unwilling to publish the challenger's criticisms.

While we find that candidates are able to frame negative media coverage, critical coverage also depends upon the closeness of the contest. In fact, in both the incumbent and the challenger models, the competitiveness of the race is the most important factor explaining the number of criticisms published in the news. For both incumbents and challengers, there is about a one-to-one correspondence between changes in poll standings and changes in candidate criticisms. Thus, for example, every ten-point increase in the closeness of the campaign generates an additional ten criticisms in the newspapers, on average.

The results presented in table 2.6 also indicate that presidential and gubernatorial campaigns act as a resource for Senate candidates by reducing the number of critical comments written about their candidacies. For example, incumbents who are not competing with gubernatorial candidates for coverage can expect to be criticized about twenty-one more times than senators who are running campaigns concurrently with gubernatorial candidates.

Finally, the endorsement decisions of newspapers significantly influence the tone of campaign coverage given to incumbents.[20] Newspapers that endorse incumbents print about twenty-five less criticisms, on average, than newspapers endorsing a senator's challenger (i.e., a two-point movement on the endorse-

2.6 The impact of the number of negative frames on critical coverage of opponent

| | Challenger/open loser | |
	Unstandardized coefficient (standard error)	Beta
Number of negative frames used by incumbent[a]	3.89 (2.30)*	.16
Incumbent spending[b]	1.40 (1.10)	.11
Competition[c]	−.71 (.14)***	−.48
Gubernatorial campaign[d]	−12.20 (4.70)**	−.24
Presidential campaign[e]	−4.80 (5.20)	.09
Endorsement[f]	−2.30 (2.80)	−.07
Constant	39.60 (8.30)***	
R^2	.41	
N	96	

| | Incumbent/open winner | |
	Unstandardized coefficient (standard error)	Beta
Number of negative frames used by challenger	3.10 (2.80)	.09
Challenger spending[b]	2.70 (1.50)*	.15
Competition	−.89 (.18)***	−.42
Gubernatorial campaign	−21.50 (6.30)***	−.29
Presidential campaign	−10.20 (6.90)	.13
Endorsement	−12.80 (3.80)***	−.28
Constant	60.70 (10.90)***	
R^2	.47	
N	96	

Note: The dependent variable is the number of paragraphs containing criticisms of the candidate.

  Note: All p-values are two-tailed except in the following cases, where our expectations are clearly directional: competition.

  *$p < .10$,   **$p < .05$,   ***$p < .01$

  a. Number of negative frames is an interval measure ranging from 0 to 3.

  b. Candidate spending is logged to base 10.

  c. Competition is an interval measure ranging from 0 to 72.

  d. Gubernatorial campaign is a binary variable where 1 = concurrent gubernatorial campaign, 0 = otherwise.

  e. Presidential campaign is a binary variable where 1 = presidential year, 0 = otherwise.

  f. Endorsement is an ordinal variable where 1 = incumbent/winner is endorsed, 0 = no endorsement, −1 = challenger/loser is endorsed

ment scale). However, endorsements do not affect the number of criticisms published about challengers.

In addition to looking at how specific negative frames produce negative coverage, we also examine whether the number of different negative frames influences the amount of criticisms published in the press. Do candidates who criticize their opponents in a variety of different ways encourage more negative coverage?[21] According to the findings in table 2.6, the answer to this question is yes, but only for incumbents. For incumbents, every additional negative frame employed produces, on average, four more criticisms of the challenger. Using the unstandardized coefficients to estimate the number of criticisms published about challengers, we find that when incumbents rely on each of the three negative frames, challengers can expect thirty-one criticisms to be published in the newspaper.[22] However, when incumbents do not use any of these negative frames, only about eleven criticisms are written about challengers.

The number of frames embraced by challengers does not influence the tone of the incumbents' coverage. The insignificant coefficient in table 2.6 suggests challengers are unable to produce more critical coverage of senators by relying on a series of negative frames. Perhaps the number of negative frames is unimportant for challengers because only the blame frame is "picked up on" by the press, as suggested by the findings in table 2.5.

Summary and Implications

In a representative democracy, communication between legislators and constituents is vital. It serves to inform both parties of goals, expectations, desires, and accomplishments. We know from common sense and mountains of evidence that the lines of communication between representatives and the represented are never equal in terms of individual access and influence. However, during campaigns, candidates spend enormous sums of money to communicate directly with the body politic via commercials, letters, pamphlets, public speeches, town forums, and so on. During the electoral season, citizens are provided with a plethora of information from the candidates.

The process by which information filters from candidates to citizens during campaigns is somewhat of a mystery. However, we know that voters are not paying close attention to the campaign information, especially in nonpresidential contests. And the information they do acquire comes from a variety of sources, including the candidates and an expanding number of media outlets. From a purely strategic perspective, then, candidates seeking to win elections attempt to control the information emanating from the news media. In this chapter, we found that candidates are moderately successful when they try to frame news coverage of their messages.

The findings suggest that incumbents are more effective than challengers at cajoling the press to frame topics in ways that resemble incumbents' chosen themes. However, this comparative advantage for incumbents is not overwhelming. Quite to the contrary, incumbents do not consistently or powerfully affect the media's framing of their candidacies. Instead, when reporters and editors devote space to certain frames, they are more responsive to the closeness of the election and the presence of competing campaigns than to the specific nature of incumbents' messages.

In the end, incumbents have their best chance of framing news coverage when they attack their opponents and speak clearly on issues. Editors and reporters are interested in drama and conflict in order to sell newspapers. Negative advertisements produced by incumbents capture their attention. Also, reporters, short on time and resources, find it much easier to write stories about incumbents' positions on issues when these positions are easy to locate in speeches, campaign pamphlets, and commercials.

Although incumbents achieve only modest success in framing media coverage of their campaign messages, challengers have virtually no success. We know from previous scholarship that challengers, compared to incumbents, lack money, name recognition, stature, experience, and organizational resources. To this list, we add the challenger's inability to influence how the news media frame coverage of their messages. Although challengers' inability to frame news coverage is routinely decried by challengers "on the campaign trail" (Fenno 1996), we had expectations that challengers might be able to frame coverage. Previously we had found that challengers are successful at shaping the content of the news media's coverage of their campaigns (Kahn and Kenney 1999). However, the data in this chapter, juxtaposed with our earlier work, suggest that it is far easier for challengers to influence "what" reporters cover, rather than "how" reporters cover campaigns.

Candidates who frame the news coverage of their campaigns influence how citizens evaluate their candidacies and, ultimately, how citizens cast their vote. In this chapter, we have made an initial foray into explaining which candidates are most effective at controlling news coverage of their campaign messages. However, many questions remain unanswered. For example, are reporters more likely to echo the candidates' frames when candidates are engaged in a competitive campaign? In addition, is the news media's responsiveness to the candidates' frames contingent upon the level of campaign spending? Finally, does the press's receptivity to the candidates' frames vary with the importance of office? Perhaps reporters are more responsive to the frames offered by presidential candidates, compared to the frames articulated by candidates running for the U.S. House of Representatives. We hope that scholars will explore these and other questions when examining the link between candidates' campaign strategies and news coverage of elections.

3

Obstacles and Opportunities
Factors That Constrain Elected Officials' Ability to Frame Political Issues

Teena Gabrielson

In the marketplace of American politics, the packaging of political issues is often as important as the product. Yet the recognition that there is a relationship between issue presentation and citizen attention gives us little leverage in understanding how elected officials choose to frame any particular issue at a given time. The considerations to which elected officials attend in their efforts to frame political issues have gained scant attention from researchers in the study of political persuasion. The goal of this chapter is to identify some of the key factors that constrain elected officials at the national level of American politics as they consider framing issues for partisan gain. In keeping with one of the themes of this volume, I also explore how the terrorist attacks of September 11 contributed to the framing of issues by partisans in a few of the hotly contested seats in the 2002 congressional elections. One might expect that an exogenous shock of this magnitude would dramatically change the political environment and open up framing opportunities for many elected officials. The theoretical discussion, however, suggests that there are good reasons for anticipatory elites to remain aware, if not cautious, of the factors that generally constrain their framing opportunities.

The framing of issues can be a powerful tool of political persuasion. Because most issues that come to the fore in American national politics are complex and multifaceted, they can be perceived and understood through a variety of different lenses or frames. For elected officials, this fact translates into an opportunity for political gain.[1] However, without minimizing too drastically human agency, I argue that the influence of skilled political entrepreneurs is limited by specific constraints on viable framing options. Thus, ideally, strategic politicians will anticipate the types of frames that will resonate with the attentive public given the contours of the political landscape at a particular time on a given issue.

As David Mayhew (1974) so forcefully argues, the first concern and primary goal of a representative is election (or reelection). Issue framing is one of the many resources available to candidates as they present themselves to the public in an effort to win office. But issue framing is also a useful tool in the partisan battle that is largely conducted among elites. In this context, an elected official may frame an issue in order to achieve the secondary goal of legislative success.[2] Still, the game of politics is rarely risk free. As will become clear, there are also significant costs involved in attempts to frame or reframe political issues. Thus, the decision to expend resources on issue framing can be a weighty one for elected officials.[3]

Further, as noted in the editors' introduction to this volume, political actors do not have carte blanche to simply present issues to the American public in any manner they desire. Instead, a host of factors limit the frames available to elected officials and influence the likelihood that an elected official will attempt to initiate political change through issue redefinition. While elected officials frequently pursue their goals through consensual politics, this chapter concentrates upon a few of those environmental constraints that hem in partisans as they decide whether or not to venture an issue redefinition through public discourse.[4] I focus particularly upon the public mood, the partisan composition and organization of interests of the representative's constituency, the historical lines of conflict surrounding an issue, and the level of institutionalization of an issue.[5]

Of these constraints, two are ideological measures: the partisan composition of the official's constituency and the "public mood"—a global measure of public opinion that indicates the ideological leanings of the American citizenry. Among Americanists, there has been a renewed interest in the study of partisan ideology, in part because recent works point to its power in shaping the landscape of American politics.[6] Scholars have found three situations to be true for most of American history: political conflict has been divided along one central line of disagreement between the two parties; the partisan ideologies of the two major parties have offered voters meaningful choices or clearly differentiated programs of governance; and the parties have maintained substantively consistent platforms for significant periods of time (Poole and Rosenthal 1997; Gerring 1997, 1998; Silbey 1991). These works suggest that partisan ideology plays a fundamental and enduring role in ordering the political arena by structuring American political conflict at the elite level. Thus, we should expect that elites will attempt to frame issues in ways that advance their partisan interests.

In addition, these works indicate that partisan ideology simplifies American politics for the electorate and serves to keep public officials responsive to their constituency. Certainly, few scholars would support the notion of an ideologically minded American electorate, but how many would disregard the role of partisan ideology altogether?[7] The ideological constraints outlined above highlight the modest but still significant role that the American public plays in circumscribing the framing options of elected officials. While the public's role is an important one, most scholars recognize that organized interests are a still more powerful force in American politics today. And one of the key ways in which interest groups wield their strength over elected officials is by blocking their actions or constraining their options (Hojnacki and Kimball 1999). Together, the public mood, the partisan composition, and the array of organized interests within a representative's constituency can all be considered representational constraints on the framing options available to elected officials.

Not all issues are equally open to framing or reframing attempts by elected officials. In this essay, I include two issue-specific constraints: the level of institutionalization and the history of conflict.[8] Among political scientists, institutions are often defined as rules. Institutionalization, then, can be defined as the legislative and administrative (rule-creating) processes through which an issue (and its frame) becomes embedded within a network of supportive political elites. In most cases, institutionalization is a question of degree. Some issue frames are highly institutionalized, and others are less so, while still other issue frames may be relatively new or lack the support of political elites. Speaking generally, a highly institutionalized issue frame will be characterized by some of the following traits: it will have maintained elite agreement for a significant period of time; it will have numerous laws and administrative rulings that reflect and secure it; it will be supported by a wide array of political elites, including interest groups, members of the bureaucracy, and elected officials; and it will enjoy widespread public support. Highly institutionalized issues generally will be more difficult to reframe than newly emerging ones because there will be a host of political elites who are committed to the existing issue frame and who have a stake in the values and treatment recommendations that it supports.

However, temporality is also important to institutionalization (Orren and Skowronek 1994). When determining whether or not to frame or reframe an issue, elected officials must consider not only the level of support an issue frame holds among political elites but also the manner by which that support was attained. The last factor—the history of conflict on a particular issue—draws attention to the larger historical context and how elite consensus on an issue frame emerges.

The "Public Mood"

Researchers in American politics have long posited the importance of public mood in constraining elected officials' behavior (Cobb and Elder 1976; Kernell 1993; Kingdon 1984; Stimson 1991; Stimson, MacKuen, and Erikson 1994; Tulis 1987). Broadly, this concept has been defined as the "prevailing public sentiment as to what constitutes appropriate matters for governmental attention" and restricts those items on the decision-making agenda (Cobb and Elder 1976, 21).[9] More recent work on the concept of public mood has lent some tractability to this otherwise rather nebulous concept. Public mood is defined as an aggregate, or a global measure of public opinion that provides the broad outlines of the polity's ideological proclivities, constructed from a host of issues that map in parallel on a scale of policy liberalism, thus marking the prevailing mood of the citizenry in ideological terms (Stimson 1991, 2002; Stimson, MacKuen, and Erikson 1994). The concept of public mood is a macro or global measure of the ideological tendencies of the citizenry at a given point in time. For example, using this measure scholars have plotted the movement of the American public from a liberal peak in the early 1970s to the significantly more conservative period of the early 1980s (Stimson, MacKuen, and Erikson 1994, 32).

On rare occasions, the mass public initiates change on a political issue and elected officials respond; far more often the public acts as an effective block on elected officials' behavior. The public mood delineates an issue space that constrains elected officials from advancing issue frames at the extremes of the ideological spectrum. Yet the public mood is not static; within its dynamic space there are distinctive shifts of consequence. Therefore, the public mood not only constrains elected officials from constructing issue frames at the ideological extremes; as it moves it also gives greater or lesser play to more moderate liberal and conservative ideas. For example, at a given time moderately conservative positions may concur with the public mood, while at another time these appeals will fall flat. Thus, while the public mood hovers around the median, the shifts within that issue space are of consequence for the framing of issues by elected officials. When the public mood evidences a strong shift toward one end of the ideological spectrum, appeals by strong conservatives or liberals are likely to be more frequent and more successful.[10] Yet partisans can be very effective in attaining their goals without a strong ideological shift if they correctly gauge public mood and frame issues in a manner that resonates with that mood.

In setting out some of the key factors that constrain elected officials, the notion of public mood is a critical one because it offers a broad gauge of the ideological position of the citizenry on a host of issues. This general information can be very useful to elected officials as they seek to frame issues for partisan gain. While partisan attachments are themselves dynamic, both partisanship and ideology provide the most stable and enduring dimensions guiding political conflict. Thus, anticipatory elected officials will attempt to frame issues in the partisan or ideological manner that will best achieve their goals. Framing appeals are highly likely to take on ideological coloration, especially when addressed to a national audience, because partisanship and ideology are key attachments guiding political conflict. For those reasons, public mood is instructive as to what types of frames are likely to persuade at any given time. While issue-specific information will be important to an elected official's decision to frame or reframe an issue, an accurate assessment of the public mood can help an elected official build a framing strategy across several issues. Similarly, just as an elected official must begin with his or her own constituency (a point discussed below), in national politics, a sound assessment of the ideological leanings of the citizenry as a whole can be instrumental to electoral and legislative success.

Miscalculating the Public Mood

Given this description of the public mood, elected officials must anticipate the ideological tenor of the attentive public in order to advance an issue frame that resonates with the public and therefore evokes the desired response. Elected officials are constrained by the public mood: if they advance a frame that falls outside of this issue space, there may be negative repercussions that adversely affect their primary goals. The most benign outcome of misjudging the public mood is the failure to attract attention and political change on the issue. However, the official who has expended significant resources in the pursuit of this goal faces a further ramification: an enduring perception of failure among the attentive public, perhaps even extending to his or her political party. This perception of failure among members of the public may dampen the probability of future success and may irreparably tarnish the elected official's ability to persuade. Last, and most devastatingly, by misinterpreting the public mood and publicly endorsing an issue frame on that misperception, an elected official may open a previously closed door for the opposition. In this situation, an attempt to benefit translates into a loss of grand scale as the opposition wins access to the attentive public and persuades through an issue frame that promotes their own goals.

For example, in the early months of his first term, President Bill Clinton decided to make good on a campaign promise by proposing to lift the ban on gays in the military. While Clinton was aware of strong opposition in several quarters, a misreading of the public mood contributed to the resulting compromise on this policy ("don't ask, don't tell"). By losing the battle over the ban on gays in the military, Clinton may have inadvertently exposed a vulnerable issue for Democrats and signaled this weakness to the opposition. Looking back on his presidency in an interview for *Rolling Stone*, Clinton discussed the administration's handling of the gays in the military policy as a strategic error, one that rested upon both a superior Republican strategy and his administration's miscalculation of the public's response. Clinton stated: "Republicans made this issue their opening salvo. And they understood—and exactly what I know now—how what we do here plays out in the country. But because it was one of my campaign commitments, I refused to back off. The message out in the country was, 'We elected this guy to turn the economy around, and instead, his top priority is gays in the military.'"[11]

Similarly, many scholars and pundits have argued that House Republicans ran headlong into ideological territory that disadvantaged them with the attentive public after the 1994 elections. After regaining control of the House of Representatives for the first time in forty years, the Republicans proposed a very conservative legislative agenda that included a balanced-budget proposal; term limits for national representatives; and welfare reform that would "discourage illegitimacy and teen pregnancy by prohibiting welfare to minor mothers and denying increased AFDC for additional children while on welfare, cut spending for welfare programs, and enact a tough two-years-and-out provision with work requirements to promote individual responsibility."[12] House speaker Newt Gingrich's language was more stark: "We'll help you with foster care, we'll help you with orphanages, we'll help you with adoption."[13] Proposals such as this one were inconsistent with the ideological tenor of the American public. As Linda Killian (1998, 414) writes: "One of the biggest mistakes the freshmen made was in misreading their mandate. It's true that no Republican incumbent lost in 1994. That undoubtedly said something about the mood of the voters and their dissatisfaction with the way Clinton and the Democrats had been running the country. . . . [But] the Republicans did not have the sweeping mandate for change they thought they did. What happened to the Republican revolution is that it never existed in the first place except in the minds of Newt Gingrich and the freshmen." In this instance, the failure of the Republican leadership (and many elected officials of the majority party) to accurately assess the public mood resulted in policy proposals that swerved too far to the right for the average American voter.

These two examples share another striking feature: in both cases, the miscalculation of the public mood stemmed from partisan interpretations of election results. While election results themselves can serve to constrain the framing alternatives of political actors—particularly those in the minority party—these examples illustrate the dangers inherent in interpreting election results, especially for the winners. After winning the election in 1992, President Clinton remained focused upon the economy but also pursued policy objectives that fell outside of the acceptable parameters of public opinion. In 1994, the Republicans' historic electoral wins were interpreted as a mandate for change.

In contrast, immediately after the 2002 congressional elections, it appeared that President George W. Bush has learned the lesson these examples recommend. In the days after the elections, President Bush maintained a careful tone in interpreting the election results, stating: "If there is a mandate in any election—at least in this one—it's that people want something to get done. They want people to work together in Washington, D.C., to pass meaningful legislation which will improve their lives."[14] Bush's linguistic prudence, however, was not accompanied by a timid legislative program. While avoiding an ideologically extreme interpretation of the elections as a demand for more conservative public policy, the president advanced a conservative legislative agenda by framing the election in pragmatic terms. As White House press secretary Ari Fleischer said of the elections: "It is a big victory. There's a lot of work that the American people want Democrats and Republicans to team up on that's not getting done. . . . Those days may be over."[15] This frame immediately draws attention to the long-held American values of a strong work ethic, bipartisan cooperation, and a government that works for the people, while it avoids the negative evaluations that so frequently accompany partisan appeals. These examples underscore the role of public mood as a constraint upon the framing options of elected officials.

Partisan Composition and the Organization of Interests

Just as the public mood acts to constrain elected officials in their framing appeals to the attentive public at the national level, the ideological leanings and organization of interests within a representative's constituency do so at the local level. The partisan composition of an elected official's constituency contributes to the decision of whether or not to publicly endorse and promote a particular issue frame. Much like the public mood, the ideological tendencies of a representative's constituency will constrain the frames available to that official on a particular issue at a given time. Further, these considerations will take precedence over the public mood, given the primary goal of reelection.[16] However, not all members of an elected official's constituency constrain the framing options available to that official.

Representatives are constrained by (and responsible to) their constituencies due to the primary goal of reelection. An elected official will be wary of publicly endorsing an issue frame that he or she perceives to run counter to the interests of the voters within the district. Furthermore, the intent behind constructing an issue frame is to change the manner in which individuals understand that issue by emphasizing different values, arguments, and treatment recommendations regarding that issue. Both of the groups of interest—voters and those who are likely to be persuaded by an issue frame—are a subset of the larger constituency. Members of these groups hold the reins that guide elected officials as they decide whether or not to pursue issue redefinition.

Issue Framing and the Attentive Public

For framing efforts to affect individual attitude change, individuals must both be aware of the message and be influenced by it (Zaller 1992, 1996). Therefore, those individuals who do not engage in the public discourse surrounding political issues will not be aware of, much less persuaded by, the packaging of political issues. In contrast, the politically sophisticated are most likely to be attentive to public discourse and therefore are arguably the most susceptible to the effects of framing. But they are also more likely to be armed with defenses against the packaging of political issues. The more informed are also more likely to have strong political predispositions and a broader array of categorized information from which they may draw in decision-making processes.[17] Therefore, the efforts of elected officials to reframe issues and thereby change attitudes are most likely to be resisted by the most politically sophisticated—or strongly ideological—members of the mass public (Jacoby 2000). To be sure, the evaluative dimension under consideration will still evoke a new set of considerations, arguments, and values, but for sophisticated, strong partisans these considerations are most likely familiar and easily discounted. Thus, it is the less ideological but attentive and voting members of the public who are the targets of elected officials' efforts in framing and reframing political issues.

Further, recent research suggests that partisans are wise to expend their efforts on this segment of the population. On the issue of government spending, scholars have found that how one frames the issue—in general or more specific terms—influences not only the overall distribution of public opinion but also individual-level attitude change. For nonideological attentive voters, how governmental spending issues are framed influences their decision on whether or not to support such spending. Broad, general frames tend to trigger negative associations with the government and thereby diminish the likelihood of support, whereas frames that specifically delineate who would benefit from such spending tend to elicit a positive response (Jacoby 2000). Thus, it is no surprise that Democrats and Republicans tend to talk about the issue of governmental spending in fundamentally different ways—by doing so, each seeks to build party support among this critical subset of voters.

Other research suggests that the logic that motivates Democrats and Republicans to frame the issue of government spending differently may apply more widely. In a recent paper, James Stimson seeks to explain the following puzzle: "While we have seen that most Americans prefer a government that does more rather than less—they are, that is, operationally liberal—asked to describe their political identity, almost two of three choose the label 'conservative' over the label 'liberal'" (2002, 30). For Stimson, the key to unlocking this puzzle lies with a critical segment of the American population that identifies symbolically as conservative and operationally as liberal. Among this small but electorally significant group both broad conservative appeals and specific, targeted, liberal spending messages are attractive. As such, they form a key constituency of persuadable voters—one that further encourages the creation of partisan frames on a variety of political issues.

The Organization of Interests

While the attentive public is crucial to the decision-making process of an official, the power of organized interests within a representative's constituency is weighted more heavily. Within a representative's district, organized interests play a more substantial role in constraining the available framing options. By definition, organized interests promote political goals, and issue framing is a central strategy in the realization of these goals. Unlike a representative's constituency, organized interests maintain the resources and skills necessary to keep abreast of and affect change on issues related to their goals. Organized interests are the embodiment of the attentive public and wield resources crucial to elected officials' electoral success. Thus, interest groups frame issues for their own benefit and ideally would encourage elected officials to accept and endorse these frames. Yet interest groups are more effective in providing a block on elected officials' behavior rather than in encouraging positive action, like endorsing a particular position or the framing of an issue in a way that would benefit the group. In this, their ability to impose constraints resembles that of the public mood.

Interest groups can have a profound influence in constraining the issue frames available to elected officials by creating a situation in which the negative repercussions of endorsing a particular frame will significantly outweigh any possible gain. Three factors play a crucial role in determining interest-group influence over the public position taken by an elected official. These are the size of the group's membership within the elected official's constituency, the extent to which the group participates in grassroots lobbying or communication with the official, and the size of past contributions given to the member in election campaigns (R. Smith 1993, 188). When an interest group maintains a sizable membership within an official's constituency, communicates with the official, and contributes to his or her campaign coffers, it greatly diminishes the probability that the official will defect from the group's position.[18]

This power was recently demonstrated in California by interest groups that included the American Civil Liberties Union of Southern California and the Disability Rights Education and Defense Fund. Bill Lockyer, attorney general of California (an elected position), successfully petitioned the U.S. Supreme Court to hear a case in which a California doctor had sued the state for violating the Americans with Disabilities Act (ADA) by refusing to grant him a license due to clinical depression. In this case, the state sought immunity from damages under Title II of the ADA. In an unprecedented action, the U.S. Supreme Court dismissed the case upon Lockyer's request. As Charles Lane reported for the *Washington Post*, "[disability] activists lobbied Lockyer to scuttle the case, telling him that otherwise they would not support him if he runs for governor in 2006."[19] In this instance, organized interests were able to block the actions of an elected official—actions that threatened both the group's policy goals and their preferred issue frame.[20] Here, the threat of a strong grassroots lobbying effort, conducted in part through interest-group alliances and sophisticated Internet-based technologies, successfully halted the actions of an elected official that otherwise might have significantly eroded the application of a civil rights frame to disability issues.

The constellation of interests that support elected officials both through their membership and through their contributions plays a decisive role in the framing options an elected official can publicly endorse while still remaining in good standing with the group. Interest groups are able to mobilize latent dispositions within an official's constituency, drawing on their relationship with the attentive public and making palpable their power as a constraint on the framing options available to elected officials.[21] The mobilization capabilities of the American Association of Retired Persons, one of the most revered organized interests in American politics, evidence the strength of protest groups in constraining the positions available to elected officials. Yet in the decision-making process regarding whether or not to publicly construct an issue frame, elected officials must weigh the power of the group against the likely response of the attentive public.[22]

An elected official seeking to focus national attention on a particular issue frame will be constrained by the public mood, the ideological leanings of his or her constituency, and the distribution and power of organized interests. As stated earlier, most issues, with one glaring exception, will be accompanied by an array of organized interests with opposing positions. Exempt from this statement are groups focused upon consumer or public interests. The numbers and strength of these groups pale in contrast with the corporate sector, and thus the field of viable framing options is significantly biased toward corporate and upper-class interests (J. Berry 1989; Schlozman and Tierney 1986). Thus, interest groups provide a constraint on the framing options available to elected officials by both their presence and their conspicuous absence.

Quite often an official will be hemmed in by opposing interests of equal strength within his or her constituency, making it much harder to take action on the issue, let alone control the conflict or place it on a national agenda.[23] Yet the nature of the issue can still determine the official's position. Even in the face of opposing organized interests, a particular issue may be strictly framed in partisan or ideological terms, confining the range of choices available to an elected official. Further, the primary industry or material interest of a region or district (the importance of technology to the Silicon Valley, farming to the Midwest, tobacco to parts of the South) may further constrain elected officials' positions on particular interests.

In each of these representational constraints, a window of opportunity appears in which the official could bring an issue forward in a particular frame. The window is created by a coincidence between the public mood and the ideological leanings of the representative's constituency where formidable opposing interest groups are silent. When these factors coalesce, the opportunity arises for the elected official to pursue an issue framing in accordance with his or her political goals. As stated earlier, we should expect these representational constraints to predominate in the elected official's decision to capitalize on this window, but issue-specific constraints—such as the level of institutionalization and historic lines of conflict—may severely constrict the opening.

The Level of Institutionalization and the Historic Lines of Conflict

The level of institutionalization of a particular issue and the historical lines of conflict surrounding it are related but analytically distinct concepts. Both of these factors contribute to the relative flexibility of the environment surrounding specific issues. In brief, once a frame is institutionalized, it becomes more difficult to dislodge or replace it. Thus, institutionalization constrains elected officials' framing options. Similarly, the process through which elite consensus is attained (a prerequisite to institutionalization) also helps determine how plastic an issue is. If consensus emerges through public debate, the issue frame will be more resilient to redefinition than if it is attained through "insider" elite bargaining.

Institutionalization involves the legislation of public policy and the creation of subgovernments to implement and oversee that policy. With institutionalization, the values, arguments, and treatment recommendations indicated by an issue frame become entrenched in a network of supportive political elites (interest groups, congressional members, bureaucrats, etc.) who can then further protect, insulate from opposition, and promote that frame. The substantive material of the frame also becomes embedded in the public's shared understanding of a particular issue, making institutionalized frames particularly enduring.[24]

For an issue to become institutionalized, at least momentary consensus is required. Evidence suggests that elite consensus leads to a shared public understanding of an issue and the winnowing of a diversity of frames regarding an issue to one predominant frame (Zaller 1992, 1996; Chong 1996). Consensus reduces the salience of political issues because contention and conflict arouse attention. Once a consensus has been reached on the framing of a particular issue, institutionalization of that issue then becomes much more probable. However, the consensus that leads to institutionalization of an issue frame is the product of a process. This process can be understood as the history of conflict surrounding a particular issue. It is important to distinguish between the end (institutionalization of an issue frame) and the means (the history of conflict on an issue) because each constrains elected officials somewhat differently.

For example, in the first decade of the twentieth century one of the key political battles shaping American land policy was whether the issue should be framed in terms of conservation and "wise use" or in terms of the preservation of American wilderness. This conflict, waged publicly, included such key individuals as President Theodore Roosevelt and the founder of the Sierra Club, John Muir. In the end, the conservationists carried the day, with significant and continuing implications for American land use today.[25] In this example, both the public nature of the conflict over land-use issue frames and the institutionalization of the conservationist frame are constraining factors. However, in most cases, it is not so much a question of whether an issue is institutionalized but rather to what degree. Newly emerging and newly institutionalized issues—such as human cloning or stem-cell research—are much more vulnerable to reframing attempts than are older, more entrenched issues such as social security. To quote James Madison, older issues enjoy "that veneration which time bestows on everything."[26]

Although the frames of reference on highly institutionalized issues are more secure than those that are not institutionalized, organized oppositions may still develop, leading to the reframing of the issue. Research indicates that a highly institutionalized issue may come under fire by organized opposition. Preconditions include the development of new information regarding the issue, an exogenous shock that brings the issue to the fore, gradual change in the political landscape, or the demise of elite consensus on the issue (Baumgartner and Jones 1993).[27] Under these conditions, the framing options available to those defending the status quo will be severely constrained in contrast to those available to the opposition. In these cases, the challengers may construct numerous frames designed to shed new light on the issue, whereas the proponents of the status quo must rely on the power of the previous frame to rebut these new considerations. Thus, the information context available to the opposition is much more fluid than that surrounding the proponents of the institutionalized issue frame.

The exceptions above underscore the fact that many political issues are of enduring interest to the American polity and are repeatedly considered in public debate. But it must be noted that in order for conflict to recur and an issue to evolve over time, particular evaluative dimensions must be more stable than others, allowing for new issues or issue redefinitions to be mapped onto these more enduring attachments. The most enduring of these are ideological.[28] Although an elected official might relish the opportunity, only a very small proportion of issues begin with a clean slate, and even new issues are linked to similar issues of the past in order to gain some purchase on how they might best be handled and understood. For example, the relatively new and controversial issue of stem-cell research has been grafted onto existing conflicts regarding both abortion and the ethical dimensions of medical research.[29] Each of these existing issue areas provides frames of reference and supportive elites who have been pressed into service in the partisan battles over a new issue.

The historical lines of conflict on an issue can be categorized into three very broad types: first, recurring conflict may harden into two distinct opposing perspectives; second, in recurring conflict an issue may be frequently reframed; and third, there may be elite consensus. In the first type of conflict, a plethora of framings has been winnowed down to two primary perspectives, which usually represent the two partisan camps.[30] Because the ideological line of conflict is the most stable one, most issues map onto this divide. As such, particular issue positions, and even particular issues, come to be understood as better handled by one or the other of the two major parties. The abortion debate exemplifies this path of conflict: over time the issue hardened into two primary positions (pro-life, pro-choice), with each perspective strongly favored by Republicans and Democrats, respectively. Under these conditions, the framing options available to elected officials are severely constricted, and the likelihood of the issue being reframed and gaining focused attention is quite limited. Another issue that, historically, has conformed to this pattern is that of gun control. However, as Karen Callaghan and Frauke Schnell suggest, the exogenous shock of the September 11 terrorist attacks may have created new framing opportunities for elected officials on this issue.[31]

The second path of conflict identifies issues that undergo recurring conflict but frequently experience a reframing. In these instances, the lines of conflict are less clear; advocates and opponents of standing policy are more difficult to decipher; and the information environment is decidedly messier than in the previous example, where the ideological dimensions of the debate are much starker. It must be clear that this is a question of degree; rarely will an issue arise that elicits national attention in which the ideological dimension is not present. However, when an issue is reframed frequently, several issue dimensions gain attention. The issue area of drug policy demonstrates this quite well. Taking a cue from Richard Nixon, President Ronald Reagan's "War on Drugs" reframed the issue of drug policy from a public-health issue to one of law and order. With this framing, a "drug czar" was appointed, an abstinence campaign was launched by the First Lady, and significant resources were extended toward reducing the supply of drugs within the United States.[32] Decades later, this frame has come under attack from both the left and the right. As stated by the Drug Policy Alliance, an organization created in an effort to "broaden the public debate on drug policy": "Everyone has a stake in ending the war on drugs. Whether you're a parent concerned about protecting children from drug-related harm, a social justice advocate worried about racially disproportionate incarceration rates, an environmentalist seeking to protect the Amazon rainforest or a fiscally conservative taxpayer you have a stake in ending the drug war."[33] Today, the issue area of drug policy is comprised of numerous, competing frames, each highlighting a different dimension of the issue. For example, drug use can be framed as a societal problem, one that contributes to social ills such as poverty, neglect and abuse of children, crime, and homelessness, among others. In this frame, the focus is upon reducing American demand for drugs through various programs such as treatment centers and after-school and extracurricular programs for young adults. The movement to legalize marijuana as a medicinal drug has added another frame and dimension to public discussions regarding American drug policy. This frame highlights the drug's healing properties; distinguishes appropriate from inappropriate uses; and identifies legitimate users, growers, and distributors.[34] As the quote above indicates, these are just two of the most prominent frames that are now deployed by political elites in an effort to shape Americans' understanding of drug policy. Under recurrent conflict of this type, the framing options available to elected officials will be wider, offering them a greater degree of flexibility in the positions that they advocate and to which they adhere. In contrast to the last example, the relative flexibility associated with conflict of this type also provides greater opportunity for consensual politics.

The third pattern of conflict is that of elite consensus. Either elite consensus can be the product of previous conflict through public debate, or it can be attained through "insider politics." These two types of consensus are likely to differ in the extent to which they provide openings for future conflict and hence distinguish different levels of protection through institutionalization. Where consensus emerges through public debate and therefore gains the attention of the electorate, the issue frame will be more resilient to redefinition, given the previous levels of support. As stated earlier, frames include values, and these values will become embedded in the shared public understanding of the issue when consensus involves the attentive public. While elected officials will construct frames that include values for both genuine and strategic reasons, their primary concern is political gain. Where political gain tends to bind elected officials more closely to the ideological and partisan dimensions guiding conflict, the values embedded in issue frames will be more enduring with the mass public.[35]

In addition to the constraints imposed by public adherence to issue-frame values, representational constraints on elected officials will be much stronger where consensus has emerged through public debate. Here, elected officials are more likely to have taken a public position on the issue and to have received endorsement for this position by constituents and organized interests. Hence, when the public is more involved in an issue-frame consensus, changing course midstream will be more difficult than it would be under conditions of less scrutiny.

In contrast, in an insider strategy, a shared understanding of an issue comes through the quiet compromises of political elites made inside the insulated corridors of government. This type of consensus fails to attract the scrutiny of the attentive public, issue frames are not debated over the public airwaves, and issue salience is low. Issue frames agreed upon by political elites through insider politics invoke the privileges of institutionalization but lack the public commitment of those discussed through public debate. These issues provide more framing flexibility for elected officials because the information context is less constricted regarding the values, arguments, and treatment recommendations associated with the issue. Here, the incentive for issue reframing lies with elected officials opposed to the status quo.

Thus, issues that undergo recurrent conflict with frequent reframings provide the most flexible conditions for issue redefinition by elected officials. Where these reframings do not involve national attention, the level of flexibility will be enhanced because the representational constraints will be relaxed. Yet even in the case where these reframings are waged in public debate, the recurring nature of such conflict will provide a greater degree of flexibility for future attempts at issue redefinition by elected officials. In contrast, elected officials have the least flexibility on issues that undergo recurrent public conflict where that conflict hardens into two opposing camps. Here, the information context is rigidly defined, and the range of framing options is drastically reduced.

Framing Constraints and the War on Terrorism

The terrorist attacks of 2001 had a profound effect upon American politics. They gave rise to an outpouring of public emotion, patriotism, and presidential support. As citizens proudly displayed the American flag, they mobilized in support of their president. From an unremarkable 51 percent the week of September 7–10, 2001, President George W. Bush's approval ratings skyrocketed to 90 percent in the wake of the terrorist attacks.[36] On Capitol Hill, the reaction was one of remarkable unity. Members of Congress came together in support of the nation both symbolically and legislatively. On the evening of September 11, lawmakers assembled on the steps of the Capitol and together sang "God Bless America" before many issued statements resolving to work together to defend the nation.[37] In the following days and weeks, the congressional agenda shifted dramatically from issues such as campaign finance reform, social security, and a patients' bill of rights to disaster relief, an airline bailout, airport security, and homeland defense.[38]

By the end of the 107th Congress in December of 2001, representatives had passed nine bills and three joint resolutions related to the terrorist attacks. Some of those bills found their way through a legislative process generally known for procedural complexity and partisan stalemate with amazing speed and astonishing levels of support. For example, the airline bailout was introduced and signed into law within one day, and the U.S.A. Patriot Act of 2001, a weighty and quite controversial piece of legislation, cleared the Senate by a vote of ninety-eight to one, with one abstention.[39] Congressional support for the president's program was initially so high that some commentators expressed concern regarding the health of the deliberative process in the legislative body. As Anthony Romero, executive director of the American Civil Liberties Union, stated, "Unfortunately, this week there has been a rush to change our nation's laws without any meaningful opportunity for deliberation or debate on how either our security or our freedom would be affected."[40]

The shift in agenda outlined above was paralleled by a drive to reframe issues in light of the terrorist attacks. Not only did congressional attention turn from domestic issues to matters of security and foreign policy, but old issues were made new through reframing. In the immediate aftermath of the attacks, the "rally around the flag" effect opened the door to a storm of legislative proposals consistent with conservative preferences on issues such as wiretapping, military tribunals, airline security, presidential authority on trade, and drilling for oil in the Arctic National Wildlife Refuge.[41] Thus, the terrorist attacks opened up opportunities for elected officials to reframe particular issues with the hope of achieving legislative success. However, as I assert at the outset of this essay, issue framing can be a useful component of strategies for both legislative and electoral success.[42]

As William Jacoby explains: "Reliance on one issue frame rather than another does not, in itself, require any outlay of tangible resources. However, it does influence the distribution of public responses to that issue. Thus, issue framing as a political strategy involves minimal costs, and it has the potential to provide sizable benefits" (2000, 751). But like any tool, issue framing will be more useful in some situations than others. Specifically, issue framing is likely to be an advantageous strategy in competitive elections for several reasons. First, if issue framing is to have an effect on election returns, the candidates must discuss (and differ over) the framing of political issues. On this score, researchers have found that candidates are much more likely to focus on the issues, rather than personal characteristics, in tight races (Kahn and Kenney 1999, 72). Second, the power of issue framing rests in its ability to change public opinion.[43] As outlined above, those who are most likely to be influenced by issue framing—the nonideological attentive public—are a small but significant subsection of the electorate that may tip the scales in favor of one candidate over another in a close election. Third, for issue framing to reach those voters, candidates must expend resources in order to get out their message, and heavy spending is much more likely in competitive than in noncompetitive elections and, while the gap is closing, in Senate versus House elections.[44]

The midterm elections of 2002 were the first national general elections since the terrorist attacks of September 11, 2001. Leading into those elections, the partisan composition of the American electorate remained closely divided, affording no clear advantage to either party.[45] Still, the political climate had changed since the 2000 elections. According to a Gallup poll, the most enduring effects of the terrorist attacks on public opinion were in Americans' ranking of terrorism as an important issue; President Bush's approval ratings; attitudes toward immigration; and, to a lesser degree, evaluations of the Republican party.[46] After the earlier high of 90 percent, President Bush's approval rating remained a substantial 65 percent in October of 2002.[47] As voters considered their congressional vote, Gallup found that more looked to national issues and questions of foreign policy to decide than had in previous elections. Terrorism, the crisis in the Middle East, and a possible war with Iraq all ranked highly, as did domestic concerns about education and the economy.[48] Polls also showed that while the favorability rating of the Democratic party remained at roughly 56 percent over the last year, that of the Republican party improved from 47 percent in September of 2001 to 53 percent in October of 2002. Over the same period, the Republican party's unfavorable ratings dropped from 48 percent to 35 percent while those of Democrats moved from 38 percent to 30 percent. Thus, in the year following the terrorist attacks, the image of the Republican party became more positive, and negative evaluations of all partisans declined among the public at large.[49]

In electoral politics, it was the Republicans who were best positioned to capitalize on these factors through issue framing. The following example explores how three victorious Republican senatorial candidates responded to this new political climate: Elizabeth Dole of North Carolina, Saxby Chambliss of Georgia, and Jim Talent of Missouri.[50] Each of these candidates ran in an incredibly tight race, and all referenced the terrorist attacks of September 11 in different ways and to varying degrees in their campaigns. Still, some significant patterns did appear.

At times, candidates used the terrorist attacks in order to draw attention to new issues such as legislation on homeland security; at others, to reframe existing issues—for example, drilling for oil in the Arctic National Wildlife Refuge or the importance of implementing a missile-defense program. However, in the electoral context, the discussion of issues is prompted by the larger goal of winning an election. Thus, candidates also used the terrorist attacks more broadly to frame the election itself. In traditional issue framing, the frame of reference defines the problem, provides causal interpretation, draws attention to a set of values, and identifies a treatment recommendation for the problem at hand. In the election frames, candidates made reference to the terrorist attacks in order to spotlight some aspect of the democratic process and to illuminate how the candidate would contribute to that end, whereas his or her opponent would not. Four election frames emerged in a canvass of these candidates' speeches, press releases, debate and interview transcripts, and political ads; I refer to them as "Follow the Leader," "Weak Record," "Obstructionist Senate," and "Bipartisan Politics." While issue and election frames are analytically distinct concepts, in practice candidates wove them together in an attempt to deliver a compelling message.

After September 11, one of the most notable opportunities for Republican candidates was the promise that President Bush's popularity held for their success. Candidates sought to make this promise a reality by using the "Follow the Leader" election frame. This frame associates the candidate with the president and suggests to the voter that the president's initiatives have a greater likelihood of success with the candidate, rather than his or her opponent, in office. Jim Talent offered an example of this frame in its most general form: "He's a president worth following. I'm looking forward to going to the United States Senate and supporting him." Elizabeth Dole went a step further by coupling this general frame with reference to the terrorist attacks in order to underscore the importance of presidential leadership. She stated: "In the months since September 11th, politicians in both parties have risen to the level of statesmanship. . . . In the midst of war and recession, Americans nevertheless assert their belief that our country is on the right track. Why? . . . Because today politics has a purpose, and we all have a president to look up to in George W. Bush!"[51] For Republican candidates, presidential popularity was an important advantage in the 2002 midterm elections, but not the only one.

Another opportunity that emerged in the post–September 11 political environment was a rather deep shift in attention from domestic to foreign policy issues—issues on which, traditionally, voters tend to evaluate Republicans very positively (Ansolabehere and Iyengar 1994; Petrocik 1996). As evidenced above, this shift occurred among both political elites and average citizens. To take advantage of these circumstances, candidates emphasized the connections between the terrorist attacks and the importance of military strength. In an introductory ad targeted to rural voters, an emotional Jim Talent was shown delivering a speech in which he stated: "Given everything that's happened in the last six months, I want to go to the Senate and try and make sure that this nation is prepared, so that we're not attacked again, as we were on September 11th. . . . The importance of military strength isn't primarily so that you'll win the war. It's so you won't have to fight it. Because a lot of people in this world don't like us, because of who we are. As long as we are who we are and stand for what we stand for, we're going to have enemies. Boy, let's learn that lesson for good. Let's let September 11th teach us that lesson."[52] Similarly, when announcing her candidacy, Elizabeth Dole said: "The terrorist attacks reminded us of what is at stake in the current global war against evil. The federal government has no greater responsibility than the security of this nation, and as our president and his team move forward on many fronts, the nation's resolve will be challenged again and again."[53] In these examples, the candidates drew attention to American defense policy by framing it in light of the terrorist attacks. But in addition to this agenda-setting function, reference to the terrorist attacks was also made in order to frame the relatively new issue of homeland security.

In an increasingly tight race against Democratic incumbent and Vietnam veteran Max Cleland, Saxby Chambliss sparked much commentary by running an ad that began with a visual of Osama bin Laden and Saddam Hussein. In the ad, an announcer stated: "As America faces terrorists and extremist dictators, Max Cleland runs television ads claiming he has the courage to lead. . . . Since July, Max Cleland has voted against the president's vital homeland security efforts eleven times." And in a postelection interview, Chambliss gave the following explanation for his victory: "The president's very popular in Georgia. People knew and understood that Saxby Chambliss was very much involved in the homeland security issue and that the president needed the homeland security package that we passed in the House. That was one of the focal points of our campaign."[54] In both examples, Chambliss framed the issue of homeland security by referring to the terrorist attacks, either explicitly or implicitly, and then embedding it within an election frame that drew attention to the need for presidential leadership and a supportive Congress. In the first case he used "Weak Record," in the second "Follow the Leader."

The "Weak Record" election frame draws negative attention to the candidate's opponent by concentrating on the heart of the electoral process: representation. The implicit message is that the opponent does not represent the voter on critical issues. Jim Talent used this frame in order to attack his opponent, Jean Carnahan: "That's one of the reasons the Homeland Security Bill ended up getting deep-sixed. Ms. Carnahan voted against missile defense the week before September 11th and then voted to put it back the week after September 11th."[55] In the Chambliss example above, the candidate referenced the September 11 terrorist attacks to emphasize the importance of homeland security legislation and then targeted his opponent's voting record on this issue. By combining the "Weak Record" and "Follow the Leader" election frames, Chambliss was able to convey to the voter his support for the president's framing of homeland security.

One problem that Democrats faced on this issue was providing a convincing explanation to voters for the discrepancy between their voting record and their stated commitment to homeland security. In this instance, the constraining role of organized interests becomes apparent. Most Democrats, including Max Cleland, backed a version of homeland security that provided for greater worker protection, an element strongly supported by organized labor, a key Democratic constituency. But loyalty to organized labor put Democrats at odds with a popular president and clouded their commitment and actual leadership on an issue critical to voters.[56]

Just as the September 11 attacks opened up framing opportunities on the new issue of homeland security, they also created an opportunity for candidates to reframe existing issues. In the Missouri debate, Jim Talent expressed his support for oil drilling in the Arctic National Wildlife Refuge this way: "the alternative is to continue importing oil from people who hate us." Similarly, in a discussion of election issues, Saxby Chambliss argued that homeland security and the economy were intimately related: "Right now there is some uneasiness among an awful lot of Americans, whether it is flying or visiting large metro areas. People just aren't spending as much money. If we could get a homeland security bill passed and get that structure in place, I think people would have more confidence and start spending and traveling more."[57]

In other instances, candidates housed issue reframings inside the "Obstructionist Senate" election frame. Like the "Weak Record" frame, this frame draws negative attention to the candidate's opponent, but instead of concentrating on representation, it focuses on the institutional role the candidate would play if elected. The "Obstructionist Senate" frame identifies the candidate's opponent as a roadblock to the passage of important legislation supported or initiated by the president. Along these lines, Elizabeth Dole reframed the economy in terms of the terrorist attacks and placed it squarely within this election frame: "Putting the economy back on track will require the same kind of resolve, discipline and focus that is now being applied to the war we wage on terrorism. To do anything less on the economic front would be a dramatic failure of leadership. The Senate should pass an economic stimulus package to help get our economy moving again, but recently the Senate leadership abandoned the bill, and walked away from the workers."[58] Likewise, Jim Talent used the "Obstructionist Senate" frame in reference to the issue of taxes: "We need to say to Senator Daschle, 'Stop trying to divide us,' because . . . tax relief for individuals is good for business, and tax relief for business is good for individuals." And in a very revealing example, Dole used the same strategy to reframe the issue of abortion. She stated: "It is this sense of mission—this binding unity—that has done so much to redefine our public life since September 11. We have been reminded, and we have shown the world that we are one nation, one nation under God. We must not let this moment pass quickly into the history books. With such a window of opportunity I pray that our country can right some recent wrongs! . . . It is tragically wrong that the liberal Democrat leadership in the United States Senate will not take up House-passed legislation to ban partial birth abortion. A bill that *this* President would sign into law!"[59] As the Dole example vividly shows, the above passages illustrate the framing opportunities that these candidates perceived to exist during the 2002 election season. However, the last election frame I will discuss, "Bipartisan Politics," suggests that these candidates also practiced a degree of restraint and saw themselves as constrained by the public mood of their constituencies.

There is no doubt that the September 11 attacks were an exogenous shock, the force of which immediately altered the landscape of American politics. However, understanding the more enduring ramifications of that shock for the political system requires closer analysis. If we conceptualize the public mood broadly as an indicator of those issues that Americans believe the government should address, it is fair to say that the terrorist attacks shifted Americans' attention away from the domestic issues that dominated the 2000 presidential campaign, such as education and social security, and toward issues of security and foreign policy. However, if we use the more specific and ideological conception of public mood identified above, the link between the terrorist attacks and public attitudes is much less clear and direct. As the polling by Gallup indicates, early evidence does not suggest that the attacks sparked a more global or persistent shift toward conservatism among Americans. More important for this essay, like President Bush (whose view is outlined above), the candidates under review did not see the September 11 attacks as a justification for an ideological interpretation of the elections. Instead, they focused on the necessity for an action-oriented bipartisan politics, which they argued could only be delivered if they, instead of their opponents, were elected into office.

The "Bipartisan Politics" frame alludes to the terrorist attacks of September 11 in order to underscore the need for statesmanship and productive legislation. It draws upon Americans' antipathy for a legislative process that is often depicted as one of petty bickering and strategic maneuvering conducted for the good of organized interests. In contrast, this frame promises the voter a representative who will work for the people's interests and strive for the common good in a time of national uncertainty. After his victory, Jim Talent stated, "I'm ready to go to Washington and get to work, and I want to go to Washington to work together." Echoing President Bush, Saxby Chambliss interpreted the elections this way: "What we're going to do is I think the American people sent a very clear message that they want Congress to work with the president, not be an obstructionist of the president. They want to see the president's agenda enacted into law and I think you saw that all across America last night." Throughout her campaign, Elizabeth Dole frequently stressed the theme of bipartisanship. In announcing her candidacy she commented, "Wherever I have gone in the course of my travels around this state, I have found a bipartisan desire for a different kind of politics, a positive campaign worthy of the challenges we confront and the sacrifices being made in defense of American democracy." In a speech to the NAACP convention in North Carolina she stated, "If our children are never too young to learn, then let it be said that our politicians are never too old, or set in their ways, to learn the value of bipartisan collaboration. In the wake of September 11 we rediscovered what I call the politics of purpose. In our grief and resolve, old divisions melted."[60]

As in President Bush's cautious interpretation of these elections, the emphasis upon bipartisanship shows candidates intent upon avoiding ideological language. In the case of Bush, evidence indicates that his political team recognized the power of the public mood as a constraint on the framing options available to elected officials. As the *Washington Post* reported in reference to the Senate elections: "White House officials said they were aware of the danger of overplaying their hand. 'Fifty-one is much better than 49, but it isn't 60, so it's not like things will just fly through the Senate.'" Other legislators also recognized the partisan and ideological constraints that continued to play in the post–September 11 political climate. As Senator Susan Collins, a moderate Republican from Maine, stated in an interview with the *National Journal:* "I think both the White House and the Republican leadership in the House and Senate are very aware of the need to avoid hubris and over-reaching. . . . I noticed that everyone from the president to our leaders in the Senate have been very temperate in their comments, post-election, and have pledged to work hard on the very large, unfinished agenda."[61]

The "Bipartisan Politics" election frame used by these elected officials demonstrates the nuances of the political environment after September 11. While the terrorist attacks did create framing opportunities for elected officials, obstacles still remained. As the *Cook Political Report* summed up the 2002 elections: "It was hardly the seismic shift in the political landscape that many have claimed. The results do not reflect any significant movement in public attitudes. Fundamentally the United States remains an evenly divided nation and as a result, most of our national elections, more likely than not, will be competitive."[62] In such an environment, strong ideological appeals run the risk of alienating voters. Thus, conservative candidates took note of the partisan and ideological constraints at work and moderated their language by framing the elections in terms of bipartisan leadership and legislative action.

Issue Framing and Public Deliberation

By bringing attention to the dynamic and complex nature of issue redefinition, and further elucidating the sphere of action in which elected officials can reasonably be expected to act, I have tried to draw a more realistic, although less optimistic, picture of our current political system and the power and flexibility available to elected officials within that system. In American politics, the fragmentation of power is not the only restraint upon legislative action. Politicians are also limited by apparent opportunities that prove to be problematic. For example, the partisan and ideological factors that initially constrained the candidates and led them to create less ideological election frames such as "Bipartisan Politics" may actually continue to hem these elected officials in as they pursue future legislative and electoral goals. One of the striking features of the election frames outlined here is their general applicability: all are familiar ones in American elections. However, what was different about their use in the 2002 election cycle was that reference to the terrorist attacks gave these frames much greater weight; in essence, September 11 served to underscore the necessity of an energetic national executive and a supportive legislative branch.

However, once in office, the above candidates will find themselves immersed in the very competitive and narrowly divided partisan and ideological climate of legislative politics. In such a climate, and especially where the Republican party holds both houses of Congress and the executive branch, meeting the call to leadership and legislative action promised in the election frames is sure to be difficult. In this case, the above frames, intended to moderate ideological extremism and secure an election victory, may actually reinforce the tendency among voters to expect too much of their elected officials.

While political elites are constrained by a number of factors, history itself confines our ability to track new ways of understanding the issues facing the American polity. The very way we understand and interpret issues also confines us because of the enduring quality of the values institutionalized in public policy and the legacy of our previous discussions about particular issues. The Homeland Security Act of 2002, passed after the midterm elections, established the Department of Homeland Security. This critical step in the institutionalization of the issue of homeland security will surely shape the issue environment and the opportunities available for future framings of that issue. Although we cannot separate our historic shared understandings of particular issues, we reduce our ability to relate these issues to new contexts if we fail to recognize the power of the past in our current debates. If we acknowledge this limitation on public discourse, we may facilitate more fruitful and open public discussions on current issues, enhancing the possibilities of democratic politics.

One of the most fundamental benefits of a democratic system is the free sharing of information and public deliberation over political issues. If we assume that public debate on political issues is beneficial because it leads to better public policy, as well as a more informed citizenry, we want officials to be able to reframe issues and therefore bring alternative arguments, values, and treatment recommendations to the fore. Given the cognitive limitations of individuals, issue frames are necessary; they bring some coherence to multifaceted issues that impinge upon many aspects of political life. But looking at a problem from several different angles generally helps one understand it better. In the same sense, public deliberation regarding political issues benefits from the construction of a variety of issue frames. Where the information context surrounding an issue is most open and fluid, we find the greatest possibility for redefining issues and considering them differently. Yet the ideological and partisan dimensions that guide conflict for elected officials tend to constrain the information context. At the very center of democratic politics lies the balance between programmatic politics and an environment that is most conducive to public debate.

PART II

The Impact of Elite Discourse on Citizens

4
Democratic Debate and Real Opinions

Donald R. Kinder and Thomas E. Nelson

In our analysis, frames lead a double life. As much of the extant literature suggests, frames are arguments and justifications embedded in political discourse. In this use, frames are either rhetorical weapons created and sharpened by political elites to advance their position or, perhaps more often, journalistic habits, convenient "handles" for succinctly conveying the essence of a story (Gitlin 1980; Gurevitch and Blumler 1990). In both uses, frames are a central part of political debate.

At the same time, frames also live inside the mind; they are cognitive structures that help citizens make sense of politics (Scheufele 2000). Frames provide order and meaning, making the world beyond direct experience seem natural. Without frames in mind, citizens are likely to be bewildered and overwhelmed by the swarm of problems that animate political life; to them politics will appear as "one great, blooming, buzzing confusion" (James 1981, 462).

Our purpose here is to establish that frames, conceived of in this fashion, are consequential: that public opinion depends in a systematic and intelligible way on how, *and especially whether,* issues are framed in democratic debate. More specifically, we will show that public opinion deteriorates in the absence of popular debate. When elites fail to provide citizens with frames that might aid their understanding, public opinion is impaired.

Of the many different theoretical approaches to the framing concept, we favor the constructivist persuasion within sociology and communication studies, which seeks to understand how objective conditions become transformed into "social problems" (e.g., Entman 1993; Gamson 1992; Neuman, Just, and Crigler 1992). We borrow most—this is a polite term for it—from the work of William Gamson and his associates (Gamson 1992; Gamson and Lasch 1983; Gamson and Modigliani 1987). Gamson presumes, as we do, that politics is in part a competition of ideas. Every issue is contested; advocates of one persuasion or another are always trying to define the issue their way. Thus the debate over abortion might be framed in terms of a woman's right to control her own body or in terms of the baby's right to life. Weapons treaties with what used to be the Soviet empire might be understood as either an effort to reduce the risks of a nuclear holocaust or a test of Communist intentions and aspirations. Government programs that benefit black Americans may be thought of as leveling the playing field in light of continuing discrimination or as handing blacks advantages they have not earned. A more intrusive and vigorous government security apparatus might be framed as a prudent response to terror or as ethnic profiling. As these examples suggest, frames are rarely evenhanded: they define what the essential problem is and how to think about it; often they suggest what, if anything, should be done to fix it.

Background Assumptions

Informing our project are long-standing disputes about the capacity of ordinary people to participate in their own governance. Democracy—rule by the people—is justified only on the assumption that average citizens are, taken all around, qualified to govern themselves. At the core of arguments for democracy is what Robert Dahl calls the presumption of personal autonomy: "In the absence of a compelling showing to the contrary, everyone should be assumed to be the best judge of his or her own good or interests" (1989, 100). The same point is reflected in John Dewey's insistence that asking people what they want, not telling them what they need or what is good for them, is "an essential part of the democratic idea" (quoted in Thompson 1970, 15).

Many perceptive analysts of politics have questioned whether citizens really are up to the demands of democracy. Walter Lippmann, Joseph Schumpeter, and most recently Philip Converse have all expressed strong reservations about the political capacity of ordinary citizens in modern mass society. Converse made his case with evidence: he concluded his analysis of national surveys carried out in the 1950s with the charge that most Americans glance at public life innocent of ideological concepts and unguided by any broad outlook on government policy.

Most troubling for democratic sensibilities was the specific indictment of "non-attitudes," the claim that "large portions of an electorate do not have meaningful beliefs, even on issues that have formed the basis for intense political controversy among elites for substantial periods of time" (Converse 1964, 245). Some citizens seemed to possess genuine opinions and to hold onto them tenaciously, but they were usually outnumbered by those who either confessed their ignorance outright or, out of embarrassment or misplaced civic obligation, concocted an opinion on the spot. Such flimsy fabrications should be regarded, according to Converse (1964, 1970), not as real attitudes but as "non-attitudes."

It may be that Americans are innocent of sweeping ideological ideas, but they are hardly innocent of personal and political considerations that bear on matters of public debate. The American political mind is not so much empty as it is teeming with potentially relevant considerations: the interests at stake, feelings of resentment or sympathy toward social groups implicated in the issue, general views on equality and the intrusive (or commendable) interventions of government, and no doubt more (Feldman and Zaller 1992; Kinder and Sanders 1996; Lane 1962). This point is perhaps best illustrated in Jennifer Hochschild's (1981) in-depth discussions with ordinary Americans about justice in politics, in the workplace, and at home. On the one hand, the people Hochschild interviewed display the same symptoms that Converse detected: inconsistency, hesitation, ambivalence, confusion, and so on. On the other hand, their fundamental problem is not that they have no ideas about taxes or unemployment or income distribution but that they have too many. They suffer not so much from a shortage of relevant considerations as from an impoverished ability to integrate them. What they lack, perhaps, are frames. What they need, perhaps, is democratic debate.

Method and Hypotheses

How can such a claim be tested? We assume that by examining the kinds of alterations in opinion that are induced by systematic alterations in the way that questions are posed—or *framed*—within a survey we can learn how changes in public opinion are induced by changes in the setting beyond the survey, in the ongoing, intermittent conversation between elites and publics that is central to the democratic process. By framing issue questions in different ways, we intend to mimic or reenact this natural process of political debate (Kinder and Sanders 1990; Nelson and Kinder 1996).

With this purpose in mind, we designed three question-wording experiments and embedded them within the 1989 National Election Study (NES), carried out in the summer and fall of 1989. In NES parlance, this was a "pilot study," part of an ongoing effort to test new instrumentation for possible incorporation into future National Election Studies. Participants who had completed both the preelection and postelection interviews from the previous (1988) National Election Study (and who had provided their telephone numbers) were eligible for selection into the 1989 NES. Participants were randomly drawn from this target population, with oversampling inversely proportional to level of political information, in order to yield a final sample that would more adequately represent the American adult population. In all, telephone interviews were completed with 614 Americans of voting age during July; nearly 500 of these were questioned again, also over the telephone, in September.[1]

For our purpose, the special attraction of the 1989 NES was that it enabled us to carry out three parallel experiments. In each, we compared public opinion on three major policy disputes elicited in one of two ways: either by questions that refer to the rival frames that dominate elite discourse (the "framed" condition) or by questions that do not (the "stripped" condition). Each of the experiments therefore mimics the distinction between public opinion with and without democratic debate. The framed treatment reenacts the political condition in which citizens witness a debate between opposing elites, each pushing an alternative definition of the issue. Meanwhile, the stripped treatment simulates the political condition where there is no elite debate. Frameless, citizens are left on their own in formulating what the issue is about.

Our experiments are the real thing: that is, participants in the 1989 NES were *randomly assigned* to the framed or stripped condition. Random assignment ensures that any observed difference between conditions is due to differences in the treatments themselves. Absent random assignment, there is no way to guarantee equivalence of groups before the treatments are applied. In a single stroke, then, random assignment sweeps aside a host of possible alternative interpretations. It is, as Cook and Campbell once put it, "the great *ceteris paribus* of causal inference" (1979, 5).[2]

Like all empirical methods, experimentation has liabilities as well as strengths. When it comes to *internal validity*—providing unequivocal evidence on causal relationships—experiments have no equal. But on matters of *external validity*—providing assurance about the generalizability of results—experiments are less persuasive. Concern about the external validity of experimental results takes various expression, but the standard complaint, and the most powerful, questions the typicality of experimental subjects—who, after all, are usually college students (Hovland 1959; Sears 1986). This line of argument may pose a serious challenge to some experiments, but it does no damage to ours. By situating our experiments within a national survey (one, moreover, that went to unusual lengths to ensure that its sample represented the national population of voting-age citizens), we neatly avoid this common liability. For a study of public opinion, we are examining precisely the population of real interest.

We undertake three experiments in parallel, each centered on a different political dispute. Each comes from a different location in the landscape of contemporary American political contention. First is the deeply felt issue of abortion, selected as an example of the agenda of social issues advanced by religious conservatives; second is U.S. relations with the Soviet Union, the preeminent preoccupation of postwar American foreign policy at the time these data were collected; and third is the federal government's obligation to black Americans, an example of a persistent and controversial aspect of American social welfare policy.

To get our particular experiments off the ground, we first had to identify the frames prevailing in public discourse and then translate them into vernacular appropriate to a national survey. This required consulting the text of Supreme Court decisions in pivotal cases, speeches delivered by public officials and prominent activists, the views expressed in political journals, and more. Whenever possible, we took advantage of investigations undertaken by others, particularly those by Gamson and Modigliani (1987), Gamson and Lasch (1983), and Luker (1984). Based on this work, we took the relevant frames to be *a woman's right to control her own body* versus *the sanctity of human life* in the case of abortion; *reducing the risks of war* versus *Communists cannot be trusted* in the case of cooperating with the Soviet Union; and *continuing discrimination* versus *undeserved advantage* in the case of government aid to blacks. In the end, after much discussion, some tinkering, and a review of pretest results, we formulated the questions in the following way.

Abortion

Framed

There has been some discussion about abortion during recent years. Some Americans oppose abortion; they think of themselves as "pro-life"; they believe that abortion is murder. Other Americans believe that a woman should have the right to an abortion; they think of themselves as "pro-choice"; they believe that whether or not to have an abortion must be the woman's choice, not the government's.

Stripped

There has been some discussion about abortion during recent years. Which one of the opinions I am about to read you best agrees with your view on abortion?

1. By law, abortion should never be permitted.

2. The law should permit abortion only in case of rape, incest, or when the woman's life is in danger.

3. The law should permit abortion for reasons *other than* rape, incest, or danger to the woman's life, but only after the need for the abortion has been clearly established.

4. By law, a woman should always be able to obtain an abortion as a matter of personal choice.

Cooperating with the Soviet Union

Framed

Our next question concerns the relationship between the United States and Russia. Some Americans feel that we should try to cooperate more with Russia, in order to reduce the chances of a nuclear war. Other Americans believe that we should be much tougher in our dealings with Russia because Russian leaders are Communists, and they still want to take over the world.

Stripped

Our next question concerns the relationship between the United States and Russia. Some people feel we should try to cooperate more with Russia, while others believe we should be much tougher in our dealings with Russia.

Do you have an opinion on this, or haven't you thought much about it?

Do you feel we should try to cooperate more with Russia, get tougher in our dealings with Russia, or is your opinion somewhere in between?

Should we try to cooperate a lot more or somewhat more?

Should we get a lot tougher or somewhat tougher?

Government Assistance to Blacks

Framed

Some people feel that the government in Washington should make a special effort to improve the social and economic position of blacks, because blacks still don't have the same opportunities to get ahead as everyone else. Others feel that the government should not make any special effort to help blacks—that blacks should help themselves, just as other groups have done.

Stripped

Some people feel that the government in Washington should make every effort to improve the social and economic position of blacks, while others feel that the government should not make any special effort to help blacks.

Do you have an opinion on this issue, or haven't you thought much about it?

Do you feel the government should or should not make a special effort to help blacks, or is your position somewhere in between?

Should the government help blacks to a great extent or only to some extent?

Should the government make any effort at all to improve the position of blacks?

Notice that the framed and the stripped versions of each of the three questions ask about the identical policy, and they offer the same response options. The only difference is that in one condition, the issue comes framed, packaged in the rival arguments that dominate elite discourse, while in the other, the issue comes stripped of any such reference. We expected that opinion elicited under framed conditions would differ systematically from opinion elicited under stripped conditions, that it would display the benefits of democratic debate. More specifically, we expected:

1. that in the framed condition, opinion would be more widespread: when asked the framed version of the question, more citizens would express an opinion

2. that in the framed condition, opinion would be more stable: when asked the framed version of the question, more people would take the same position from one occasion to the next

3. that in the framed condition, opinion would be better anchored: when asked the framed version of the question, people would express views predicted better by the group resentments and political principles that the frame highlighted

In these ways, framed opinions should more closely resemble the real opinions that democracy would seem to require.[3]

Results

Before our hypotheses about framed versus stripped opinions can be tested, it is necessary first to establish that survey participants randomly assigned to the two conditions are actually comparable. It would of course complicate things if one group was more liberal, for instance, than the other. With this concern in mind, we undertook a series of comparisons, examining the two groups on a full roster of standard demographic and political variables. The results are reassuring on the point that the two groups really are comparable, that the only feature that sets them apart is the experimentally induced one: some citizens were asked to think about abortion, cooperation with the Soviet Union, and government assistance to black Americans under relatively enriched circumstances, while others were asked to think about the same policies under relatively impoverished conditions.[4]

The Expression of Opinion

That citizens are reluctant to provide answers to some of the questions they encounter in the course of a political survey is due, at least in part, to the way questions are posed to them. In particular, citizens might not know quite how to think about an issue when it comes at them free of context. But when the issue is presented within a familiar frame, they might more readily give an answer. With a familiar and friendly frame in mind, citizens should be better equipped to integrate over various competing considerations, to overcome ambivalence, to arrive at an overall position.

To test this hypothesis, we simply partitioned those survey participants who declared that they had no opinion on the three issues from those who declared that they did, irrespective of what their opinion might be. We did so separately within the framed and stripped conditions, to see whether opinions were more likely to appear when the issue was framed. The results, shown in table 4.1, largely conform to our hypothesis. On two of three issues—U.S. relations with the Soviet Union and assistance to blacks—the expected framing effect appears, with significantly fewer "don't know" responses when the issue is framed. The lack of a framing effect for the abortion issue can perhaps be written off to the virtual absence of "don't know" responses there: of 614 people questioned on abortion, just 9 failed to provide an answer.[5]

More opinions aren't necessarily a good thing, of course. Are the additional views expressed under the framed condition real opinions? Or are they flimsy fabrications, created by the momentary presence of persuasive-sounding frames? We cannot resolve this question decisively with the evidence in hand, but we are inclined toward the former characterization—that the opinions are real and should be taken seriously—on three grounds. For one thing, opinions elicited under the framed condition were no less extreme. In our three experiments, frames did *not* yield a harvest of answers that pile up suspiciously in the center.[6] For another, when we repeated the analysis summarized in table 4.1, after first controlling for whether or not participants had expressed an opinion on a comparable issue when questioned in the 1988 NES survey, we found that frames were not any more effective among those who failed to express a view in 1988.[7] And finally, frames produce more opinions even among the comparatively well-informed.[8] In short, frames facilitate the expression of opinions among citizens in general, not just among "know-nothings." Frames, it would seem, help citizens find their political voice.[9]

4.1 Percentage expressing an opinion on abortion, relations with Russia, and aid to blacks when the issue is framed versus when the issue is stripped

	Framed	Stripped
Abortion	99.4	99.3
(N)	(311)	(298)
		$\chi^2 = .002$, n.s.ccc
Cooperating with Russia	74.2	67.7
(N)	(299)	(313)
		$\chi^2 = 3.16$, $p = .076$
Aid to blacks	69.7	57.7
(N)	(297)	(312)
		$\chi^2 = 9.51$, $p = .002$

Source: 1989 National Election Study

The Stability of Opinion

It was the observation of flagrant instability in public opinion that led Converse to the troubling conclusion that on many pressing matters of public debate, citizens possessed not real attitudes but non-attitudes. Here we suggest that unstable opinions may be a reflection in part of fluctuations in the way the issue is framed or, more likely, the absence of a guiding frame altogether; if citizens are left to their own devices, their views on government assistance to blacks might be shaped on one occasion by concerns over interests, at another time by ideas about equality, and on still a third occasion primarily by feelings of group solidarity or resentment. Such cycles might be broken by framing the issue in a consistent fashion, as we did in the 1989 NES. Citizens were questioned first in July and then again in September, and on both occasions they were asked about each of the three issues in the identical way. If the frames were in fact successful in inducing people to think about the issue in the same way, then opinion should be more stable across the two interviews in the framed than in the stripped condition.

Alas, it seems not to be. Our calculation of the percentage of survey participants expressing exactly the same view in July and in September, separately under framed and stripped conditions, provides another case of a plausible hypothesis running into an inconvenient fact. By this test, the presence of frames does little to enhance the stability of opinion. These results are on display in table 4.2. As revealed there, framed opinions do show more stability than their stripped counterparts on each of the three issues, consistent with our expectation, but the differences are small. In statistical terms, the differences are impossible to distinguish from no difference at all. Much the same conclusion obtains if we compare Pearson correlations or compute the absolute change in opinion. With different issues, or using different formulations, frames may increase opinion stability, but we see little evidence of that here.[10]

4.2 Stability of opinion on abortion, relations with Russia, and aid to blacks when the issue is framed versus when the issue is stripped *(% consistent)*

	Framed	Stripped
Abortion	73.7	69.8
Cooperating with Russia	54.3	53.7
Aid to blacks	59.6	55.3

Source: 1989 National Election Study

The Antecedents of Opinion

Our final analysis examines the extent to which opinions are rooted more securely in their putative antecedents under framed conditions, where citizens are guided to consider those antecedents invoked by the rival frames, than under stripped conditions, where citizens are more on their own. The most general expectation would be that the pattern of antecedent relationships discovered in the framed condition would resemble the pattern of relationships in the stripped condition, but in amplified form. Tiny relationships would grow more visible, modest relationships would become strong, and strong relationships would become stronger still. Moving from the stripped condition to the framed would be the equivalent of switching from a black and white television to color: we would be looking at the same picture, but presented in a more vivid and arresting way. Or alternatively, perhaps the effects of framing would be specific and contingent. Then we would see increases in particular relationships. In forming their views, citizens would draw especially heavily on those antecedents that the rival frames highlighted.

To find out, we undertook two identical regression analyses for each of the three issues. Within each pair, one regression was based on those survey participants who were presented with the issue embedded in rival frames, while the other was based on those who were presented with the issue without frames. Each pair of equations included the same set of plausible antecedents. For the purpose of analyzing opinion on abortion, for example, these antecedents included measures of moral conservatism, religious traditionalism, attitudes toward the pro-life movement, and attitudes toward feminists. Comparable and occasionally overlapping sets of antecedent variables were developed for the issues of relations with the Soviets and government assistance to blacks (see table 4.3). In almost all cases, antecedent variables were represented in the regressions by multiple-item scales, with individual items taken from the 1988 NES. (The scales are described in detail in the appendix.) Each equation also included, for purposes of control, a standard set of demographic and political variables: age, region (South), education, race (black), gender (male), ideological identification, and party identification.[11]

Table 4.3 presents the results for each of the three issues in the form of unstandardized regression coefficients. For each issue, there are two columns of coefficients, one (on the left) corresponding to the framed condition and one (on the right) corresponding to the stripped condition. For the sake of convenience, we coded all variables on the 0–1 interval.

With the most general expectation in mind, we should see coefficients increasing in absolute magnitude as we move from the stripped column to the

4.3 Antecedents of opinion on abortion, relations with Russia, and aid to blacks when the issue is framed versus when the issue is stripped

	Abortion		Cooperating with Russia		Aid to blacks	
	Framed	Stripped	Framed	Stripped	Framed	Stripped
Limited government	.23	.20			.09	.17
	(.09)	(.09)			(.08)	(.08)
Moral conservatism	−.25	−.15				
	(.09)	(.10)				
Religious traditionalism	−.38	−.39				
	(.08)	(.08)				
Attitudes toward feminists	.43	.45				
	(.11)	(.12)				
Evaluation of pro-life movement	−.20	−.28				
	(.06)	(.06)				
Anti-Communism			.22	.12		
			(.06)	(.06)		
Attitudes toward the military			.12	.20		
			(.08)	(.08)		
Evaluation of Gorbachev			−.29	.21		
			(.06)	(.06)		
Equal opportunity					.22	.16
					(.10)	(.10)
Attitudes toward blacks					.80	.41
					(.12)	(.12)
Attitudes toward the poor					.01	−.16
					(.08)	(.08)
Constant	.87	.89	.34	.47	.14	.45
	(.12)	(.11)	(.09)	(.09)	(.12)	(.12)
N	293	282	265	286	260	267
R²	.38	.37	.32	.32	.37	.22
Standard error	.26	.28	.20	.20	.22	.23

Source: 1989 National Election Study

Note: Table entry is the unstandardized regression coefficient with standard errors in parentheses. Blanks indicate that variables were excluded from the equation. Each equation also includes measures of age, region (South), education, race (black), gender (male), level of political information, ideological identification, and party identification, all taken from the 1988 NES. On the issue of aid to blacks, the analysis is based on whites only. All variables are coded on a 0–1 interval.

framed. But as table 4.3 shows, we generally do not see that. Sometimes the coefficients get bigger, sometimes they get smaller, and often they stay about the same size. Likewise, neither R² nor the standard error of the regression (both found at the base of table 4.3) supports the general expectation. Wrapping issues in frames does not simply produce a more highly resolved picture of the sources of opinion.

There are, however, results in table 4.3 that point to the importance of frames—and therefore to democratic debate. The case is clearest for opinion on government help to blacks. Recall that in the framed condition, support for government assistance was justified on the grounds that American society failed to provide equal opportunities to blacks. Meanwhile, opposition to government help was justified on the grounds that blacks must take individual responsibility for their own lives, as other groups had done. Encouraged to think about government assistance in this way, citizens should attach more weight to their assessment of the moral qualifications of black Americans than they otherwise would. And they did. Racial sentiments had a bigger impact on opinion in the framed condition than in the stripped. The difference is large and statistically significant.[12] The emphasis on blacks' individual responsibility seems to have induced a "group-centric" approach to this issue (Nelson and Kinder 1996).

Framing the question in the way that we did also seemed to diminish the importance of other possible considerations. While racial sentiments were being brought to center stage, other ways of seeing the question were being shunted aside. In particular, opposition to government intervention as a matter of principle was less important under framed than under stripped conditions, and so was sympathy for the poor. As table 4.3 indicates, the effect of limited government, noticeable in the stripped condition, becomes invisible in the framed condition; meanwhile, sentiments toward the poor are quite prominent in the stripped condition but fade away in the framed condition.[13] These results suggest that when frames draw attention to some considerations, they deflect attention away from others.

The same point is made with public opinion toward U.S cooperation with the Soviet Union. Notice first that the Cold War rhetoric of the U.S.–Soviet frame appeared to enhance the importance of citizens' views toward Gorbachev and Communism. Framing the issue in this way appears to have turned cooperation with the Soviets into a referendum on Soviet intentions. To the extent that citizens approved of Gorbachev and were reluctant to see Communism as the evil empire, they were willing to support cooperative relations.[14] At the same time, framing the issue in this way may have diminished the relevance of evaluations of the U.S. military to the issue.[15] Thus, as before, frames both highlight certain considerations and push others to the side.

Third and last is the issue of abortion. As table 4.3 reveals, views on abortion are rooted in religious and moral convictions and in assessments of the principal social movements that have clashed over the issue. These relationships are powerful, and they are largely unaffected by whether or not the issue was embedded in a frame. There is a hint that moral conservatism matters a bit more when abortion is framed as a choice between the sanctity of life and the right of women to control their own bodies than when the issue is stripped of this frame, but we should not make too much of it.[16] The larger picture here, as throughout, is the resilience of public opinion on abortion. Abortion's exemption from framing may reflect the conspicuous and deeply felt debate that has unfolded in American politics over the last two decades. Perhaps on this issue, most Americans really know what they think: that is, they have internalized a single frame, one way of thinking about the issue, and are therefore no longer reachable by elites seeking to define the issue of abortion differently.

Implications

Members of Congress, corporate publicists, organized interests, presidents, and more are engaged in a perpetual contest of words and symbols. They are always trying to define issues advantageously, in ways that advance (or protect) their position. In a democratic society, this means that advocates tune their arguments with the general public in mind. This war of frames becomes available to ordinary people in a variety of ways: by the reporting of daily events in television news programs, newspapers, and radio; by editorials, syndicated columns, political talk shows, cartoons, newsletters, and the like; and, most directly, by press conferences, debates, advertisements, and speeches. Through all these channels, citizens are showered with frames, bombarded with suggestions about how issues should be understood. In the process, some issues are spotlighted, while others, perhaps equally important, are ignored.

Here, in a series of three experiments, we have asked whether the presence of such a debate contributes to an informed public opinion. Do framed opinions, compared to their stripped counterparts, resemble more the opinions that exponents of democratic government hope for? The answer is yes. We found that enriching the question with a frame enables citizens to express a view, that framed opinions appear to be as sensible and solid as those that do not require such assistance, and that opinions expressed in the presence of frames are fastened more securely to their premises. The effects are not overwhelming, but they are quite consistent, and they are produced by modest interventions. All that we have done is add several well-formulated phrases, and yet this addition visibly enhances the structure of public opinion. In this concluding section, we take the implications of our results off in three directions: democratic debate, the nature of opinion, and recipes for question writing.

Frames and Democratic Debate

A persistent theme in democratic theory is the importance of cool and reasoned discussion. John Stuart Mill, to take one prominent and influential example, placed debate over the common good at the heart of democracy. Without extensive discussion, according to Mill, we simply cannot grasp what might be worth doing, nor, just as important, can we learn from our mistakes: "There must be discussion, to show how experience is to be interpreted.

Wrong opinions and practices gradually yield to fact and argument: but facts and arguments, to produce any effect on the mind, must be brought before it. Very few facts are able to tell their own story, without comments to bring out their meaning. The whole strength and value, then, of human judgment, depending on the one property, that it can be set right when it is wrong, reliance can be placed on it only when the means of setting it right are kept constantly at hand" (1992, 20).

The claim that democracy requires or should aspire to orderly and widespread discussion receives extensive attention in contemporary writing as well. Consider, as prominent cases in point, Robert Dahl's (1989) democratic criterion of "enlightened understanding," the requirement that democratic institutions provide citizens with adequate and equal opportunities for discovering their own interests, or the utopian proposal of Jürgen Habermas (1982) on behalf of "ideal speech," where discussion is free and equal and practically endless and where consensus emerges only as the result of the force of better arguments.

If democracy depends mightily upon conversation—if it is "government by discussion," as Bagehot once wrote—then issue frames take on special importance. For frames might provide at least a partial solution to the ancient complaint that democracy requires of citizens more than they can supply. Frames supply a common vocabulary, one that enables elites and citizens to take part in the same conversation. Frames allow elites to speak clearly to citizens. Indeed, it would be odd if it were otherwise, since frames are created with this aim prominently in mind. Our experimental results suggest the benefits of democratic debate to public opinion.

At the same time, our results also suggest a more sinister side to the framing enterprise. Consider the results in table 4.3 regarding government assistance to black Americans. Recall that in the framed condition, support for government assistance was justified on the grounds that American society failed to provide equal opportunities to blacks, while opposition to government help was justified on the grounds that blacks must take individual responsibility for their own lives. Encouraged to think about government assistance in this way, white opinion turned out to be dominated by racial sentiments. In the stripped condition, in the absence of a frame that turned the issue into a referendum on black character, public opinion was far less single-minded. Attitudes toward blacks still played an important role, but they did not overwhelm other considerations. Instead, public opinion reflected a diversity of ingredients: views on equality, beliefs about limited government, sentiments toward the poor—all had their say. The lesson here is that frames sharpen public thinking, but not necessarily in desirable directions.

More generally, insofar as frames are important to the formation of public opinion, power is transferred from ordinary people to political elites. Frames are, for the most part, created by intellectuals and activists, then brought to public attention by issue entrepreneurs and journalists. To be sure, elites construct and try out frames with public reaction very much in mind. And citizens certainly may reject frames they dislike and rework those they adopt. But by and large, citizens consume frames rather than produce them.[17]

Opinions on the Fly

Americans are far from blind to the momentous issues of the day, but they are often uncertain exactly how to think about them. The results from our experiments, as from other studies (Hochschild 1981; Iyengar and Kinder 1987; Kinder and Sanders 1990, 1996; Nelson and Kinder 1996; Sniderman and Piazza 1993; Stoker 1994; Tourangeau and Rasinski 1988; Zaller 1990, 1992; Zaller and Feldman 1992) suggest that most Americans, on most issues, do not really possess opinions, at least as that term is usually understood. That is, citizens do not possess a well-formed, crystallized position that, should the occasion arise, can be easily located and automatically reported. Citizens lack preformed opinions, but they are in possession of considerations out of which opinions can be constructed.

Such constructions can be quite meaningful. As we have seen here, most Americans appear to have in mind an assortment of ingredients out of which genuine and serious opinions on abortion, cooperation with the Soviet Union, and government programs for blacks can be fashioned. Exactly which opinion gets constructed out of these materials depends in part upon which of the materials come most prominently to mind. Not only because opinions on public issues are typically rather lightly considered but also because the complete set of relevant ingredients is too cumbersome to consider all at once, public opinion tends to reflect less the complete repertoire of citizens' interests and convictions and more which aspects of their interests and convictions happen to come to attention.

The two contributors to this chapter have been of two minds about the likely psychological mechanisms underlying framing effects. One of us (e.g., Kinder and Sanders 1996) has emphasized how frames "prime" certain considerations, giving them a privileged position in memory among all possible thoughts that relate to an issue (see also Zaller 1992). A primed consideration should be especially likely to affect issue opinions, relative to other possible influences (which might not even enter into active thought at any given moment). The other author (e.g., Nelson and Oxley 1999) has suggested that framing also influences the relative *importance* we attach to considerations, especially when we are aware of multiple, conflicting values or other ideas relevant to the issue. We can't be sure which psychological route was followed by most of the participants in these experiments, although the general research design ("framed" versus "stripped") appears more congenial to the former, "priming" phenomenon. In the stripped version, respondents might simply feel unqualified to present a legitimate opinion and so opt out of the question entirely. The framed version, by contrast, might remind respondents of reasons to favor or oppose the topic in question. The operative term here is "remind"—the priming hypothesis rests on the assumption that the frames simply call to mind ideas that previously had been associated with the issue. It is also possible, of course, that the frame actually implants new opinions by suggesting reasons to favor or oppose the issue that had not yet occurred to respondents. The precise effect doubtless varies from person to person, depending on the amount of attention given to the issue before the interviewer phoned.

Both because opinions can be rooted in a variety of considerations and because which considerations are given special attention may depend on how issues are being discussed and framed, citizens may sometimes run into trouble when trying to say exactly what they think. From this point of view, it is not so much that people have a single opinion in mind as it is that they have several possible opinions (cf. Sherif, Sherif, and Nebergall 1965). Granted, a few citizens do in fact hold well-crystallized positions of the classical sort. If we were to interview a member of the National Security Council about U.S. policy toward Russia, we would readily discover that she is in possession of a real opinion in the traditional sense—a deeply felt, well-defended one. However we put the question, her position would be the same: her internalized frame would override whatever frames we momentarily attached to our queries. In cross-sectional samplings of the general public, cases such as this probably show up at little more than trace levels. At the other extreme, of course, is the non-attitude. Even on the most contentious and prominent of issues, some citizens will be unable to construct a real opinion. If they happen to be asked, they will either confess to no interest or, out of embarrassment, fabricate a response, one so rickety and ill constructed that it promptly collapses as soon as the conversation moves on. Most cases lie in between: most of us, on most topics, possess not a single opinion, tenaciously held, nor a non-opinion, cooked up for the moment, but a range of opinions, each a more or less sensible reflection of our interests and convictions.

The conception of public opinion we are offering here can be read as an effort to put the public back in public opinion. By public opinion we mean to refer not just to the opinions of the broader public but to opinions that are made through public discussion—between elites, between elites and ordinary citizens, and among citizens themselves (Converse 1987; Peters 1995). A complete understanding of public opinion requires both a close examination of the intricacies of individual information processing and a detailed investigation of the circulation of ideas in society and the activities of opinion makers.

Recipes for Question Wording

That a policy can be framed in different ways to highlight or downplay certain of its features, and that different frames can influence what public opinion turns out to be, obviously complicates the business of gauging public sentiment accurately. If policies are typically framed in different ways in the political context outside the survey, we should certainly expect that the policy descriptions we use inside the survey will influence opinion as well. Our experiments show that they do, thereby demonstrating why the design of issue questions is one of the most vexing problems faced by survey researchers.

Our remedy for this problem may seem peculiar, but it follows directly from our results on framing: issue questions should incorporate the frames that prevail in contemporary political debate. Because such debate is almost always partisan and contentious, our recommendation moves against the conventional view that would have us compose innocuous questions. In the conventional view, questions should be sanitized, stripped of arguments, symbols, and reasons, anything that might sway citizens to one side or the other. Our advice, instead, runs to questions that are surrounded by arguments, symbols, and reasons. Like the political debate they are intended to mimic, issue questions should be provocative and contentious.

Better to surround issue questions with representations of the prevailing political culture than to strip them of this familiar and significant context. Better still to manipulate this context in systematic and relevant ways, in order to probe the dynamics of public opinion. Our experiments illustrate the point that surveys not only measure public opinion but also shape, provoke, and occasionally create it. This is a problem and a headache, but as we have tried to show here, it is an opportunity as well. Those of us who design surveys find ourselves, unavoidably, in roughly the same position as elites who create and promote the terms of political discourse. Both parties must decide how public issues are to be thought about and discussed. By examining the kinds of alterations in opinion that are induced by systematic alterations in the way that questions are framed within the survey, we can learn how public opinion is shaped by the conversation that takes place between leaders and citizens in democratic societies.

Appendix A

Scales and Items

I. Equal opportunity: Cronbach's alpha = .66

    A. Our society should do whatever is necessary to make sure that everyone has an equal opportunity to succeed.

    B. We have gone too far in pushing equal rights in this country.

    C. This country would be better off if we worried less about how equal people are.

    D. It's not really that big a problem if some people have more of a chance in life than others.

    E. If people were treated more equally in this country, we would have many fewer problems.

    F. One of the big problems in this country is that we don't give everyone an equal chance.

II. Attitudes toward blacks: alpha = .57

    A. Racial resentment

        1. The Irish, Italians, Jews, and many other minorities overcame prejudice and worked their way up. Blacks should do the same without any special favors.

        2. Over the past few years, blacks have gotten less than they deserve.

        3. It's really a matter of some people not trying hard enough; if blacks would only try harder, they could be just as well off as whites.

        4. Generations of slavery and discrimination have created conditions that make it difficult for blacks to work their way out of the lower class.

    B. Thermometer rating of whites minus thermometer rating of blacks

III. Moral conservatism: alpha = .62

    A. The world is always changing, and we should adjust our view of morality to those changes.

    B. We should be more tolerant of people who choose to live according to their own moral standards even if they are very different from our own.

    C. This country would have many fewer problems if there were more emphasis on traditional family ties.

    D. The newer lifestyles are contributing to the breakdown of society.

IV. Religious traditionalism: alpha = .77

    A. Would you say your religion provides some guidance in your day-to-day living, quite a bit of guidance, or a great deal of guidance?

    B. Here are four statements about the Bible, and I'd like you to tell me which is closest to your own view. Just give me the number of your choice.

        1. The Bible is God's word, and all it says is true.

        2. The Bible was written by men inspired by God, but it contains some human errors.

3. The Bible is a good book because it was written by wise men, but God had nothing to do with it.

4. The Bible was written by men who lived so long ago that it is worth very little today.

5. Other; please specify.

C. About how often do you pray—several times a day, once a day, a few times a week, once a week or less, or never?

D. Do you consider yourself a born-again Christian?

E. Do you identify with Christian fundamentalists?

V. Limited government: alpha = .61

A. Some people think the government should provide fewer services, even in areas such as health and education, in order to reduce spending. Suppose these people are at one end of the scale, at point 1. Other people feel it is important for the government to provide many more services, even if it means an increase in spending. Suppose these people are at the other end of the scale, at point 7. And of course some other people have opinions somewhere in between, at points 2, 3, 4, 5, or 6. Where would you place yourself on this scale, or haven't you thought much about this?

B. There is much concern about the rapid rise in medical and hospital costs. Some people feel there should be a government insurance plan that would cover all medical and hospital expenses for everyone. Others feel that all medical expenses should be paid by individuals and through private insurance plans like Blue Cross or other company-paid plans. Where would you place yourself on this scale (of 1 to 7), or haven't you thought much about this?

C. Some people feel the government in Washington, D.C., should see to it that every person has a job and a good standard of living. Others think the government should just let people get ahead on their own. Where would place yourself on this scale (of 1 to 7), or haven't you thought much about this?

D. Next, consider a different pair of statements. Which is closer to your own view?

1. The government should try to ensure that all Americans have such things as jobs, health care, and housing.

2. The government should not be involved in this.

VI. Anti-Communism: alpha = .72

A. The United States should maintain its position as the world's most powerful nation even if it means going to the brink of war.

B. Any time a country goes Communist, it should be considered a threat to the vital interests and security of the United States.

C. The United States should do everything it can to prevent the spread of Communism to any other part of the world.

VII. Attitudes toward feminists: alpha = .47

    A. Thermometer rating of feminists

    B. Identification with feminists

    C. Recently there has been a lot of talk about women's rights. Some people feel that women should have an equal role with men in running business, industry, and government. Others feel that women's place is in the house. Where would you place yourself on this scale (of 1 to 7), or haven't you thought much about this?

VIII. Attitudes toward the military: Pearson r = .35

    A. How important is it for the United States to have a strong military force in order to be effective in dealing with our enemies? Is it extremely important, very important, somewhat important, or not at all important?

    B. Thermometer rating of the military

IX. Attitudes toward the poor: alpha = .49

    A. Thermometer rating of the poor

    B. Thermometer rating of welfare recipients

    C. I am going to read two statements. Please tell me which one is closer to your own view.

        1. Most people are poor because they don't work hard enough.

        2. Most people are poor because of circumstances beyond their control.

5
Terrorism, Media Frames, and Framing Effects
A Macro- and Microlevel Analysis

Frauke Schnell and Karen Callaghan

On September 11, 2001, the United States experienced domestic terrorism on a scale unparalleled by any event in its history. Three airplanes hijacked by members of the Al Qaida terrorist network crashed into the World Trade Center and the Pentagon; a fourth plane headed for Washington crashed before hitting its target. The terrorist attacks killed nearly three thousand people and set in motion a series of events that would change the worldview of American citizens and alter the course of American history.

Even the most casual observer of U.S. politics would agree that the tragic events of September 11 had a dramatic impact on American attitudes, values, and behavior. For instance, in the aftermath of 9/11, pollsters and social scientists have observed decreased support for civil liberties; increased attendance at institutions of worship; and significantly enhanced anxiety about biological, chemical, and nuclear terrorism.[1] They also have found that Americans generally feel less secure; although some fears spawned by the attacks have eased, a strong majority of Americans still expect another large-scale act of terrorism inside the United States.[2] In addition, the terrorist attacks have altered attitudes toward Islamic citizens, and attitudes toward the United States have changed dramatically among the Islamic public in the Middle East. The "war on terror" has also been used as a catchphrase for political purposes. Candidates competing in the 2002 and 2004 elections frequently evoked images of the terrorist attacks, America's response, and the patriotic symbolism it entails.

Along with these attitudinal and political changes, the terrorist attacks changed the public debate on a variety of political issues, including military expenditures, civil liberties, and the constitutionality of flag burning. In the post–9/11 political climate, opposition to a constitutional amendment banning flag burning is easily interpreted as a critique of America's renewed sense of patriotism and renewed appreciation for the American flag.[3] In a similar vein, the events on September 11 and the subsequent domestic and international "war on terrorism" had a profound impact on the debate over the gun control issue. Specifically, the new metaphors of terror and terrorism have reframed and emotionalized the debate. This changed public discourse about gun control provides a provocative issue for analysis.

Gun control is an ideal issue to explore the impact of exogenous events on framing and subsequent public opinion, not only because of the abrupt shift in elite frames that occurred, as we demonstrate shortly, but because of the stability of American public opinion on this issue. Gun control attitudes are relatively stable and thus fairly resistant to change. Furthermore, although Americans tend to be moderate on most political issues, they hold strong, intense opinions on gun control.[4] Given the stability and intensity of public opinion, Americans will be less likely to alter their opinions due to a change in issue frames, unless the frames are very provocative. In this respect, this analysis represents a strong test of the impact of focusing events. Furthermore, arguments pertaining to the issue are clearly understood by "average" citizens: the issue requires no particular expertise to form an opinion. Thus, asserting as we do that issue frames linked to 9/11 altered Americans' thinking about gun control is a considerably stronger claim than one that involves frames on more complex or less salient issues.

This macro- and microlevel analysis contributes to the framing literature in three specific ways. It assesses the impact evolving issue debates have on public opinion. Do older, already established frames continue to shape attitudes toward the issue? Or are they easily displaced by newer frames that reflect a changed political reality? Prior research has examined how political players use events strategically to gain leverage; how aggregate-level opinion changes in response to an event (e.g., Page and Shapiro 1992; Birkland 1997; Wolsfeld 2003; Zaller 2001); and how context moderates framing effects where context is defined in terms of interpersonal conversation, elite debate, political information, and source credibility (e.g., Druckman forthcoming; Price and Na 2000; Callaghan and Schnell 2005; Sniderman and Theriault 1999). Up until now, no studies have explored how exogenous events alter framing debates and influence individual-level opinions.

This study also broadens our understanding of frames and framing effects by considering some novel dependent variables. These variables allow us to explore the impact of frames on citizens' issue priorities, emotions, group-based evaluations, and behavioral intentions.

Finally, it places framing research in a realistic communications environment. In addition to comparing pre– and post–9/11 frames, we test the impact competing or "dual" frames have on public opinion. Most studies assume that citizens can be easily swayed from one side of an issue to the other depending on how the issue is framed. In other words, public opinion is constructed by elites; its outcome depends on how they choose to characterize an issue. The underlying assumption is that most people hold ambivalent attitudes and "possess opposing considerations on most issues that might lead them to decide the issue either way" (Zaller and Feldman 1992, 585). Thus, different frames can evoke different predispositions and different attitudes. This constructionist perspective, however, fails to mirror most policy debates. In reality, people are exposed to more than one-sided arguments. Frames are frequently countered by opposing frames offering a new set of perspectives as elites compete to frame and reframe political issue debates to their liking (see Sniderman and Theriault 1999; Druckman forthcoming). Furthermore, the deeply ingrained norm of objectivity encourages journalists and editors to include multiple views on issues; thus, articles or broadcasts often include both sides of an issue.[5] In order to approximate the reality of political communication, this study examines the impact dual frames have on public opinion. We ask: how do citizens respond to the issue of gun control when they are presented with a two-sided or dual frame? If framing effects are weakened, then frames may be less consequential than most scholars have previously thought.

Focusing Events, Frames, and Framing Effects

Political communications do more than simply offer mere facts for discussion. They also give influential cues on how a policy issue is to be interpreted. These cues are not static, however. New issues excepted, existing policy frames are constantly revised by politicians, interest groups, the media, and other political elites as they adapt the issue frame to changes in the political and social environment. For example, during the 1994 congressional campaign, political rhetoric about welfare issues was dramatically changed. The new frames focused on excessive welfare entitlements and the belief that welfare erodes responsibility and is financed by the poor working class (Staeheli, Kodras, and Flint 1997). In a similar vein, the debate surrounding gun control has changed over time as politicians, interest groups, and the media have tried to shape the issue to their advantage. Much of the time this was a slow change. That is, until 9/11.

Scholars have long suggested that critical or "focusing" events can alter or reframe the substance of a policy debate (Kingdon 1984; Birkland 1997; Cobb and Elder 1983). They include natural catastrophes, hijackings, assassinations, and the like in their list of "critical events." Political entrepreneurs use these events as resources to influence public policy and mobilize public opinion. For instance, the much-publicized oil spill from the tanker *Exxon Valdez* into Prince William Sound on the Alaska coast in 1989 highlighted environmental concerns and gave increased visibility to political entrepreneurs sympathetic to the protection of Arctic wildlife. Environmentalists could now frame and re-frame the debate over oil drilling in Alaska to their benefit.

Exogenous events as a cause of issue framing possess a key characteristic absent from other forces—abrupt change. They introduce a fundamental dif-ference in frames inconsistent with or unrelated to previous frames and thus have the capacity to reshape public opinion on the issue. Immediately follow-ing the event, political actors advance a new angle or interpretation of the pol-icy issue that promotes their policy goals. By highlighting specific aspects of a current policy issue and relating them to the event, political players can ad-vance their interests and goals. In this way, political context and the political opportunity structure play a key role in determining how an issue will be framed for public consumption.

Once a focusing event occurs, the news media become "massive search en-gines" looking for dramatic ways to frame issues linked to the events (Wolsfeld 2003, 229). Normal journalistic routines are suspended, as selected frames dominate coverage for extended periods. Media attention to "event-related" frames assures them a prominent place on the public agenda.

The Gun Control Debate Pre– and Post–9/11

There is no doubt that 9/11 was one of the major focusing events in post–World War II American domestic and foreign policy. It was extensively covered by the media; it revealed failures in many different policy areas (e.g., airport security, homeland security, foreign policy); and it sparked a prolonged debate among interest groups, government, and parties to search for new solu-tions to the terrorism problem. What significance did this focusing event have for public debate on gun control? Did 9/11 alter the frames elites offered the general public and the direction they could lead the public to turn? Finally, whose frames penetrated media coverage?

Media Frames on Gun Control Pre–9/11

Early frames on gun control focused on the constitutional rights issue and the argument that governmental regulations infringe on personal liberties. Throughout U.S. history, "rights" issues have occupied a very special place in Americans' minds. As David Harding (quoted in Glendeon 1991, 23) notes, in American society, rights are spoken of reverentially; "specific rights and liber-ties seem almost to constitute a pantheon for our nation's secular religion: the law." He adds that "if the liturgy of this faith is litigation, its most sincere form of prayer is certainly 'rights talk.'" Harding defines "rights talk" as "the sim-ple tendency of Americans to elevate any especially prized activity to the status of a right in order to convince others, and perhaps themselves, that the freedom to perform that act is both inalienable and inviolable."

Up until the 1970s, public discourse on gun control focused on rights issues.[6] For the most part, however, Americans paid little attention to gun control. Few gun control laws were passed.[7] Most people still objected to strict gun control laws on constitutional grounds and continued to do so for the next forty years.

In the wake of urban riots in the late 1960s and the assassinations of Senator Robert Kennedy and Reverend Martin Luther King Jr., the gun control debate was redefined. Supporters of gun control asserted that strict gun laws were a cure for rampant crime and violence. As crime rates rose, or at least the media's reports on them did, a new and different issue frame emerged: "Crime and the Culture of Violence." For example, reporter Tom Brokaw reminded Americans in his leadoff segment headed "Society under Siege" that "society, of course, is under siege from gangs, guns and violence" (NBC Nightly News, November 22, 1993) and that "bloodshed is no stranger to many American cities and towns as they try to cope with the rise in violent crime (NBC Nightly News, January 23, 1994).

Meanwhile, opponents of gun control continued to concentrate on the principles of freedom embodied in the "Constitutional Rights" frame. Thus, gun control now encompassed both ideological concerns about the proper role of government and specific concerns about crime and violence. The political conflict was intense and highly emotional, fueled by tradition and fears and widely divergent concepts of personal liberty and the limits of government responsibility. Which side won the framing debate in the media during this period?

In an earlier analysis of interest-group and media framing of the gun control issue, we found that television news coverage of gun control by the major networks was dominated by the pro-control "Guns Promote a Culture of Violence" frame, which claimed 47 percent of all network news frames (Callaghan and Schnell 2001a).[8] Frames rooted in NRA terminology (e.g., "Constitutional Rights," "Guns Deter Crime," "Guns Don't Kill, People Do") received hardly any exposure (less than 16 percent). The remainder of the news frames were "media-generated."[9]

However, in the wake of the Columbine High School shooting in April 1999, usage of the already prominent "Crime and Violence" frame further increased, either because the event fit nicely with journalists' reporting style (i.e., one that emphasizes drama and conflict as an element of good reporting) or because journalists received more pro-control cues from a mass public that was decidedly liberal on the issue. As crime and violence increased in American society, political hostility to opponents of gun control soon developed.

Interest-Group Frames and the Terrorist Link

In the post–9/11 period, the dominant interest groups—the Brady Center to Prevent Handgun Violence (formerly called Handgun Control, Inc.) and the National Rifle Association (NRA)—have dramatically altered their approach to the gun control debate. Our analysis of interest-group frames is based on the systematic examination of all press releases posted on the respective group Web sites. In the six-month period after 9/11, the Brady Center posted thirty-nine press releases, while the NRA posted eleven.[10]

Clearly, terrorist frames have now become central to the Brady Center's communication strategy. Fully 38 percent of their press releases in the six months after the attack linked gun control to terrorism through issue framing. A commonly cited argument is that lax gun laws help terrorists: "As demonstrated by recent attacks, terrorists will use any weapons—explosives, firearms, and even knives—to carry out their deadly schemes. Congress must close gaps in our laws—such as the gun-show loophole—that criminals, potentially terrorists, exploit to obtain such weapons" (Brady Center press release, September 20, 2001).

After the September 11 terrorist attacks, Attorney General John Ashcroft refused the FBI's request to use National Instant Criminal Background Check (NICS) records to determine whether individuals on the "suspected terrorist" list had been approved to buy guns. Sarah Brady, wife of former Reagan press secretary Jim Brady and now chair of the Brady Center, expressed these views: "Thanks to Attorney General John Ashcroft guns will now end up in the wrong hands" (Brady Center, July 23, 2002). Brady further argued: "For terrorists around the world, the United States is the Great Gun Bazaar. Guns are being used to commit acts of terrorism and to resist law enforcement efforts at apprehension and arrest. In short, guns and terrorism go together. What we need to protect Americans at home and abroad are common sense gun control measures that prevent terrorists from acquiring guns" (Brady Center, September 30, 2002).

The NRA adopted a slightly different framing approach. It argued that the injection of terrorist frames into the gun control debate constituted crass political opportunism at its calculated worst. To the NRA, gun control groups and the media were shamelessly manipulating acts of war to promote a political agenda: "The national public policy debate had plunged to a new low . . . [making] an outrageous attempt to link terrorist strikes against this country to a national tradition as old as America itself—gun shows. . . . It's time for full disclosure" (NRA press release, October 26, 2001). The NRA further argued that personal liberties were becoming a casualty in the war against terrorism.

Moreover, NRA press releases emphasized the right to bear arms "for our national defense" and noted the significance of the recent upsurge in gun sales: "True American public opinion is telling its own story. Since the attacks of September 11, media outlets have been filled with reports of Americans purchasing their first firearms and learning to use them safely and responsibly for self-protection" (NRA press release, October 26, 2001).

Although 36 percent of their press releases in the six-month period after 9/11 discussed terrorism-related issues, the NRA adopted a more defensive framing strategy. Rather than taking a specific stance on guns and terrorism, the NRA emphasized its support for the fight against terrorism, while distancing itself from the "Guns Stop Terrorism" theme. However, by emphasizing the recent surge in gun sales and concerns about "our national defense," it too helped to link the gun control debate to terrorism, albeit implicitly.

Post–9/11 Media Frames

In an interview with *ABC Evening News,* a first-time gun buyer reported that she had purchased a gun because of "the fear of the unknown and what could possibly happen." In the same broadcast, Tom Christy, the manager of the Firing Line, in Denver, explained that "definitely a lot more people have been coming in [to gun shops] who are first-time buyers, who I guess as a result of the [terrorist attacks] have just figured maybe the government is not enough to protect its citizens and maybe they should do something for themselves" (*ABC Evening News,* February 28, 2002).

The *ABC Evening News* (March 19, 2002) also quoted NRA spokesperson Andrew Arulanandam: "It's a natural feeling that after 9/11, people want to be proactive and take necessary action to protect themselves and their loved ones in these uncertain times."

On the other hand, supporters of tougher gun laws talked about the necessity of closing the so-called gun-show loophole and warned that terrorists could exploit the slack enforcement and oversight of gun shows.[11] They also warned of the risk guns pose to children and cited the story of a three-year-old Virginia boy who accidentally killed himself with a handgun his father purchased for protection after the terrorist attacks.

These excerpts represent a *new* element or frame in the debate over gun control that was hardly seen in the media before last September. Our claim is based on a systematic content analysis of all Nexis transcripts for *ABC World News Tonight* and *CBS Evening News* programs for a six-month period.[12] For this analysis, we searched the database for all articles containing the following words: *guns, gun control, weapons, assault weapons, Brady Law, terrorism,* and *terrorists.* Our results show that in the post–9/11 media debate, more than half of all gun control–related broadcasts aired in the six months after the terrorist attacks were linked to the terrorism theme. Of the sixty-nine gun-related news stories, 54 percent linked the issue to terrorism by discussing a wide range of topics: the prospects for relaxed gun laws, the pros and cons of arming pilots, the rise in the sale of firearms, guns and airport security, Attorney General Ashcroft's decision not to conduct gun-purchase background checks for post–9/11 detainees, attempts of terrorism suspects to purchase guns, the gun-show loophole, and the possibility of U.S. weapons falling into the hands of Taliban fighters. Forty-six percent of the broadcasts ($N = 32$) focused on traditional gun-related frames, most frequently violence in schools and the workplace, court challenges and NRA victories, lawsuits against gun manufacturers, and the perils of guns in the hands of children.[13]

In contrast, the network news made *no specific reference* to guns and terrorism in the six months before September 11. The CBS and ABC evening news programs featured twenty-six stories about gun control and related issues. The central theme in that period was gun-related crime and violence in schools (e.g., Columbine). Other topics covered included lawsuits against gun manufacturers, gun-buyback programs, the keeping of records of gun sales, criminal background checks, and the decline in gun sales.[14] In sum, the "Crime and Violence" theme dominated media coverage of gun control in the period before 9/11. However, after 9/11 this frame was replaced by more prominent "War on Terrorism" themes that linked pro- and anti-control arguments to the September 2001 terrorist attacks.

In *Agendas, Alternatives, and Public Policies* (1984), John Kingdon proposes two models of the development of public policy issues. One model suggests that the developmental process is evolutionary, akin to natural selection. Policy issues gradually emerge, while those that do not meet certain criteria slowly die away. The alternative model posits a sudden, dramatic, and often unanticipated change—what Baumgartner and Jones (1993) refer to as "punctuated equilibrium."[15] As applied to the framing debate, the evidence we provide here supports the notion that focusing events can suddenly alter framing debates at the macrolevel of American politics. Although the development of gun control themes proceeded slowly throughout much of U.S. history, sudden and substantial change occurred after September 11, 2001.

But to picture the full impact of events, we need to link these frames to microlevel changes in preferences and opinions. In the next section we report the results of an experimental study that simulates public response to news frames on terrorism and gun control.

Experimental Study on the Impact of Terrorism Frames

To assess the impact of terrorism frames on the public's attitudes, emotions, and political behavior, we conducted a laboratory experiment during the summer of 2002. Our subjects were undergraduate students ($N = 160$) from two public universities in the Northeast (the University of Massachusetts, Boston; and West Chester University, Pennsylvania). The typical participant was a white (63 percent) woman in her late twenties from a middle-class background (family income of sixty thousand dollars or greater). Politically, she labeled herself a liberal (46 percent) Democrat (41 percent) with a strong interest in politics and following the news.[16] The only criterion for selection was U.S. citizenship. Given our focus on constitutional rights issues and our interest in the political mobilization of frames, participants who were not U.S. citizens were excluded from the analysis.[17]

Participants were informed that the study was about the public's perception of a variety of public policy issues; they were then assured that their responses would be anonymous. The surveys were then randomly distributed to the study participants.

Manipulating News Frames on Gun Control

A key feature of the experiment is the creation of realistic stimuli that mirror the dominant frames in American political discourse.[18] These frames are derived theoretically from our previous content analysis of media coverage and interest-group rhetoric. We created different versions of a newspaper article about an academic conference on the most pressing political issues of the day. The article, entitled "Gun Control Still the Issue," was formatted to appear as an excerpt from a major newspaper. The article explained that gun control was a key issue discussed at the conference, and the experimental framing passages were embedded within the context of the report about the conference (see the appendix). While the conference was fictitious, the story was modeled on newspaper reports of actual conferences. The physical appearance of the article was carefully crafted after newspaper copy, and subjects were given the opportunity to read and think about the article at their leisure, thus enhancing the external validity of the research situation (e.g., Cook and Campbell 1979). In an attempt to avoid confounding article subject matter, linguistic cues, and issue frames, we held the essence and language of each article constant.

Each version of the article began with a description of the conference. A political reporter reviewed the stories for content, style, and consistency across articles. In writing the news articles, we made every effort to simulate real coverage with slight editorial changes to emphasize the particular issue frame(s) being used. Importantly, each news article presented an equal number of arguments on the topic, and all were about equal in length.[19] The frame manipulation occurred by varying the gun control arguments within each article. By manipulating the frame of the article while keeping other factors like headlines and most aspects of the text constant, we are able to draw valid conclusions about the relative effects of different gun control frames.

We selected the media's most popular issue frames before and after 9/11. Based on our content analysis of media frames on gun control, we identified the most prominent framing passages to be those presented in table 5.1.

Specifically, the "Constitutional Rights" frame depicts gun control as a fundamental right of the individual to possess and bear arms, protected by the Second Amendment. The "Crime and Violence" frame attributes the tide of violence in society to the lack of adequate gun control and the proliferation of weapons among criminal elements in society. The "Guns Cause Terrorism" frame focuses on lax gun laws and the possibility of guns being acquired by terrorists. The major argument in the "Guns Stop Terrorism" frame is that guns in the hands of well-trained, law-abiding citizens can help to protect the country. Finally, participants in the "Dual Frame" were presented with opposing arguments: guns might be useful for self-protection, but they also might end up in the hands of terrorists. These conditions mimic the political communication environment in the real world.

Our participants were assigned randomly to one of the five framing passages or were assigned to a control condition where they received no framed passage but merely answered a political opinion survey.[20] The control group provides a baseline, unadulterated measure of public opinion on gun control. We also took several important steps to guard against "demand characteristics"—that is, cueing the participants about what we expected of them. First, we informed subjects that the study was on public perceptions about a variety of contemporary issues. Besides gun control, we asked for their opinions on other current domestic and foreign issues (e.g., cloning, the environment, immigration, abortion, AIDS research, global warming, relations with China).

5.1 Old frames (pre–9/11)

Gun control frames	Gun rights frames
Crime and Violence	Constitutional Rights

New frames (post–9/11)

Gun control frames	Dual frames	Gun rights frames
Guns Cause Terrorism	Guns Can Cause Terrorism as Well as Prevent It	Guns Prevent Terrorism

Second, to deemphasize the prominence of our experimental manipulations, we embedded the key questions in a lengthy questionnaire. Third, the questions immediately following the news article were unrelated to gun control to further reduce demand characteristics; rather, they focused on the readability of the passage. Finally, we embedded the framing manipulation in a news story about a conference. Our efforts were rewarded. After completing the experiment, subjects were asked if they had formed an opinion about the study's intent. No subject surmised the experiment's purpose.

After they had read the newspaper article, we asked subjects to make a series of judgments on gun control and related issues, to state their attitudes toward groups involved with the issue and their fears about terrorism and crime and violence, and to answer a few demographic questions.

Expectations about Terrorism Frames

What is the expected impact of our experimental frames? Obviously, we expect attitudes toward gun control to vary depending on the arguments put forward in the frames. However, due to the negative affect typically associated with terrorism after 9/11, we expect the terrorism frames to produce the largest opinion differences between the frames and the control group.

Media coverage during this period focused on the government's inability to combat terrorism through established channels. Thus, the "Guns Stop Terrorism" theme, which presents the self (not the government) as the agent of resolution ("If government will not solve the larger terrorist problem, then citizens must take action"), will reduce support for strict gun control laws, compared to the control group. This theme may remind individuals of their powerlessness, both personally and collectively. The "Guns Cause Terrorism" frame offers an opportunity to resolve the problem through the reform of laws ("If we act by restricting guns, the problem will get better"). In this case, support for strict gun control laws should be increased, compared to the control group. Framing effects will still appear for other frames, but they will not be as provocative.[21] No doubt, crime and violence and constitutional rights have been part of the gun control debate for a long time; however, the continuity of a frame over time does not guarantee its effectiveness. Although in other work we found that presenting gun rights as an extension of formal constitutional rights or a problem of crime and violence produced significant framing effects (Callaghan and Schnell 2000, 2001a), if framing effects depend on political context, we do not expect a stable response to these frames in the post–9/11 climate.

In addition, we expect the frames to influence group evaluations, issue importance, and values. Specifically, we expect the "Terrorism" frames to evoke issue priorities that are closely related to the fight against terrorism (e.g., national defense or homeland security). On the other hand, the "Crime and Violence" frame should activate issues closely related to this frame (urban crime, school violence). Appealing to fears about terrorism will produce issue priorities more closely linked to this frame than in other conditions.

We also expect that issue frames will elicit emotional reactions. Emotions play a significant role in shaping political attitudes and behavior. For instance, emotions can influence citizens' assessment of political candidates (Abelson et al. 1982; Marcus, Neuman, and MacKuen 2000), and they are linked to cross-domain phenomena like motivation to act (e.g., Rudolph, Gangl, and Stevens 2000; see also Mackie 2002). Given that emotions like fear and anxiety are strongly aroused by events, we expect that frames linked to the heinous attack on 9/11 may have the greatest impact on emotional reactions.

Further, since emotions can inspire political protest and other forms of political participation (e.g., Butler, Koopman, and Zimbardo 1995), we expect the terrorism frames to have the largest impact on subjects' behavioral intentions, compared to the other conditions.

Affectively laden responses to group associations are also possible. After the attack on the World Trade Center and the Pentagon, in which Islamic radicals killed nearly three thousand people, discussion about Islamic extremism filled the airwaves. Although the events of 9/11 arose from the extreme ideological beliefs held by splinter groups of Al Qaida and Taliban fundamentalists, not from mainstream Muslim opinion, Muslims became principal actors in the story of 9/11. Given that an individual's response to groups reflects not only that person's experience with the group but also the media's presentation of the group, media frames on the war on terrorism with implicit links to the Muslim hijackers may generate negative effects toward Muslims.

We also consider whether gun control frames influence affect toward the NRA, one of the most prominent, long-standing groups involved in the gun control debate. The "pro-control" frames ("Crime and Violence" and "Guns Cause Terrorism") may elicit a negative response to the NRA, while the "anti-control" frames ("Constitutional Rights" and "Guns Stop Terrorism") may elicit a positive response to the group. It is also possible that framing effects for group associations are less pronounced during "non-event" debate periods. In this case, the impact that the frames have on affect toward the NRA across all conditions may be similar to the control group.

Finally, we expect framing effects to be weaker in the "Dual Frame," compared to the other terrorism frames. As we have argued, presenting both arguments and thus mirroring the complexities of the public debate is likely to result in less pliable opinions. When attention is not restricted to only one side of an issue, citizens can make choices consistent with their underlying principles (Sniderman and Theriault 1999). The initial frame induces citizens to think in terms of that frame by making the given domain accessible in memory, which in turn influences their attitudes and opinions. The result is likely to be a more "neutral" evaluation of the argument (see also Druckman 2001a, forthcoming; Levin, Johnson, and Davis 1987). It is of course possible that when the frames are presented together, one (the most provocative) will be more salient and push attitudes in that direction.

Impact of Terrorism Frames on Political Beliefs and American Values

Table 5.2 presents the mean attitudinal response to gun control across framing conditions. Support for gun control laws is measured on a 50-point scale (scored 1, "strongly disagree," to 50, "strongly agree"). In partial support of our hypotheses we found that two frames, "Guns Stop Terrorism" and the "Dual Frame," decreased individual support for gun control laws compared to the control group. Conversely, the "Guns Cause Terrorism" frame increased support for gun control, though not significantly. The "Constitutional Rights" and "Crime and Violence" frames also did not have significant effects on public policy support.

Furthermore, the "Guns Stop Terrorism" and the "Guns Cause Terrorism" frames generated the most negative affective *reaction to Muslims*.[22] Apparently, the attack on 9/11 raised questions about Islamic extremism for some Americans. The media, as information providers, may have helped create this cognitive linkage by discussing this group consistently within the context of 9/11. How do our results square with Gallup opinion data showing a positive spike in Americans' attitudes toward Muslims after 9/11? We can only speculate that the terrorism frames crystallized underlying negative attitudes toward Muslims. Aggregate-level opinion measures do not necessarily show this, especially since political elites like President George W. Bush and others made many rhetorical attempts to disassociate U.S. Muslims from the terrorist attackers.

None of the frames significantly influenced affect toward the NRA compared to the control group. We suspect that affect toward the NRA and other groups was more susceptible to framing effects after the shooting at Columbine High School in April 1999—that is, it takes an exogenous event closely linked to the group to push attitudes and group-related affect in the direction of the frame.[23] Thus, political context or political opportunity structure, as well as the public opinion climate or political culture, seems to play a role in determining when framing effects occur.

If issue frames heighten belief importance (see Nelson, Clawson, and Oxley 1997; Nelson and Oxley 1999), certain groups of subjects (i.e., those exposed

5.2 The impact of terrorism and non-terrorism frames on attitudes toward gun control

Dependent variables	Old frames		Terrorism frames				Model	
	Constitutional Rights	Crime & Violence	Guns Cause Terrorism	Guns Stop Terrorism	Dual Frame	Control	F-value	Probability
Support for strict gun laws (1–50-pt. scale)	34.12 (26)	34.65 (24)	40.33 (25)	28.39* (24)	29.00* (28)	34.00 (33)	.81	.49
Rank of national security values	−1.49 (21)	−1.05 (21)	−2.42** (20)	−1.99* (19)	−1.14 (27)	−1.19 (29)	1.68	.14
Positive affect toward Muslims (0–10-pt. scale)	4.58 (26)	4.83 (24)	4.04* (25)	4.29* (24)	5.64** (28)	4.79 (33)	1.68	.14
Positive affect toward the NRA (0–10-pt. scale)	4.47 (26)	4.23 (24)	4.40 (25)	5.00 (24)	5.00 (28)	4.62 (33)	.49	.78

Note: Cell entries are means for each condition; numbers in parentheses are cell Ns. Means with an asterisk are statistically different from the control group using ANOVA contrast analysis (pooled variance estimates).
 *$p < .10$,   **$p < .05$,   ***$p < .01$ (one-tailed test)

to the terrorism frames) should place a high priority on *defense-related values.* To test this hypothesis, we asked subjects, after they had read the newspaper passages, to rank-order a list of eight values according to personal importance. The defense-related values included love of country, a world free of war and conflict, freedom, national security, and family security. The remaining values items tapped "non-security"-related goals. These included hard work and self-reliance, a world of beauty, and love of the arts.[24] For this measure we subtracted the mean ranking of national-security and defense-related values from the other items. Thus, a high negative score indicates the importance of values related to national defense. Conversely, a high positive score reflects the importance of non-terrorism-related values.

As table 5.2 shows, subjects exposed to the "Guns Stop Terrorism" and the "Guns Cause Terrorism" frames gave a higher priority (lower rank) to values related to the war on terrorism compared to the control group. This predicted skew did not manifest itself in the "Dual Frame."

In addition, the pre–9/11 "Crime and Violence" and "Constitutional Rights" frames also failed to make defense-related values a high priority. As Inglehart (1984, 564) has argued, over the last several decades the basic value priorities of Western publics have shifted from a materialistic emphasis on physical sustenance and safety to a "postmaterialistic" emphasis on self-expression and "the quality of life." He traces this shift to the unprecedented levels of economic and physical security of the postwar era. But Inglehart was writing before the United States experienced its first major attack on the mainland by foreign agents since the War of 1812. In the aftermath of 9/11, national-defense values should have greater relevance overall. As expected, the value priorities across all conditions lean in this direction (all means are negative). However, the terrorism frames significantly enhanced these effects. Given that individuals' basic priorities are largely fixed by adulthood (Inglehart 1984), these findings are impressive.

Terrorism Frames and National Problems

Further evidence of the power of terrorism frames can be found in an assessment of how they influence issue priorities. Do subjects who read a news story linking terrorism to gun control believe national-security and defense-related issues are more important than those who read a framed passage devoid of any references to terrorism? Conversely, is crime control perceived to be the dominant issue facing Americans today for individuals exposed to the "Crime and Violence" frame? Finally, what are the issue priorities of individuals overall? To address these questions, we asked subjects to indicate what they believed to be the most important issues facing the United States today (up to five issues were recorded). First, we scaled the responses according to the number of "terrorist-related" concerns they mentioned (e.g., national security, biological terrorism, CIA and FBI failures in terrorist intelligence gathering, problems with homeland security), compared to the "non-terrorism" issues they mentioned (e.g., social welfare, corporate accountability, the environment). Then we rescaled the same responses for the number of "Crime and Violence" issues subjects mentioned (e.g., crime, violence, violence in schools), compared to non-crime-related issues. Presumably, the first issues they noted were the most readily available and thus politically significant. Therefore, we refined the issue-priority measures by weighting subjects' responses according to the order in which they were mentioned. We also controlled for the verbosity of the individual subjects (i.e., the number of issues mentioned) by computing a weighted proportion of the total number of issue items that fell into each of the two issue categories.[25]

As seen in table 5.3, the terrorist frames significantly influenced the perceived importance of issues related to U.S. national security. The mean for subjects in the "Guns Cause Terrorism" frame was .40, while the mean for the control group was .23. Subjects assigned to the "Crime and Violence" and "Constitutional Rights" frames mentioned fewer national-security issues and placed them at the bottom of their list. The means for these framing conditions (.26 and .14, respectively) were not statistically different from the control group's mean (.23). These frames, however, elicited concerns about crime as an important national issue. The "Guns Cause Terrorism" frame also enhanced beliefs about the importance of crime as a national issue (mean = .17). This is

5.3 Most important problem by framing conditions

National defense mentioned as U.S.'s most important issue *(F-value: 3.97, p <.002)*

Constitutional Rights	Crime & Violence	Guns Cause Terrorism	Guns Stop Terrorism	Dual Frame	Control
.26	.14	.40***	.40***	.36**	.23
(23)	(20)	(23)	(22)	(31)	(26)

Crime and violence mentioned as U.S.'s most important issue *(F-value: 1.46, p <.20)*

Constitutional Rights	Crime & Violence	Guns Cause Terrorism	Guns Stop Terrorism	Dual Frame	Control
.13*	.13**	.17**	.08	.09	.04
(23)	(20)	(23)	(22)	(31)	(26)

Note: Cell entries are mean weighted proportions of the total number of "most important issue" mentions in that issue category. Numbers in parentheses are cell Ns. Means with an asterisk are statistically different from the control group using ANOVA contrast analysis (pooled variance estimates).
*p <.10,   **p <.05,   ***p <.01 (one-tailed test)

not surprising since the framed passage intentionally included a "Crime and Violence" subtext (see the appendix).

In sum, while frames matter for the assessment of national concerns, *frames linked to terrorism matter even more*. The shift in issue priorities induced by these frames is quite dramatic. It also suggests that frames have an important, and previously unidentified, "agenda-setting" function. *Agenda-setting*, a term coined by McCombs and Shaw (1972), refers to the relationship between the order of importance given by the media to political issues and the significance attached to these same issues by citizens and politicians. Research shows that issues deemed important by Americans are those that merit media attention (e.g., Iyengar and Kinder 1987). Our results demonstrate that media frames on terrorism produced a significant agenda-setting effect. Moreover, since agenda-setting (and priming) effects have been shown to be fairly resistant to change over time (Iyengar and Kinder 1987), these findings suggest that framing effects have the potential to endure (see Druckman forthcoming for another view).

The Impact of Frames on Political Participation

In this section, we explore the effect of terrorism frames on people's intention to engage in political activities. *Behavioral political intentions* were assessed with several questions about the subjects' intended political activities: to vote, to become better informed, or to tangibly support the right to bear arms (e.g., donate money, volunteer their time, attend a rally, sign a petition).

As table 5.4 shows, the "Guns Stop Terrorism" frame had the most consis-

5.4 The impact of terrorism and non-terrorism frames on political behavior

Participation in "right to bear arms" interest-group activities

Donate money (less than $25) *(F-value: 2.22**)*

Constitutional Rights	Crime & Violence	Guns Cause Terrorism	Guns Stop Terrorism	Dual Frame	Control
4.34***	3.43	4.00	4.42***	3.63	3.69
(26)	(23)	(25)	(24)	(24)	(33)

Volunteer time *(F-value: 3.38***)*

Constitutional Rights	Crime & Violence	Guns Cause Terrorism	Guns Stop Terrorism	Dual Frame	Control
4.65***	3.50	4.12	4.58***	3.83	3.79
(26)	(23)	(25)	(24)	(24)	(33)

Attend the rally *(F-value: 2.30**)*

Constitutional Rights	Crime & Violence	Guns Cause Terrorism	Guns Stop Terrorism	Dual Frame	Control
4.58**	3.65	4.08	4.50***	3.92	3.94
(26)	(23)	(25)	(24)	(24)	(33)

Sign the petition *(F-value: 1.18, ns)*

Constitutional Rights	Crime & Violence	Guns Cause Terrorism	Guns Stop Terrorism	Dual Frame	Control
3.88	3.56	3.08	3.88	3.25	3.30
(26)	(23)	(25)	(24)	(24)	(33)

Other political actions

Learn more about gun control *(F-value: 2.61**)*

Constitutional Rights	Crime & Violence	Guns Cause Terrorism	Guns Stop Terrorism	Dual Frame	Control
29.51	26.79	26.60	26.50*	36.00	27.89
(24)	(23)	(25)	(24)	(25)	(29)

Vote in the 2002 election *(F-value: .79, ns [1–4-pt. scale])*

Constitutional Rights	Crime & Violence	Guns Cause Terrorism	Guns Stop Terrorism	Dual Frame	Control
1.75	1.87	1.60	1.96*	1.93	1.68
(24)	(23)	(25)	(24)	(28)	(29)

Note: Cell entries are means for each condition; numbers in parentheses are cell *N*s. Means with an asterisk are statistically different from the control group using ANOVA contrast analysis (pooled variance estimates). Interest-group activities scored 1, "willing," to 5, "unwilling." Learn more scored 1, "strongly disagree," to 50, "strongly agree." Vote scored 1, "very likely," to 4, "very unlikely."

*$p < .10$,   **$p < .05$,   ***$p < .01$ (one-tailed test) tent impact on subjects' willingness to engage in political activities. For example, subjects were more willing to donate money (mean = 4.42), volunteer time (mean = 4.58), and attend the rally of an interest group supporting the right to bear arms (mean = 4.50) than those in the control group (means = 3.79, 3.94, and 3.40, respectively). The "Constitutional Rights" frame also increased willingness to participate in the group's activities. The "Guns Cause Terrorism" theme did not reduce the likelihood of subjects' political participation.

The terrorism frames negatively influenced subjects' intentions to vote and learn more about the issue of gun control, though only the "Guns Stop Terrorism" mean was statistically significant. This might seem paradoxical. On one hand, our subjects are willing to engage in interest-group politics. On the other, they are disenchanted politically and are less inclined to vote. Apparently, people do not always engage in politics in a uniform fashion. Put another way, evocative frames can produce divergent results: political engagement and withdrawal.[26]

Framing Effects and Emotional Response

What is the emotional impact of frames? Obviously, not all frames are charged with similar amounts of affect. As we argued earlier, over the past forty years, gun control was seen as either a mechanism to reduce crime and violence in American society or a violation of constitutional rights. In the wake of 9/11, the "old frames" may be less evocative. To test this hypothesis, we asked subjects to indicate the level of anxiety caused by a series of terrorism-related threats, including nuclear, biological, or chemical attacks and suicide terrorism (scored 1 to 4, "none" to "extensive"). These responses were aver-

5.5 The emotional impact of terrorism and non-terrorism frames

Fear about terrorism *(F-value: .718, p <.61)*

Constitutional Rights	Crime & Violence	Guns Cause Terrorism	Guns Stop Terrorism	Dual Frame	Control
2.42	2.52	2.80*	2.60	2.70	2.64
(24)	(21)	(21)	(24)	(26)	(29)

Fear about crime and violence *(F-value: 2.58, p <.05)*

Constitutional Rights	Crime & Violence	Guns Cause Terrorism	Guns Stop Terrorism	Dual Frame	Control
1.96**	2.33	2.61	2.06**	2.09*	2.41
(24)	(21)	(21)	(24)	(26)	(29)

Note: Cell entries are means for each condition; numbers in parentheses are cell *N*s. Means with an asterisk are statistically different from the control group using ANOVA contrast analysis (pooled variance estimates).
*p <.10,   **p <.05,   ***p <.01 (one-tailed test)

aged to form a "fear of terrorism" scale. Additionally, we asked subjects to indicate the level of anxiety caused by crime-related threats, including stabbings and armed robbery (scored 1 to 4, "none" to "extensive"). These responses were averaged to form a "fear of crime" scale. Table 5.5 presents the results.

As table 5.5 shows, all frames do not evoke the same type and amount of affect. The fear of physical insecurity related to terrorism is significantly heightened in the "Guns Cause Terrorism" frame ($p \leq .10$). However, the "Guns Stop Terrorism" frame reduced subjects' fear of terrorism, although the mean is not statistically different from the control group. The "Constitutional Rights" frame also had a similar effect.

The second row in table 5.5 shows that subjects in the "Guns Stop Terrorism" (mean = 2.10) and the "Dual Frame" (mean = 2.09) conditions became less concerned about street-related crime and violence. So did subjects in the "Constitutional Rights" frame (mean = 2.00).

Thus, terrorism frames can evoke deep-seated anxiety reactions about future terrorist attacks and also influence long-standing concerns about "street-level" crime and violence. These frames appear to be more emotionally involving than the other frames.[27]

Discussion

Our analysis shows that 9/11 as a focusing event changed media coverage of the gun control issue. More than half of the broadcasts about gun control aired in the six months after the terrorist attacks were linked to the terrorism theme, either because the media incorporated the frames put forward by interest groups or, more likely, because these frames provided much-desired drama and sensationalism. Further, our results also highlight the significant relationship between focusing events and framing effects. As we have shown, 9/11 produced a substantial frame change that in turn influenced citizens' policy support, group-related affect, issue priorities, emotions, and issue activism. Generally, old, already established frames were not as effective as the new "guns and terrorism" themes. The most effective frame was the anti-control frame "Guns Stop Terrorism," probably because of the emotions this frame elicits.[28] Moreover, the impact of the "Dual Frame" on public opinion was often close to the "Guns Stop Terrorism" frame. Thus, this theme proved to be the most provocative. Apparently, two opposing frames in the same news article do not always cancel each other out and lead to a more neutral evaluation of the issue at hand; instead, some themes are more powerful than others. By the same token, the media do not always include both sides of an issue, especially when reporting on the gun control issue (e.g., Callaghan and Schnell 2001a). Thus, from this perspective, framing effects are still quite pervasive.

Our results square nicely with recent changes in gun-related attitudes and behavior. Up until 9/11, a substantial majority of Americans favored additional gun control laws. In the post–9/11 period, however, the percentage has declined. According to an ABC News poll, 46 percent of respondents strongly favored strict gun laws in January 2001. By May of 2002, this figure had dropped to 39 percent. At the same time the number of gun sales has increased.[29] Although the number of background checks conducted in 2001 is generally lower than in 2000, this trend sharply reversed after September 11. In fact, there was a double-digit percentage increase in September and October (10 percent in September to 22 percent in October), compared to the same months in the previous year. The number of background checks conducted from January to June 2000 increased 1.8 percent in 2001.[30] Thus, our results are consistent with recent changes in mass public behavior and attitudes.

Our analysis also gives some insight into the underlying psychological mechanisms responsible for framing effects.[31] While fear of crime and violence is still important, the threat of terrorism produced even more anxiety. While heightened fear and anxiety generally diminish the effectiveness of persuasive communication, emotional appeals can still be very effective if the preventive measures suggested by the communication are efficacious (Janis 1967; Levanthal, Watts, and Pagano 1967). Thus, the peculiar significance of the "Guns Stop Terrorism" frame (compared to the other terrorism frames) is that it points to the helplessness of the government and puts individual citizens in charge of our national defense. As Donahue, Cai, and Mitchell (2001, 209) note, terrorist attacks disrupt the order of reality. Consequently, citizens begin to search for a way to restore the order that has been suspended (see also Perry and Pugh 1978). Apparently, the "Guns Stop Terrorism" frame satisfies this desire.

Our results also shed light on the complex relationship among focusing events, interest groups, the media, and the public. Political entrepreneurs use focusing events to influence public policy and mobilize the public (Kingdon 1984; Schattschneider 1960). As we have shown, terrorism-related frames became the centerpiece of the Brady Center's communication strategy after 9/11. Although the theme suggesting that "terrorists are helped by lax gun laws" was promoted by the news media, it did not resonate that strongly with the public. On the other hand, our content analysis of NRA press releases suggests that the NRA was reluctant to advance the evocative "Guns Stop Terrorism" frame. We can only speculate as to the gun lobby's rationale behind this decision. Quite possibly, the NRA realized that this argument might spark further discussions about a link between guns and terrorism. The NRA might also have been aware of the potential public opinion success of this frame. Clearly, the idea that armed Americans possess the capability to keep the nation safe from terrorism struck a chord with the public. And since a frame's success hinges upon the credibility of the spokesperson (e.g., Druckman 2001b), the "Guns Stop Terrorism" argument may be more persuasive if it is *not* associated with the gun lobby.[32]

Finally, what do our results imply about the power of events to arouse a normally indifferent public? The attack on 9/11, an event unparalleled in U.S. history, profoundly altered political rhetoric, including gun control discourse, and it affected public opinion and priorities. Did it also alter political behavior and activate involvement with the issue? The answer is yes. Constructing a link between gun control and terrorism mobilized our respondents to become "issue" activists but did not persuade them to participate in traditional political activities, that is, voting. The "Guns Stop Terrorism" frame increased participants' willingness to donate money, volunteer time, and attend the rally of a gun rights group. However, it slightly decreased our respondents' willingness to vote in the 2002 election. Of course, voting does not provide citizens the opportunity to become directly involved in forestalling terrorist attacks, compared to other activities. Whether or not citizens became mobilized to press for change depends—mobilization is selective and related to the levels of anxiety the frame elicits.

Terrorist Frames and the Future of the Gun Control Debate

For many years, scholars have argued that the two sides of the gun control dispute have achieved a basic stalemate: gun control activists have won some relatively minor regulations, and gun control opponents occasionally have repealed these laws. The most prominent example is the Brady Handgun Violence Protection Act of 1993, which was rescinded in 1997 as each side gained and lost. In fact, in 1998, some scholars predicted that gun control politics was unlikely to change in the near future (Bruce and Wilcox 1998). That was before 9/11.

In the post–9/11 period, American opinion on gun control policies has moved in a more conservative policy direction. Even the key actors who dominate national institutions (e.g., President George W. Bush, Attorney General John Ashcroft) are not as favorable toward gun control laws as they once were and indeed have supported rolling back existing legislation. Finally, as we demonstrate here, the dominant news frames on gun control have also shifted in a "pro-gun" direction. Thus, it seems reasonable to conclude that the attacks on 9/11 destabilized the policy advantage of gun control advocates. But it was not the skilled policy entrepreneurs on the pro-gun side of the issue who took advantage of the window of opportunity and reframed the debate for the public. The news media played the major role. After 9/11 they reframed gun control by making explicit links between the issue and terrorism, although no cues about this link were provided by the anti-gun lobby. Whether this reframing of the issue was caused by journalists' and editors' changed assessment of the reality of the issue or by attempts to further sensationalize the issue remains undetermined.

As Kingdon (1984) has argued, different evolutionary models apply to public policy debates at different time periods. Just as biologists posit an evolutionary process of slow change, so too the gun control debate slowly changed prior to 9/11. Then there was a sudden and substantial change as new terrorism themes emerged. Of course, gun control frames had emerged previously in sudden leaps, as in the "Mob Violence" frame of the 1930s (see note 7), but their lifespan was fleeting. Terrorism is now a predominant theme of twenty-first-century American politics and a historical marker for generations of American citizens. Thus an important question is: when does this policy-framing window on gun control close? That is, when will terrorist frames lose their dramatic potency? The answer is, when the events of September 11 and the subsequent war on terrorism do not press with such immediacy on Americans' thinking. But this is not likely to occur in the near future. There are new color-coded alert levels issued by the Department of Homeland Security for each new holiday or event. There is a no-fly zone over the Super Bowl. The fear that generalized across the American public on September 11 remains and will continue to make terrorist appeals on policy issues like gun control evocative.

Appendix: Experimental Passages

"Crime and Violence" Frame

Gun Control: Still the Issue

Washington, D.C., May 29—What are the pressing social policy issues of the day? According to participants at the twenty-fifth annual meeting of the American Policy Institute, gun control is high on the agenda. In his annual address, Dr. Lawrence Stein, president of the institute, said that guns contribute to the culture of violence that is slowly but steadily destroying the nation. Stein noted that America's high homicide rate is related to the unique access Americans have to firearms: "Guns serve little other purpose but to kill, and the recent school and office shootings are evidence of our culture of violence."

Participants at the Georgetown Hilton conference, who came from a wide variety of academic backgrounds, including health and social science professionals, pointed toward recent statistics and international comparisons. These clearly show that a gun in the home is forty-two times more likely to kill a friend than an intruder. Every day thirty American children are killed or wounded by guns. Murder rates in the United States are much higher than in Canada, Europe, or Japan.

"The only answer to these devastating statistics lies in gun control laws that make it more difficult for criminals to obtain weapons," one political scientist said. "The level of gun-related violence in America is not acceptable; let's get on with the business of saving lives. This can only be done by stopping the proliferation of firearms and by passing strict gun control laws. These common-sense gun laws will make it more difficult for criminals to acquire guns; they will make our neighborhoods safer from gun violence and will protect American children."

Perhaps no topic is more uniquely American than gun control. Guns are deeply woven into the fabric of this culture. What was made clear at the meeting is that the issue of gun control remains high on the nation's agenda. And as the speakers said, the spiral of violence caused by guns needs to be stopped. Only then can a civil society endure.

"Constitutional Rights" Frame

Gun Control: Still the Issue

Washington, D.C., May 29—What are the pressing social policy issues of the day? According to participants at the twenty-fifth annual meeting of the American Policy Institute, gun control is high on the agenda. In his annual address, Dr. Lawrence Stein, president of the institute, said that the framers of the U.S. Constitution clearly recognized the right of citizens to carry arms and defend themselves. That is why they went out of their way to include the crucial individual right to bear arms in the Second Amendment.

Stein noted that gun ownership is a right that Americans possess over the people of almost every other nation, where the governments are afraid to trust people with arms: "You cannot defend the U.S. Constitution and at the same time limit people's rights to carry arms," Stein says. Law-abiding people have the right to own guns—for hunting, target shooting, and, last but not least, for self-protection.

Participants at the Georgetown Hilton conference, who came from a wide variety of academic backgrounds, including health and social science professionals, agreed that the authors of the Bill of Rights wrote the Second Amendment to safeguard the individual right to keep and bear arms.

"To support the Constitution is to guarantee the right of individuals to keep and bear arms," one political scientist said. "Early Americans fought a brave war to free themselves from a dictatorial English king. They understood the right to keep and bear arms was about the power to protect and defend our rights, and ultimately the power to resist and overthrow a tyrannical government. Americans weren't fooled, and they won't be fooled today. When it comes to firearms, the U.S. Constitution means exactly what it says."

Perhaps no topic is more uniquely American than gun control. Guns are deeply woven into the fabric of this culture. What was made clear at the meeting is that the issue of gun control remains high on the nation's agenda. And as the speakers said, the Second Amendment guarantees a fundamental right to bear arms; it is nonnegotiable and a crucial building block for freedom in a democratic society.

"Guns Cause Terrorism" Frame
Gun Control: Still the Issue

Washington, D.C., May 29—What are the pressing social policy issues of the day? According to participants at the twenty-fifth annual meeting of the American Policy Institute, gun control is high on the agenda. In his annual address, Dr. Lawrence Stein, president of the institute, said that the recent surge in gun sales after the September terrorist attacks will only result in the proliferation of weapons and more gun-related violence against innocent citizens. Stein noted that the nation already has undertaken important steps to defend its citizens from further terrorist attacks: "Law enforcement has been given the tools they need to investigate and deter terrorist attacks. Equally important, American troops are fighting terrorism abroad. Guns, however, won't protect Americans from terrorists armed with viruses or nuclear bombs."

Participants at the Georgetown Hilton conference, who came from a wide variety of academic backgrounds, including health and social science professionals, agreed that recent legislation has not addressed the problem of easy access to firearms. "Our firearm laws allow individuals to amass large-scale deadly arsenals that can be used against innocent citizens and against our soldiers."

"For terrorists around the world, the United States is the Great Gun Bazaar," one political scientist said. "Guns can be used to commit acts of terrorism or to resist law-enforcement efforts at apprehension and arrest. In short, guns and terrorism go together. Thus, proposals that fail to address easy access to firearms are clearly inadequate. What we need to protect Americans abroad and at home are common-sense gun control measures that prevent terrorists from acquiring guns."

Perhaps no topic is more uniquely American than gun control. Guns are deeply woven into the fabric of this culture. What was made clear at the meeting is that the issue of gun control remains high on the nation's agenda. And as the speakers said, ensuring homeland security means combating the threat of terrorism in all its possible forms, with all its potential weapons, especially guns.

"Guns Prevent Terrorism" Frame
Gun Control: Still the Issue

Washington, D.C., May 29—What are the pressing social policy issues of the day? According to participants at the twenty-fifth annual meeting of the American Policy Institute, gun control is high on the agenda. In his annual address, Dr. Lawrence Stein, president of the institute, said that the recent terrorist attacks on the World Trade Center have shown the public that the government, police, and the military simply cannot be there all the time to keep them safe from danger and defend them from terrorism. Stein noted that 9/11 was a wake-up call, showing Americans how vulnerable they are to terrorism: "Americans need to understand that they must take responsibility for their own safety. The best deterrent against terrorism is to let honest law-abiding citizens carry guns."

Participants at the Georgetown Hilton conference, who came from a wide variety of academic backgrounds, including health and social science professionals, argued that citizens are often the most important line of defense against terrorism. Weapons in the hands of the public can prevent acts of terror. Skillfully trained citizens and armed pilots must assist in the fight against suicidal terrorists who threaten the nation's safety.

"Arms discourage and keep the invader and plunderer in awe; only they can preserve our liberty," one political scientist said. "The first target in homeland security should be the terrorists. If America is to remain the bright doorway of freedom to the world, we must defend our freedom in its hour of maximum danger. We must allow citizens to carry arms to protect themselves and their country."

Perhaps no topic is more uniquely American than gun control. Guns are deeply woven into the fabric of this culture. What was made clear at the meeting is that the issue of gun control remains high on the nation's agenda. And as the speakers said, we must move the front lines of the fight against terrorism to where they belong: the right to carry firearms for self- and national protection.

Dual Frame

Gun Control: Still the Issue

Washington, D.C., May 29—What are the pressing social policy issues of the day? According to participants at the twenty-fifth annual meeting of the American Policy Institute, gun control is high on the agenda. In his annual address, Dr. Lawrence Stein, president of the institute, said that the recent terrorist attacks on the World Trade Center were a wake-up call, showing Americans how vulnerable they are to terrorism.

Participants at the Georgetown Hilton conference, who came from a wide variety of academic backgrounds, including health and social science professionals, took different positions on the role of gun control in the fight against terrorism.

One political scientist said that Americans need to take responsibility for their own safety. "The best deterrent against terrorism is to let honest law-abiding citizens carry guns. If America is to remain the bright doorway of freedom to the world, we must defend our freedom in its hour of maximum danger. We must allow law-abiding citizens and pilots to carry arms to protect themselves and their country. Arms discourage and keep the invader and plunderer in awe; only they can preserve our liberty," the speaker said.

Other presenters warned that the recent surge in gun sales after 9/11 will only result in the proliferation of weapons and more gun-related violence against citizens. "The United States is the Great Gun Bazaar for terrorists, and their deadly arsenals can be used against soldiers and innocent citizens," the speaker said. "Let law enforcement investigate and deter terror attacks. Guns in the hands of Americans won't protect them from terrorists armed with viruses or nuclear bombs. What we need are common-sense gun control measures that prevent terrorists from acquiring guns."

Perhaps no topic is more uniquely American than gun control. Guns are deeply woven into the fabric of this culture. What was made clear at the meeting is that the issue of gun control remains high on the nation's agenda. And as the speakers said, the proliferation of weapons can contribute to terrorism, but by the same token, well-trained citizens can aid in the fight against it.

6

Super-Predators or Victims of Societal Neglect?
Framing Effects in Juvenile Crime Coverage

Franklin D. Gilliam Jr. and Shanto Iyengar

An impressive array of scholarly research demonstrates that language has a profound influence on human thought (see Carroll 1956; Seidel 1975; Sanford 1987; Rosch 1973; Lakoff 1987). In the realm of political communication, the use of particular forms of presentation or modes of discourse (also known as "frames") strongly influences perceptions of public issues, events, and leaders (Iyengar 1991; Neuman, Just, and Crigler 1992; Gamson 1992). For example, the public is more likely to endorse increases in government welfare spending when the beneficiaries are said to be "poor people" rather than "people on welfare" or "black people" (Bobo and Kluegel 1993; Gilens 1996; Gilliam 1999; T. Smith 1987).

Of course, the most common forum for the presentation of public issues is broadcast news. The overwhelming majority of broadcast news reports are "episodic" or event oriented, focusing on concrete acts or live events rather than general contextual material. Television news coverage of poverty, for instance, is much more likely to deal with the predicament of particular poor people than with current economic trends or social welfare policy issues (Iyengar 1991; also see Gilens 1996). A similar pattern has been noted in news coverage of terrorism; information about specific terrorist acts is not matched by information about underlying historical, social, or economic antecedents (Altheide 1987). In short, as depicted in television news programs, political issues are invariably particularized. Few issues match crime for the pervasiveness of the episodic news frame; in network newscasts the ratio of episodic to thematic stories is approximately nine to one (Iyengar 1991). The pattern is even more skewed in local television newscasts, the most frequently encountered form of news (Roper Starch Worldwide 1994). Local news coverage of crime is almost universally episodic (Budzilowicz 2002; Yanich 1998). In the Los Angeles media market the typical thirty-minute local newscast includes three reports on crime, cumulating to approximately four minutes (out of twelve minutes devoted to "news") of coverage (see Gilliam et al. 1996). In this respect at least, Los Angeles is not an outlier; one study of local news in fifty-six cities indicates that crime accounted for one-third of all broadcast news (Klite, Bardwell, and Salzman 1997).

In addition to the dominance of the episodic news frame, crime coverage is also characterized by two qualitative attributes—an emphasis on violent crime and an interest in individual perpetrators and victims. As seen in the news, most crime is violent—"if it bleeds it leads" is the order of business. In Los Angeles, for instance, while murders represent only 2 percent of all felony crimes, stories about murders account for some 30 percent of crime news coverage (see Gilliam et al. 1996). Crime coverage also features information about particular attributes of the perpetrators and victims, in particular their race or ethnicity and age (Entman 1993; Gilliam 1998; Gilliam and Iyengar 2000). Race and ethnicity are clear visual cues, especially since news reports often feature photographs or composite sketches of the suspect and/or victim. While visual or verbal descriptions of suspects are typically less revealing of their age, higher rates of juvenile crime are reflected by an increase in news coverage of youth gangs and gang-related criminal activity in which the suspects are either explicitly or implicitly described as juveniles or young adults (Gilliam et al. 2001).

We anticipate that public reaction to crime is heavily influenced by the news media's portrayal of perpetrators as racial minorities or juveniles (especially as gang members). More specifically, we expect that viewers' attitudes toward crime are not so much based on general principles as on racial and age-related stereotypes.[1] Thus, we expect that if subjects are presented with otherwise identical news reports on violent crime that feature alternatively white and non-white perpetrators, those subjects who are exposed to the non-white perpetrators version will express greater fear of crime and support for punitive criminal justice policies. Independent of the perpetrator's race, we expect similar results on the gang/non-gang dimension (i.e., higher levels of fear and punitiveness in the gang version of the news story).

Juveniles and Non-Whites as "Super-Predators"

Throughout the early and mid-1990s pundits warned of an impending youth-crime epidemic (DiIulio 1995). To many observers (e.g., Bennett, DiIulio, and Walters 1996), the increasing frequency of juvenile violent crime signified that America was now home to a new breed of so-called super-predators—amoral, radically impulsive, and brutally cold-blooded preadults who murder, assault, rape, burglarize, deal deadly drugs, engage in gang warfare, and generally wreak communal havoc (Bennett, DiIulio, and Walters 1996, 27; Berkman 1995). As proof, analysts noted that teenage homicides and violent-crime arrests doubled between the mid-1980s and the mid-1990s, the number of gun homicides tripled, and juvenile gang murders quadrupled (Bennett, DiLulio, and Walters 1996). Indeed, talk of violent, remorseless teen "super-predators" quickly became part of the public discourse. As criminologist James Fox observed, "Unless we act today, we're going to have a bloodbath when these kids grow up" (quoted in Garrett 1995).

To be sure, the immediate surge of youth crime through the mid-1990s was concentrated among members of particular racial and ethnic minority groups. According to the U.S. Department of Justice, *Office of Juvenile Justice and Delinquency Programs,* for example, "black youth were responsible for the majority of the increase between 1986 and 1994" in homicides nationwide. In California, a state that experiences about twice its expected share of teen murders, the overwhelming preponderance of teenage violent crimes between the mid-1980s and the mid-1990s was committed by blacks and Latinos (California Commission on the Status of African-American Males 1996). Strengthening the connection between ethnicity and youthful criminality even further is the disproportionate number of minority youths who are involved with urban street gangs (Curry and Spergel 1992; Hagedorn 1991; M. Klein 1995; Vigil 2002). For example, gang-related homicides accounted for 18 percent of all homicides in Los Angeles County in 1978, but by 1994, the figure had risen to 43 percent. Likewise, the gang-related homicide rate for fifteen- to nineteen-year-old African American males was 60.5 per 100,000 population during 1979–81; for the 1989–91 period; the rate was 192.4 per 100,000.

Public alarm over juvenile crime through the mid-1990s was heightened by extensive media coverage. Of course, young people (especially minority youth) who engage in criminal violence are especially newsworthy (see Males 1996; Dorfman et al. 1995); senseless acts of violence by "glassy-eyed, remorseless" teenagers in gang attire (V. Berry and Manning-Miller 1996) satisfy the media's programming needs. As general trends in American public opinion suggest, the growing reach of local news contributed to increased support for punitive remedies aimed at youth offenders (Dorfman et al. 1995; Gilliam 1998). For instance, the public called for more aggressive law enforcement, and in response policy makers across the country proposed and adopted more severe sanctions on adolescent crime, such as incarceration in adult facilities, trying juveniles as adults, the death penalty, and "three strikes" legislation (Alderman 1994; Jacobius 1996; Tang 1994; Walinsky 1995). Thus the rate of juvenile crime and the increased visibility of juvenile crime to the public through the news media—frequently featuring non-white teenagers engaged in the most violent of acts—were thought to have contributed to the high levels of public concern for crime.

In summary, the reality of violent crime in the mid-1990s was that an individual's age and ethnicity could realistically be considered "threatening" attributes. Our objective in this chapter is to examine the extent to which the public's attitudes toward crime reflect these cues. More specifically, we test the proposition that people become more fearful of crime and more committed advocates of punitive measures for dealing with violent crime when the news media frame the issue in ways that highlight the juvenile and non-white attributes of perpetrators.

Methodology

We treat the two relevant characteristics of individual perpetrators (race and youth) as orthogonal factors in a fully crossed experimental design. A recently broadcast news story dealing with increased police patrols in the city of Long Beach provided the experimental stimulus. The story described armed police patrols of high-crime areas and the eventual arrest of two males. We manipulated the age of the suspects indirectly by depicting the police activity either as a general effort to reduce crime or, alternatively, as an attempt to curb gang-related crime. Thus, we altered the anchor's introductory lead-in so that the police operation was described as either a "crime sweep" (the words appeared on the television screen during the anchor's introduction) or a "gang sweep" (this label was substituted for "crime sweep" during the lead-in, and later the reporter referred to the suspects as "gang members"). With the exception of these two variations, the gang and non-gang versions of the news report were equivalent.

The race/ethnicity manipulation was more direct. Because the original report included police photographs of the two suspects, we were able to insert different "mug shots" corresponding to different ethnic groups. Depending on the experimental condition, the photos of the two suspects featured African Americans, whites, Hispanics, or Asians. Except for the substitution of the photographs, the news reports were identical in content and appearance.

Experimental participants watched a fifteen-minute videotaped local newscast (including commercials) described as having been selected at random from news programs broadcast during the past week. The objective of the study was said to be "selective perception" of news reports. Depending upon the condition to which they were assigned (at random), participants watched one of the following versions of the news story on the Long Beach police patrols.

1. The "crime-sweep" report that included the close-up photo of the two suspects

2. The "crime-sweep" report, but with all references to particular suspects eliminated

3. The "gang-sweep" report that included the close-up photo of the two suspects

4. The "gang-sweep" report, but devoid of any reference to individual suspects

Control participants watched the same newscast, but without any story on crime. In place of the crime report, they watched a story on a partial solar eclipse.

The design allows us to investigate a variety of questions. First, we can compare viewers' responses to news reports featuring non-white perpetrators (operationally defined as the conditions featuring African Americans and Hispanics) with their responses to coverage in which the suspects were white or Asian or to coverage in which there was no information about specific perpetrators.[2] Second, we can estimate the effects of youth-related crime on public attitudes by comparing reactions to the "gang-sweep" and "crime-sweep" conditions. Third, we can isolate the interactive effects, if any, between the youth and ethnicity factors. Perhaps viewers feel especially threatened when the crime involves juvenile gangs and the gang members are non-white.

In addition to the additive and interactive effects of perpetrator ethnicity and age, we can also assess the relative influence of visual cues (photographs of faces) and semantic cues (the "crime-sweep" versus "gang-sweep" labels) in news coverage of crime. Simple comparison of the difference in viewer responses between the "gang-sweep" and "crime-sweep" conditions that excluded pictures of the suspects with the baseline condition in which there was no reference to crime at all provides an estimate of the effects of crime coverage that lacks visual information about individual perpetrators. A parallel comparison of the gang- and non-gang-related conditions in which photographs of the perpetrator appear reveals the degree to which "pictures speak louder than words."

The report on crime was inserted into the middle position of the newscast, following the first commercial break. Except for the news story on crime, the newscasts were identical. None of the other stories appearing in the newscast concerned crime or matters of race.[3]

The experimental "sample" consisted of residents of West Los Angeles who were recruited through flyers and announcements in newsletters offering fifteen dollars for participation in "media research." The age of the participants ranged from eighteen to sixty-four. Fifty-one percent were white, 30 percent were black, 4 percent were Asian, and 7 percent were Latinos. Fifty-two percent were women.[4] The participants were relatively well educated (40 percent had graduated from college) and, in keeping with the local area, more Democratic than Republican (47 versus 22 percent) in their partisan loyalty.

The experiment was administered during the fall of 1995 at a major shopping mall in West Los Angeles in a two-room suite that was furnished casually with couches, lounge chairs, potted plants, and so on. Participants could browse through magazines and newspapers, snack on cookies and coffee, or (in many cases) chat with fellow participants who were friends or colleagues.

On their arrival, participants were given their instructions and then completed a short pretest questionnaire concerning their social background, party identification and political ideology, level of interest in political affairs, and media habits. They then watched the videotape of the newscast. At the end of the videotape, participants completed a lengthy questionnaire that included questions about their evaluations of various news programs and prominent journalists; their opinions concerning various issues in the news; their recall of particular news stories; their beliefs about the attributes of particular racial/ethnic groups; and, of course, crime. After completing the questionnaire, subjects were debriefed in full (including a full explanation of the experimental procedures) and paid.

Indicators

Our primary interest lies in examining the effects of news coverage on public opinion toward crime. Two facets of opinion are especially relevant to the "super-predator" hypothesis—fear of violent crime and support for punitive criminal justice policies. We used two closed-ended items to construct a "fear of crime index." The first was the standard General Social Survey (GSS) question on fear of victimization: "Is there any area around where you live—say, within a one-mile radius—where you would be afraid to walk alone at night?" Affirmative responses were scored as 1, other responses as 0. Second, we asked participants to rate the importance of random street violence: "Lately, there has been a lot of attention paid to the problem of random street violence. How serious a problem do you think random street violence is in your immediate neighborhood?" The response options included "very serious," "somewhat serious," "not very serious," and "don't know." Participants choosing the "very" or "somewhat" categories were given a score of 1; all others were scored as 0. The responses to the two questions were then averaged.[5]

We assessed support for punitive criminal justice policies with a pair of open-ended questions that asked participants to attribute responsibility—both causal and remedial—for the occurrence of crime. These questions were worded as follows:

People sometimes disagree about the reasons for crime. In your opinion, what are the three most important reasons why people commit crimes in the United States?

People also disagree about ways to solve the crime problem in the United States. In your opinion, what are the three most important remedies for crime?

Responses to these questions revealed a rich diversity of explanations and recommended solutions. Attributions of causal responsibility fell into three general categories. Crime was attributed either to individuals' personal characteristics (e.g., greed and immorality), to societal conditions (e.g., economic and social inequality), or to the indecisive and lenient nature of the criminal justice process (e.g., problems in obtaining convictions and adequate sentences). In the case of remedies for crime, the responses referred either to changes in societal conditions (e.g., more job opportunities) or to the imposition of more severe and punitive sanctions (e.g., stricter enforcement of the death penalty). We defined an index of punitiveness as the total number of references to punitive factors in participants' lists of causes and remedies.[6]

In order to boost the efficiency of our estimates of the effects of the experimental manipulations, we also incorporated a number of control variables into the analyses—factors known to predict individuals' views about crime and crime policy. These included participants' race and gender. Blacks and Hispanics were scored as 1 and compared with all other respondents. In the case of gender, men were assigned a score of 1. We also included measures of partisanship and political ideology (Republicans were scored as 1, all others as 0; conservatives as 1, liberals, moderates, and others as 0) and an index of racial stereotyping reflecting the degree to which participants agreed with negative characterizations of African Americans.[7] Finally, we included a question tapping participants' level of exposure to local television news (daily viewers were scored as 1 and compared with all others).[8]

Results

We began by validating the two experimental manipulations. The gang manipulation was designed to influence participants' perceptions of perpetrators as juveniles. Accordingly, at the very end of the posttest questionnaire, we directed participants' attention to the news story on crime (identified by the label "Crime in Long Beach") and asked them to recall the age of the suspects ("Thinking back to the suspects in the news story, please identify their age"). We compared the percentage of participants who recalled the suspects as over the age of twenty in the gang-sweep and crime-sweep conditions. As expected, there was a significant difference in recall of the suspects' age—while 60 percent of the participants in the crime-sweep conditions recalled the suspects as over the age of twenty, 60 percent of the participants in the gang-sweep conditions recalled the suspects as twenty or younger. This difference was highly significant ($p < .01$); use of the gang-sweep label did influence perceptions of the perpetrators' age.

We also asked participants to recall the ethnicity of the suspects ("Thinking back to the suspects in the news story, what was their race/ethnicity?"). Across all four levels of the ethnicity manipulation (Asian, white, African American, Hispanic), 48 percent of the participants accurately recalled the suspects' race. Excluding participants who were unable to recall anything about the suspects, the level of accuracy in recall of ethnicity increased to 57 percent. That is, participants with accurate recall of the suspects' race outnumbered those with inaccurate recall by a margin of 2.3 to 1.0. Despite the open-ended format of the recall question, and the fact that it was asked at the end of the survey instrument (a full thirty minutes after exposure to the news story on crime), the pictures of the perpetrators did convey information about their ethnicity. Participants' ability to recall the ethnicity of the suspects varied noticeably depending on the particular category of the ethnicity manipulation. As shown in table 6.1, the ratio of accurate to inaccurate identifications was highest in the African American and Hispanic conditions (67 to 5 percent) and significantly lower when participants were exposed to the conditions featuring white and Asian suspects (40 to 34 percent). This difference was statistically significant ($p < .01$).

The significant effect of the race of the suspect on accuracy of recall suggests that participants' prior beliefs about the attributes of particular ethnic groups powerfully color their interpretation of new information. We asked our participants to rate each of the four ethnic groups in terms of their tendency to be "not law abiding" and "violent." While 46 percent of the sample reported that these attributes applied "very well" or "fairly well" to African Americans and Hispanics, only 25 percent considered the attributes similarly apt descriptions

6.1 Recall of suspects' race by experimental condition

	Asian/white face	Crime story B (no face)	African American/ Hispanic face
Percentage accurate	40		67
Percentage false recognitions	34	44	5
	(99)	(93)	(95)

of whites and Asians. (For corroborating evidence concerning the similarity of whites' stereotypes about Hispanics and African Americans and the distinctiveness of whites' stereotypes of Asians, see Bobo et al. 1994.) The importance of racial stereotyping is especially apparent in the responses of participants who watched the crime report devoid of any reference to individual suspects. Forty-four percent of these participants falsely recalled a suspect, and only 4 percent of these false recognitions referred to a white or Asian. In short, news coverage of crime featuring African American and Hispanic suspects tends to confirm viewers' existing stereotypes of non-whites, while news reports in which the perpetrator is white or Asian disconfirm beliefs about whites and Asians. (For further evidence of "motivated recall," see Gilliam and Iyengar 1997.) Given the significantly higher levels of accurate recall in the African American and Hispanic conditions and the convergence of the African American and Hispanic stereotype ratings, on the one hand, and the stereotype ratings of whites and Asians, on the other hand, we decided to fold the ethnicity manipulation into two categories—non-white (the African American and Hispanic conditions) and white/Asian.

Testing the Super-Predator Hypothesis

The underlying premise of the hypothesis is that minority offenders are especially threatening to the public. Therefore, we expect that people will become more fearful and punitive when they are exposed to news stories that feature "super-predators." Table 6.2 presents the results of parallel analysis-of-variance tests for the impact of the age (gang sweep versus crime sweep) and ethnicity (non-white versus white/Asian) manipulations on the indices of fear and punitiveness. The top half of the table reveals a robust main effect of the youth-crime manipulation on fear of crime ($p < .05$). As expected, exposure to news coverage of gang-related crime boosted fear by a factor of 10 percent (in relation to news coverage of ordinary crime). Despite their heightened fear, viewers were *not* more likely to mention punitive accounts of crime when they encountered the "gang-sweep" frame. To the contrary, the gang frame made participants significantly ($p < .02$) less punitive in their approach to crime. Thus, these results provide only partial confirmation of the super-predator hypothesis; people are especially threatened by youthful offenders, but youth crime does not prompt them to prescribe harsh treatment of offenders.

The effects of the race/ethnicity manipulation are presented in the second half of table 6.2. Both measures show the expected pattern—higher levels of fear and punitiveness when the suspects were non-white—but both patterns are weak. If we subject the data to a more pointed test of the hypothesis by comparing the conditions with non-white suspects with those featuring whites

6.2 Fear of crime and punitiveness by types of crime and race of suspect

Type of crime coverage

	Gang crime	No crime coverage	Ordinary crime
Fear of crime	.58 (132)	.45 (65)	.48 (155)
		F-value: 3.91, p <.05	
Punitiveness	.80 (132)	1.06 (65)	1.18 (155)
		F-value: 3.96, p <.02	

Race of suspects

	Asian/white	No crime coverage	Non-white
Fear of crime	.50 (99)	.45 (65)	.57 (95)
		F-value: 2.21, ns	
Punitiveness	.88 (99)	1.06 (65)	1.16 (95)
		F-value: 1.36, ns	

or Asians, the results are more telling. The lower level of punitiveness when the suspect is either Asian or white is significant at the .05 level. In the case of fear, the difference is less dramatic ($p < .15$). As compared with their counterparts who encountered Asian or white suspects in news coverage of crime, participants who saw Hispanic or African American suspects were significantly more punitive and somewhat more fearful. These results thus validate the racial component of the super-predator hypothesis.

How is it that people are more fearful of crime but at the same time are less willing to favor punitive measures when presented with youthful offenders? Perhaps the study participants, following the model of criminal law, reasoned that preadults should not be held individually accountable for their actions. Moreover, gangs are collectivities, making it difficult to pinpoint responsibility. The distinctiveness of the gang label is also suggested by the finding that the significant differences in punitiveness elicited by the race/ethnicity manipulation were conditioned by the distinction between gang crime and ordinary crime. That is, we detected evidence of an interaction between reference to gang crime and the suspects' race. When the news is not framed in gang-related terms, non-white offenders elicit more punitive responses than white or Asian offenders. When the report refers to gangs, on the other hand, the ethnicity cue becomes less informative and participants make no distinction between the white/Asian and black/Hispanic suspects. In effect, the gang frame makes participants noticeably less punitive in their attitudes irrespective of the suspects' race.

6.3 Verbal versus visual framing of crime

Type of crime coverage

	Gang crime		No crime coverage	Ordinary crime	
	Pictures	*No pictures*		*No pictures*	*Pictures*
Fear of crime	.58 (88)	.59 (44)	.45 (65)	.48 (155)	.50 (106)
			F-value: 2.25, p <.06		
Punitiveness	.77 (88)	.84 (44)	*1.06 (65)*	*1.10 (49)*	*1.22 (106)*
			F-value: 2.08, p <.08		

Verbal versus Visual Cues

The analysis to this point has ignored qualitative differences in the depiction of crime. Specifically, the differences reported in table 6.3 were calculated across the conditions that featured both verbal and visual cues (the "gang-sweep" or "crime-sweep" label followed by photos of the two suspects) and conditions that provided only the verbal cue. The effects of the "verbal only" and "verbal plus visual" conditions are presented in table 6.3.

These results do little to support the maxim that pictures are more persuasive than words. In general, the addition of the photographs of the suspects did not strengthen the manipulation. In the case of gang-related crime, the presence of the visual cues, if anything, tended to reduce viewers' fear and punitiveness. On the other side of the manipulation (ordinary crime), the pattern was reversed; participants tended to be more fearful and punitive when the news story included photographs of the suspects. While none of these differences is statistically significant, the pattern suggests that the conceptual distinction between gang-related crime and garden-variety crime takes precedence over the presence or absence of visual cues concerning individual suspects. When viewers are forewarned that the crime in question is gang related, exposure to the pictures of two "gang members" serves to make them slightly less punitive. On the other hand, when viewers are not led to anticipate gang involvement in crime, exposure to the identical pictures elicits slightly higher levels of punitiveness. In our final set of tests, we isolated the participants who were exposed to both elements of the super-predator concept—juvenile and non-white offenders—and compared their levels of fear and punitiveness with all other participants. Unlike the earlier analyses of variance, this specification treats both experimental factors as simple dichotomies (gang crime versus all other conditions, non-white suspects versus all other conditions). Using this reconfigured design, we reestimated the effects of the manipulations, this time controlling for a set of individual differences generally thought to influence crime-related attitudes. These included participants' race, gender, party identification, ideology, frequency of exposure to local newscasts, and stereotypes of African Americans. Table 6.4 presents the reduced-form or "best-fit" multiple-regression analyses of the fear and punitiveness indices.

Fear of crime was equally affected by exposure to juvenile crime and nonwhite offenders. Among participants who watched the news report on gang-related crime, fear of crime increased by 9 percent; for participants who encountered Hispanic or African American suspects the increase was 8 percent. The interaction of the youth and race factors proved insignificant. That is, the effects of the suspects' race proved uniform in the gang-crime and ordinary-crime versions of the news report.

Turning to the control variables, women and blacks were especially fearful of crime. These individual differences are in keeping with the literature on victimization and fear of crime. In addition to race and gender, people who watch local news on a regular basis are more likely to fear crime, suggesting that the distinctive agenda of local newscasts has been passed on to the audience.

The right-hand column of table 6.4 displays the regression coefficients for the open-ended measure of punitiveness. The multiple controls weaken the effects of the gang crime–ordinary crime distinction considerably; the decreased frequency of punitive responses among participants who saw the report on gang crime now only borders on significance ($p < .15$). The most noteworthy result for the index of punitiveness, however, is the interaction between the two defining attributes of super-predators. This interaction occurs because of the substantial weakening of the race manipulation when the news report focuses on gang-related crime. As we noted earlier, the effects of the suspects'

6.4 Best-fit regressions for fear and punitiveness

Predictor	Fear	Punitiveness
Race of suspects	.08 (.04)	.32 (.17)
Gang crime	.09 (.04)	−.21 (.15)
Race and gang interaction		−.39 (.27)
Race of participant	.11 (.05)	.31 (.14)
Gender	−.19 (.04)	.17 (.06)
Party identification		.35 (.17)
Index of stereotyping		.20 (.19)
Constant	.58 (.06)	.47 (.18)
Adjusted R^2	.10	.11
N	352	

race virtually disappear when the news focuses on gang crime. The regression coefficient for the race manipulation in the right-hand column of table 6.4 tells us that punitive responses increased in frequency by a factor of .32 ($p < .07$) when participants saw non-white suspects in the context of ordinary crime. The interaction coefficient of −.39 ($p < .15$) indicates that when the news report focuses on gang crime, the race effect is reversed. That is, when the suspect is an alleged gang member, white and Asian suspects elicit more punitive responses (by a margin of .39) than Hispanics or blacks.

Finally, the effects of the control variables were true to form—whites, Republicans, and conservatives were in the vanguard of the punitive approach to crime. People who tune in to local news regularly were not only more likely to fear crime; they were also significantly more punitive in their outlook.

In all, our results provide mixed support for the super-predator hypothesis. We found that exposure to news reports featuring juvenile and non-white offenders triggered more responses reflecting concern about crime (as compared with groups who were exposed to crime stories featuring other categories of perpetrators), but there was no outpouring of support for punitive criminal justice policies. Our subjects actually expressed less punitive attitudes when they were exposed to juvenile offenders, no matter what the perpetrators' ethnicity. Apparently, people believed, or at least hoped, that youthful offenders could be reformed with appropriate intervention.

We offer three related accounts of the incomplete substantiation of the super-predator thesis, having to do with design, measurement, and context. An initial design concern is that our age manipulation conflates group-based and individualistic accounts of crime. The previous discussions of "super-predators" have assumed that individuals, rather than groups, are the major criminal forces. Gang crime necessarily shifts the focus to collective behavior. Even ordinary citizens seem to explain gang activity based on the harsh realities of contemporary urban environments. Most scholars of gang life suggest that a sense of group identity and the need for protection and self-esteem far outweigh criminal motives as the primary incentives for youth involvement in gangs (see, e.g., M. Klein 1995). Once the behavior of individuals is placed in the context of gang activity, the public's outlook seems to shift from the failings of individuals to the shortcomings of the broader society. The net result is that people do not endorse harsher penalties as the most effective way to treat youth crime. In other words, because gang conditions contain notable thematic content, they are not completely accurate representations of typical episodic news stories. And, as noted above, the vast preponderance of local television news is episodic in nature. A cleaner test of the super-predator thesis should feature a sole perpetrator in the experimental design.

A second design flaw has to do with the fact that we created experimental treatments featuring Asian, white, African American, and Latino youth perpetrators. There is little doubt that stereotypes about blacks (especially black youth) are still more accessible to most white Americans (Bobo et al. 1994; Entman 1992; Entman et al. 1998; Peffley, Shields, and Williams 1996; Peffley and Hurwitz 1999). While the rapidly changing demographics of America's urban landscape call into question the general utility of the black-versus-white distinction, it is still a staple of local television reporting of juvenile crime news.

Two matters of measurement may have further contributed to the tepid support for the super-predator hypothesis. First, our operationalization of crime attitudes did not specifically focus on the public's view of *youth* violent crime, and a core element of the super-predator hypothesis, of course, is the alleged perpetrator's age. Thus there is a conflation of people's general crime attitudes and their specific views on what to do about youth crime. A second, more minor concern is that our previous measure of punitive crime attitudes was crafted from a set of open-ended responses. While this surely has the advantage of obtaining more spontaneous responses, this type of measurement also introduces a fair amount of measurement error. In any event, closed-ended items directed at youth crime would be an improvement.

Our final explanation for the results is contextual. In the first instance, the rate of juvenile crime significantly declined between the mid-1990s and the beginning of the new century. For example, the national violent-crime index of juvenile arrests decreased 23 percent between 1996 and 2000 (Office of Juvenile Justice and Delinquency Prevention 2001). Nonetheless, the local television news media continued to focus on crime as a prime topic of youth-related news. In 2000, for example, the child advocacy organization Children Now commissioned Gilliam and others to perform a content analysis of youth and local television news (Gilliam et al. 2001); their data show that crime stories accounted for 53 percent of all adolescent news coverage (Bales and Gilliam 2003; see also Amundson, Lichter, and Lichter 2000). How could crime continue to dominate local-television youth-news coverage in the face of quickly falling youth-crime rates?

One answer is that the rash of tragic and violent school shootings in 1998 and 1999 trumped the fact that juvenile crime rates were in serious decline. The media frenzy and ensuing national hand-wringing after the school shootings in Paducah, Jonesboro, and Columbine continued to hold juvenile crime in the spotlight. Interestingly, the media added a new element to the youth-crime narrative—namely, a featured role for the victim of violent crime. The Children Now data, for instance, show that youth were more likely to be depicted as victims of crime rather than as perpetrators (this holds regardless of the level of violence depicted). Over three-quarters of crime stories featured juveniles in the role of victim (Bales and Gilliam 2003). This finding is in line with the results reported by Amundson, Lichter, and Lichter, who note a "heavy emphasis on crime victimization" in their study of six local news markets (2000, 11). Youth-as-crime-victims has apparently become a new element of the youth-crime frame.

In all, weakness in design and measurement, combined with a significantly changed context, accounts for the incomplete rendering of the super-predator hypothesis. With this in mind, we conducted a second study designed to overcome the liabilities mentioned above. We paid special attention to securing a more typically episodic news treatment, limiting the analysis to white and black youth, revising dependent measures to reflect views specific to youth crime, and incorporating the role of the violent-crime victim into the youth-crime news narrative.

The Role of Race, Youth, and Crime in Television News

In this study we were interested in assessing the effects of the race and crime role played by youth in crime news stories. In this instance, the stimulus was incorporated into a sixty-second crime story about an adolescent male who was murdered at an ATM. Thus we constructed a 3×3 design in which we manipulated the crime role and the presence of racial cues in crime news. Subjects were randomly assigned to one of nine conditions (i.e., white perpetrator, no perpetrator, black perpetrator × white victim, no victim, black victim). Depending upon the condition to which they were assigned, subjects watched a news story on crime that included a close-up photo of the suspect and/or victim. Using the method described above, the photo depicted either a youthful African American or a white male. The report on crime was inserted into the middle position of the newscast, following the first commercial break. Except for the news story on crime, the newscasts were identical in all other respects. None of the remaining stories on the tape concerned crime or matters of race. As previously noted, two facets of opinion are especially relevant to the "super-predator" hypothesis—fear of violent crime (particularly youth crime) and support for punitive juvenile justice policies. We operationalized fear of *youth* crime with two items. The first was worded as follows: "Who commits most of the violent crimes these days? Would you say they are committed mostly by adults or mostly by young people?" The second question asked: "Which of the following do you personally perceive as a greater threat: violent crime committed by adults or violent crime committed by young people?" Study participants who believed young people committed the most violent crimes or that youth crime posed a greater threat than adult crime were coded as 3. People who were unsure were assigned a score of 2, and those who felt that adults were more threatening received a value of 1. A scale was constructed by summing the responses to the two items and dividing by two (mean = 2.13, sd = .55, Cronbach's alpha = .73). To separate out general crime fears from fears of youth crime, we measured general fear of crime with the standard GSS question: "Lately there has been a lot of attention paid to the problem of random street violence. How serious a problem do you think random street violence is in your neighborhood?" Subjects who believed random street violence was a "very serious" problem were coded as 3, those who thought it was "somewhat serious" received a score of 2, and those who believed it to be "not very serious" were given a score of 1 (mean = 2.27, sd = .72). We measured support for punitive juvenile justice policy using a two-item index. The first item was worded as follows. "When a teenager commits a murder and is found guilty by a jury, do you think he should get the death penalty, or should he be spared his life because of his youth?" The second question asked: "In your view, should the law require fines or prison sentences for the parents of juveniles convicted of major crimes, or not?" Subjects who supported the death penalty and fines and prison were coded as 3, people who were unsure were given a score of 2, and those who believed a teenager should be spared because of his youth and did not support fines and prison were coded as 1. We created the index by summing the responses and dividing by two (mean = 1.88, sd = .64, Cronbach's alpha = .63).

For this section we performed analysis-of-variance tests to measure the impact of the youth-crime news script. Initial analysis indicated that the critical influence on crime attitudes concerned the pairing of white victim with black perpetrator. There was no statistically significant difference as a function of other configurations of race of perpetrator, race of victim, and crime role. Thus, we conducted parallel analyses for the main effects of exposure to the white victim or black perpetrator (controlling for several common individual differences including education, income, age, gender, marital status, ideology, and party identification) on subjects' crime attitudes.[9]

Table 6.5 presents the results of the second study. The top third of the table provides moderate support for our expectations. For example, exposure to the white-victim condition was associated with a significant increase in fear of random street violence and teen crime and violence. Similarly, exposure to the black-perpetrator condition increased fear of random street violence but did not have an appreciable impact on fear of adolescent crime or punitive crime solutions.

These results are produced, in large part, by the significant difference be-

6.5 Impact of TV news by crime role and race of subject

	Threat of teen crime	Punitive solutions	Fear of random street violence
All subjects *(N = 300)*			
White victim	2.36*	2.22**	1.90
Non-white victim	2.23	2.09	1.87
Black perpetrator	2.32*	2.15	1.89
Non-black perpetrator	2.25	2.12	1.88
White subjects *(N = 132)*			
White victim	2.43**	2.27*	1.96
Non-white victim	2.13	2.11	1.82
Black perpetrator	2.39*	2.29**	1.81
Non-black perpetrator	2.17	2.11	1.90
Black subjects *(N = 85)*			
White victim	2.41	2.26	1.79
Non-white victim	2.41	2.14	1.84
Black perpetrator	2.45	2.20	1.90
Non-black perpetrator	2.40	2.17	1.80

*$p < .10$ **$p < .05$

tween white and African American study participants. Thus the second third of the table examines the impact of the dominant frame on whites' crime attitudes. The results of this analysis provide more solid support for the super-predator perspective in four of the six relevant comparisons. In other words, exposure to either a white victim or a black perpetrator was related to heightened fear of youth crime and support for punitive juvenile justice policies. On the other hand, there were no measurable effects on more general fear of crime attitudes. Finally, the last third of the table repeats the analysis for black subjects. The main finding is that the manipulations do not influence African Americans' crime attitudes (see also Gilliam and Iyengar 2000). Presumably this is a result of the fact that African Americans are more likely to have a deeper pool of experiences upon which to base judgments. In other words, they do not rely as heavily on the news media for information about their community.

Discussion

Our results describe a cascade of effects that reveal subtle variations in the applicability of the super-predator hypothesis. Contrary to expectations, our study participants were reluctant to punish juvenile criminals in the context of gang involvement, regardless of the race of the perpetrator. The gang manipulation in our study effectively reduced the proportion of viewers who offered consistently punitive attributions of responsibility—those who cited inadequate deterrents and the personal attributes of perpetrators as causal factors *and* who recommended harsher and more stringent sanctions as the key to reducing crime. Once the behavior of individuals is placed in the context of gang activity, the public's outlook seems to shift from the failings of individuals to the shortcomings of the broader society. Thematic frames thus lead to societal attributions of responsibility (Iyengar 1991).

This sounds an optimistic note for policy advocates who seek to resist the popular trend toward more punitive approaches to juvenile crime. For one thing, our results indicate that the public is not monolithic in its support for "get tough" measures. Even among policy makers who favor punitive approaches to juvenile crime, there is considerable recognition that intervention at an early age (e.g., information, education, mentoring, family support) is crucial in the fight against juvenile crime (see, e.g., Bennett, DiIulio, and Walters 1996).

Nonetheless, there is still strong support for the super-predator hypothesis as the dominant youth-crime frame available to the American public. Our second study strengthened the mild findings in the first experiment. For example, among white study participants, exposure to the black perpetrator significantly increased the number of people fearful of teen crime and supportive of more punitive juvenile justice policies like placing youth in adult detention facilities. This is all the more interesting given that the black/white juvenile murder-arrest rate is at the lowest it has been in two decades (Snyder 2002).

The addition of the crime role—perpetrator or victim—as an element of the news frame yielded interesting insights. For example, exposure to white teen victims in and of itself raised fear levels and support for punitive crime policies among white participants. In other words, people gain no added leverage by knowing the identity or race of the alleged perpetrator. Simply knowing that the victim was white increased the proportion of harsh crime attitudes.

All told, our evidence suggests the following generalizations. First, both semantic and visual cues condition public attitudes on crime. The word *gang* appears to associate crime with violence and youthful perpetrators. Accordingly, people exposed to the cue become both more fearful of crime and less enthusiastic about punitive remedies. It is worth noting that the effects of the gang cue on support for punitive remedies were "color-blind"—study participants were more lenient with youthful offenders, no matter what their ethnicity. At the same time, our evidence also demonstrated considerable traces of race-based reasoning about crime. Exposure to non-white perpetrators or white victims was sufficient to move the audience in a more punitive direction. In this respect ordinary citizens seem more consistently race oriented than the judicial process. Criminal sentencing, as is well documented, is most extreme when the case involves both a white victim and a non-white perpetrator (Sidanius and Pratto 1999). The court of public opinion, however, is insensitive to perpetrator-victim permutations; the mere presence of a non-white perpetrator or white victim is sufficient to elicit an extreme "sentence."

7
Media Frames, Core Values, and the Dynamics of Racial Policy Preferences

Paul M. Kellstedt

Most Americans, regardless of their race, do not directly experience affirmative action policies, school busing to achieve racial integration, or other such governmental actions. In the 1950s and 1960s, for example, very few Americans personally witnessed the civil rights protests that defined that era. Many of these events occurred in isolated Southern rural environments, far removed from the bulk of the population. And even those that happened in larger cities like Little Rock or Montgomery, of course, had crowds that numbered, at best, in the thousands, not the millions. Yet millions of Americans vicariously experienced these events, many of which became a part of the broader American political environment, because they were mediated: millions of people who do not directly experience the day-to-day realities of political activity are nevertheless participants in the national discussion on race when they read the paper, listen to the radio, and watch television news.

And when people watch a television news report about a civil rights protest, they are not watching an unedited, hours-long, un-commented-upon video feed. They are, typically, watching a ninety-second segment full of interpretation by movement participants on both sides, most likely emphasizing conflict of viewpoints, and commentary by a reporter. This is, quite simply, the way it has to be. None of us knows when events are likely to break out, and no television or radio network is going to broadcast all such events live, all the time. And even if they did, most citizens would not have the interest to tune in for hours on end.[1] We rely on news professionals to select which stories to tell us, and which ones to omit, during the thirty minutes we allow them into our homes. Anything short of that would make the average citizen a reporter instead of a citizen.

Hence, *how* racial policy is covered in the media is potentially quite important. The decisions journalists make about whether to cloak their coverage of, say, a court decision on affirmative action in the language of diversity, in the language of reverse discrimination—or, most likely, both—provide the interpretive lenses through which citizens internalize the reality that we did not directly witness. The interpretive lenses, or frames, that journalists use help citizens incorporate new stories into preexisting cognitive structures. Frames help us to make mental connections between things we already know or believe and the things we're just learning. What makes the framing process so interesting is that, as in the case above, multiple and competing frames are typically available to a reporter.

Media Frames and Race

Contrary to the polemical nature of most rhetoric that we hear on racial issues, which would have us believe that there are only extremists involved in the debate, I believe most Americans actually see nuggets of truth to both liberal and conservative arguments on race. Most Americans, if the reader will pardon the pun, see very little that is clearly black or white but rather see many shades of gray. This perspective on the nature of racial attitudes is consistent with the best recent work on the nature of mass attitudes more generally, though it has not been applied rigorously to racial attitudes.[2]

Americans have core values that resonate with liberal arguments on race. When people hear that government needs to protect people against discriminatory and unfair treatment, that harmonizes with a part of the average citizen's value structure. And at the very same time, these same Americans have core values that are consistent with conservative arguments on race. In particular, this is the case when people hear that liberal racial policies can violate the notion that people should get ahead solely because of individual effort. The critical aspect here is that these values coexist inside people's hearts and minds, though they occasionally come into conflict.

What are these core American values? They are two centerpieces of the American ethos, *individualism* and *egalitarianism*. Individualism refers to the principle that people should get ahead on their own, pull themselves up by their own bootstraps. A person should get what he or she earns and earn what he or she gets. Assistance from government (or anyone else) is not required nor particularly desirable. Individualism has long been considered the distinguishing American value. Tocqueville saw it as the feature that distinguished America from its European counterparts, and recent research confirms its continued importance.[3] Egalitarianism, in contrast, asserts the fundamental equal value of all people. As such, every person deserves an equal opportunity to succeed in life. If particular individuals or groups are disadvantaged, the government may have a role in leveling the playing field. Research on American values has shown that substantial majorities of Americans do not choose one or the other position but subscribe to the tenets of both of these abstract values.[4]

Most Americans concede that blacks have suffered a disadvantaged history. But what, if anything, should government do about this? Here the consensus ends, and the prescriptions of individualism and egalitarianism differ. Individualism, of course, dictates that blacks, now free from the legal bonds of discrimination, must get ahead on their own without governmental assistance. In contrast, egalitarianism prescribes that all people must be given a fair chance, and therefore, to the extent that blacks have been denied an equal chance, something must be done to rectify past wrongs.

At times in our history, a particular value is highlighted at the expense of another; at other times, the situation is reversed. Media coverage of race emphasizes individualism on some occasions and egalitarianism on others, and these differences in the nature of media content over time are among the primary causes for the variation in racial policy preferences. When the cues presented by the media at any given moment are disproportionately composed of references to egalitarianism, people will be more likely to express preferences for liberal racial policies. When, at other times, the media send messages disproportionately emphasizing the value of individualism, the public will be more likely to express conservative policy preferences. My argument here is that media coverage has emphasized certain core American "values" frames, with the degree of emphasis varying over time.

This hypothesized tension between individualism and egalitarianism in media content is consistent with historical recollection. In the 1950s and early 1960s, stories in the media portrayed blacks being systematically denied their right to vote in most Southern states, black children being prevented by the police from attending school with white children, citizens being denied service at "whites only" lunch counters, and nonviolent black marchers being attacked for protesting these situations. The media's message demonstrated the inconsistency between American beliefs in egalitarianism and the way society treated blacks. I hypothesize that this type of framing led the public to express more liberal preferences on racial policy.

After passage of the Civil Rights Act of 1964, the Voting Rights Act of 1965, and the Civil Rights Act of 1968 (Fair Housing), most of the fundamental legal rights that were the stated goals of the civil rights movement had been won. But the struggle to improve the lives of black Americans continued. The focus of the civil rights movement shifted to thornier issues, namely the means to achieve desegregation (like busing) and affirmative action programs to achieve workplace and educational equality. And this shift generated a shift in the nature of media coverage of civil rights issues from egalitarian to individualistic themes. Although it is not uncommon to see stories about affirmative action that mention "leveling the playing field" or "making up for past discrimination" (i.e., using egalitarian frames), at least as often, such coverage is framed in the guise of the core value of individualism. Terms such as "reverse discrimination," "race-based quotas," and the like were used and became symbols for the view that blacks were getting something that was not earned or deserved but given. Liberal racial policies, then, sometimes transgress upon the traditional American belief in individualism. Media messages that highlight the inconsistency between the American value of individualism and liberal racial policies lead to more conservative policy preferences.[5]

Measuring Key Concepts

The hypotheses outlined above are longitudinal claims, testable through time-series analysis. In previous work, I have created a decades-long annualized series of aggregate racial policy preferences (Kellstedt 2000, 2003, chap. 3). It traces the year-to-year shifts in the public's appetite for liberal racial policies. There have been peaks of liberalism, such as the late 1960s and early 1990s, and valleys of conservatism, such as the late 1970s and early 1980s. Moreover, this movement is synchronous across issues, encompassing preferences over a wide variety of racial policies. We will use that measure for the current analyses.

A critical task remains—that of measuring (again, over time) the degree to which the media frame coverage of race in terms of individualistic or egalitarian values. Unlike public opinion and economic data, there are no available time series of media-framing data. And unlike the marginals from opinion surveys or economic data, newspaper or television prose is not readily amenable to quantification. Hence, content analysis of text becomes necessary.[6]

Of course, this approach requires the existence of electronic text as input for the program. This is a tall order, given that the period of interest runs roughly from 1950 to the early 1990s. I have chosen *Newsweek* as my primary source of media data.[7] A total of 2,087 articles from 1975 onward was obtained from Nexis.[8] Stories from 1950 to 1974 were optically scanned from library archives; in that period, there were 1,953 stories about race.

Taking the raw stories and creating a dictionary that will detect individualist or egalitarian emphasis is difficult. These stories almost never overtly trumpet the notion that "liberal racial policies can violate America's belief in individualism" or that "America's egalitarian values demand a level playing field for all races." Allusions to values are subtle, and overt references are the exception. The detection of egalitarian value cues in the content analysis involves locating several types of ideas: statements about blacks having rights equal to those that whites have or about equal rights in general; phrases focusing on fairness or equality (or the lack thereof) in various parts of the political process (e.g., voting rights); sentences referring to "equal protection of the laws" or to its counterpart, Jim Crow laws; reports of blacks seeking equal access to facilities such as buses, schools, and the like; stories referring to open housing; sentences describing bigotry directed toward blacks or hate crimes committed against blacks; statements focusing on racial discrimination in employment and laws that attempt to prevent it; and finally, stories that describe segregation. When making references such as these, the national media were framing their coverage of race in egalitarian language, portraying American society as one in which blacks are (or have been) treated as less-than-full citizens, as unequals.

Through a similar process, individualistic value cues are detected, focusing on the following themes: coverage that describes any type of government policy that discriminates against whites in its effort to help blacks; sentences that depict "reverse" discrimination; stories that portray blacks as lazy and undeserving of assistance or equality; and phrases that describe individuals (black or white) as "earning" or "deserving" the benefits or goods that they receive. These stories focus on the value of people getting ahead on their own effort and on whether people are deserving of assistance. The key issue here is merit: are people, both blacks and whites, getting what they deserve? Deservingness—of economic success, of government assistance—is determined by effort. Those who live the Protestant work ethic are exalted as virtuous, whereas those who depend (especially on the government) lack character.

Of the 2,087 *Newsweek* stories that were downloaded from Nexis, 1,606 contained at least one mention of either individualistic or egalitarian values. And from the 1,953 articles from the pre-1975 period, 1,437 mentioned individualistic or egalitarian values. Figure 7.1 displays the resulting time series of egalitarian value mentions, measured annually from 1950 to 1993. Although *Newsweek*'s coverage of race contained many egalitarian references in the 1950s, their prevalence exploded in the early 1960s and continued until the end of that decade. Egalitarian references became less common in the early 1970s, but they never disappeared altogether. Interestingly, *Newsweek* made an increasing number of egalitarian references in its coverage of race as the 1980s progressed.[9]

However, it is likely that there are other forces that also influence aggregate racial policy preferences over time; omitting these forces from the analysis would pose a serious threat to inference. Six possibly confounding (and possibly complementary) forces come to mind. First, consistent with Durr's research on policy mood, it is possible that aggregate optimism or pessimism about the future of the economy drives racial policy preferences. Durr postulates that periods of economic optimism are associated with an aggregate willingness to

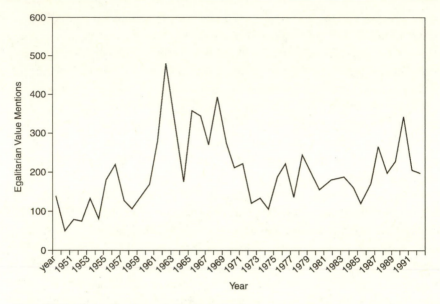

Figure 7.1. Egalitarian value frames in the media over time

pay for liberal (and often expensive) government policies. In contrast, when the outlook for the economic future is less rosy, the public becomes less enthusiastic about bankrolling a liberal government agenda. Like Durr, I will measure economic optimism and pessimism with the University of Michigan's time series on consumer expectations for business conditions in the next five years (see Durr 1993).[10]

A second alternative explanation for shifts in racial policy preferences is that public willingness to accept government intervention *on matters of race* is a function of public willingness to accept government intervention *more generally.* In this sense, policy preferences on race are viewed as a subset of a broader set of policy concerns. Changes in racial policy preferences, then, reflect changes in policy concerns generally. Stimson conceives of aggregate policy preferences in precisely this way and creates a series he calls Policy Mood. It represents the global predisposition of the mass public to endorse or reject government activism (Stimson 1999).[11]

A third alternative for explaining movements in racial policy preferences is the generational-replacement hypothesis, which arises from the work of Schuman and colleagues (Schuman et al. 1997, chap. 4). Simply put, the authors hypothesize that earlier generations of Americans were socialized into a society where bigotry and racism were expected, both from individuals and from governments. Generations socialized since the civil rights movement grew up in a country that, while still imperfect, began to include blacks as full partners in the American dream. I will measure these effects by counting the proportion of the adult population that turned eighteen during or after 1963, which was the beginning of a brief period when civil rights dominated the American agenda.[12] For years before 1963, the series consists of zeros.

Fourth, it is reasonable to speculate that other types of media frames might influence racial policy preferences. In particular, the emphasis on states' rights might be important, particularly in the 1950s and 1960s, when it (rather than individualism) was the central value conflict with egalitarianism. In this earlier period, one of the primary arguments against federal-government intrusion on behalf of blacks was that this was an area properly left to the states. Measuring the number of states' rights frames with the *Newsweek* database is straightforward.

Fifth, it is possible that racial policy preferences do not respond to a *particular type* of coverage about blacks, but to coverage of *any sort* about blacks. Perhaps it is not stories that highlight the importance of values like individualism or egalitarianism in the context of race that influence public opinion, but rather the sheer volume of stories on race that influences public opinion on the matter. Increases in the amount of coverage, I hypothesize, will generate more sympathy for blacks, thus edging support for liberal policies upward. The measure used here is simply the number of stories about race per year in *Newsweek* magazine.

Finally, it is possible that racial policy preferences are somehow influenced by shifts in actual racial policy—in a policy-feedback type of relationship. Perhaps as racial policy becomes more liberal, the public finds itself less enchanted with such policies; conversely, as racial policy becomes more conservative, the public increasingly sees the need for it. This is consistent with the thermostatic model of representation outlined by Wlezien (1995) and Durr (1993). I have developed a measure of the federal government's commitment, over time, to enforcing antidiscrimination policy and will use it here (Kellstedt 2003, chap. 4).

Results

With measures of all key constructs in hand, I proceed to evaluating the merits of my theory.[13] In table 7.1, the dependent variable is racial policy preferences, and a lagged endogenous variable is included in the standard Koyck scheme to control for the effects of previous lags of exogenous variables that are excluded from the model. In column a of table 7.1, I show the results of a bivariate dynamic regression, with racial policy preferences as the dependent variable and egalitarian media framing as exogenous. Egalitarian media fram-

7.1   The causal dynamics of racial policy preferences

	(a)	(b)	(c)
Dynamics	0.91***	0.91***	0.52***
	(0.06)	(0.07)	(0.10)
Egalitarian cues	0.01**		0.02***
	(0.00)		(0.01)
Individualistic cues		0.01	−0.02
		(0.01)	(0.01)
States' rights cues			−0.27*
			(0.15)
Number of stories on race			−0.03
			(0.02)
Policy feedback			−9.36*
			(4.92)
Economic expectations			−0.01
			(0.02)
Policy mood			0.20**
			(0.10)
Generational replacement			0.19***
			(0.05)
Constant	9.13	10.56	38.58***
	(6.66)	(7.39)	(8.75)
R^2	0.86	0.85	0.92

Note: $N = 43$ for all equations; standard errors are in parentheses.
  *$p < .10$ (two-tailed),   **$p < .05$ (two-tailed),   ***$p < .01$ (two-tailed)

ing is a significant cause of racial policy preferences. (The seemingly small unstandardized coefficient of 0.01 is a function of the large variance in the media variable. The true effects are somewhat larger. The standardized beta is 0.12, and these contemporaneous effects are magnified by strong dynamics, as these effects linger for several subsequent time periods.)

The results in column b of table 7.1 are again bivariate, but in this case the exogenous variable is individualistic media framing. Here, though, I find no significant relationship between individualistic media framing and racial policy preferences. The coefficient of 0.01 is statistically insignificant ($t = 0.80$) and in the opposite direction than was hypothesized. The fully specified model is presented in column c of table 7.1, with all three types of media framing, policy feedback, economic expectations, policy mood, the total volume of coverage on race, and generational replacement as exogenous variables. As in column a, egalitarian media framing is a significant predictor of racial policy preferences, and in this model, the effects are enhanced (standardized ß = 0.25). To translate these effects into more interpretable numbers, consider that this indicates that between 1982 and 1991, during which the GSS item on busing showed an increase in liberalism of 15 points, about 4 of those 15 points are due to an increase in egalitarian framing over the same time period.

In this multivariate context, individualistic media framing narrowly misses statistical significance ($p = 0.14$), and the coefficient this time runs in the expected (negative) direction. The coefficient of -0.02, when standardized, indicates that the effects of individualistic cues are less than half as large as the effects of egalitarian cues (standardized $ß = -0.12$). Column c also shows the effects of other types of media coverage. In particular, there is a small (and marginally significant) effect of coverage of states' rights on racial policy preferences. An increased focus on states' rights lessens support for liberal racial policies. The effect, however, is smaller even than that for individualistic coverage (standardized $ß = -0.10$). The total coverage of race in *Newsweek* is unrelated to racial policy preferences; although the relationship is in the expected direction, it does not approach statistical significance.

If anything, these findings understate the effects of media coverage on national opinion on race. It is well-known that measurement error in independent variables tends to attenuate statistical relationships, and the *Newsweek* measures used here, though the best measures available to date, surely are imperfect indicators of overall media coverage.

Other findings emerge from column c of the table. The policy-feedback variable emerges as a (marginally) significant predictor of racial policy preferences. In the multivariate context, liberal shifts in policy produce disenchantment with those policies, and opinion becomes more conservative. In addition, both policy mood and generational replacement are significant predictors of racial policy preferences. That is, as the public becomes more accepting of government action generally, it also becomes more accepting of government intervention to bring about racial equality. This represents testimony to the power of a "national mood," where preferences across a wide range of issues (including race) move in tandem through time. In addition, the effects of generational replacement are evident and strong (standardized $ß = 0.61$); as older generations that were socialized into an American society that expected discrimination against blacks become a smaller portion of the population, society becomes more liberal on racial policy. Column c of table 7.1 shows that economic expectations are not a significant predictor of racial policy preferences, and what effect can be found runs in the wrong direction.

Clearly, many forces shape racial policy preferences and have contributed to their evolution over time. Unsurprisingly, generational replacement has been important in the liberalization of American opinion on race. But the media have also played a role, as has opinion on government more generally and racial policy itself. Although it might be tempting to reduce the main finding of this chapter to a statement such as, "The media influence racial policy preferences," a more complete rendition of the findings here would recognize that the nature of media influence is extremely subtle. The national media do not make blanket statements about race like "Blacks are good" or "Blacks are bad" that the public blindly accepts as truth and incorporates into its policy preferences. This is in contrast to other areas of coverage such as the economy, where media messages are far more direct ("The economy continues to show signs of sluggishness"). In those cases, it is easy to portray media influence in a simple way: the media say something; the people believe it. Race, as usual, presents a more complex scenario. The types of messages that influence public opinion are messages that resonate with values to which most Americans subscribe. The question, then, becomes one of emphasis, whether the media tend to emphasize one core value or another. The choices are subtle, but their impact is substantial, at least with respect to public opinion.

Perhaps the most significant contribution of this analysis is the effort to explain both liberal as well as conservative shifts in racial policy preferences. Instead of limiting the focus to why Americans have become more liberal (or more conservative) on race, I have provided a framework that can explain movements in both directions.

But this research leaves many questions unanswered. Perhaps most pressing among these is to investigate the extent to which real-world events—a concept that is not put to much use in these analyses—affect racial policy preferences. Particularly in a volume such as this, which emphasizes the effects of media framing, the distinction between attributing causal priority to events that happen in the real world as opposed to the media's portrayal of those events is a critical one. Many studies have used media coverage as a proxy for the effects of events (e.g., Krosnick and Kinder 1990). The intent is never to ignore events as likely causes of opinion shifts but rather to understand the effects of them more fully by modeling the more proximate cause of opinion change, namely media coverage. But there are particularly vexing methodological problems associated with using media measures as proxies for real-world events.[14] These issues don't affect the analyses reported here, because my intent is not to use the media to measure real-world events but to use the media to measure media framing. Still, disentangling the effects of objective reality from press reporting of that reality is a key avenue for future research.

In the present case, it is natural to suspect that policy preferences are shaped by such events—riots, marches, and the like. Of course, it is possible that the true effects of these events have been captured by the media variables in this analysis. But only further research can answer this question definitively. This challenge is also a large one for another reason: the coding of raw events will not prove to be easy.[15] To take a simple example, how would an analyst code the events of the urban riots of the 1960s? Presumably, these obstacles are not insurmountable, but they require more attention than is possible here. Perhaps further work will alter some of the conclusions reached in this analysis.

Framing and Media Manipulation

We have discovered that the over-time drifts back and forth in public opinion on race are, to some extent, a function of the way that the national press has framed its coverage of racial issues. Of course, I have just used the rather bland, social science–jargon phrase "a function of" to describe the causal relationship between the press and the public. To use more normative, judgment-laden phrases, can we say that, on the basis of these findings, the press "controls" or "manipulates" public opinion? Do the effects uncovered here represent something that is potentially harmful for American democracy?

Public opinion is embedded within the system of causes and effects that is American politics. It would be naive and nearly impossible to conceive of a situation where public opinion was some kind of unmoved first mover, the Big Bang of politics, which has no causes, only consequences. Public opinion, like everything else that is interesting to social scientists, must have its causes.

There are several factors that mitigate any fears about media manipulation of opinion. The first is that public opinion, as embodied here, is not some whimsical fast mover. The typical year-to-year shifts in racial policy preferences are a point or two. What is remarkable about opinion is that these shifts continue for years on end. But the notion that the press might somehow "manipulate" opinion with a flood of stories about a particular topic, producing an immediate and permanent shift in opinion, seems to violate the nature of aggregate opinion presented here. Opinion simply doesn't move that fast.

The second reason that media manipulation might not be a problem is that public opinion, as we saw in table 7.1, is a function of plenty of things in addition to the media. In this sense, the media are one in a set of forces that influence public preferences about racial policy. It is true that they are an important piece of that causal puzzle; but they are not the only piece.

Finally, if "media manipulation" were an accurate characterization, then it would seem necessary that media coverage itself would be that unmoved first mover in American politics. But it isn't. Press coverage is not invented out of nowhere by scheming editors and reporters. It too is a function of other forces in the real-world system of American politics. The media, themselves, can be "manipulated" by skillful and entrepreneurial politicians and public figures.

Consider the genius of Martin Luther King Jr. and other leaders of the civil rights movement and how they used the tool of nonviolent public protest to attract public attention. When the press covered peaceful marches, lunch-counter sit-ins, and the like, and the violent local government reaction to the demonstrators, was there another available frame besides egalitarianism to the press? Nonviolence, in this sense, can be viewed as an ingenious method designed to lose the battle but win the war by winning the hearts and minds of the public. If the press has to cover the "who, what, where, when, and why" of an event, then a nonviolent protest often requires the press to report, for example, that many protesters were arrested (the "what") for trying to ride in the front seats of buses (the "why")—which, to many consumers of the news, is going to highlight that blacks and whites were treated unequally (in nonegalitarian fashion). When the authorities used violence in response to nonviolence, the situation only became clearer.

Of course, there are other political circumstances where the effects of media framing might not seem so innocuous from a normative perspective. In my view, the complete picture on the effects of framing, from both an empirical and a normative perspective, has yet to be painted. This volume will surely provide important elements of that picture, which I suspect will not be either completely black or white when finished, but instead filled with a variety of shades of gray.

Conclusion
Controversies and New Directions in Framing Research

Karen Callaghan

Framing has become both a coherent research paradigm and an important conceptual tool for examining the processes by which political issues are defined and debated in American politics. Yet certain areas of research remain unexplored, while others are controversial. For instance, due to changing conceptualizations of the news, researchers must broaden the type of communications studied. This means studying nontraditional forms of political communication and conducting comparative analyses. Another area worth investigating is how we model framing effects. Also important are the implications of framing for individual citizens and democratic processes. That is, what are the political costs and benefits of "frame-based" information processing? How do framing effects fit with the long-standing debate in political science about the notion of citizen (in)competence? These are some of the issues I address in this chapter.

Broadening the Types of Communications Studied

When a newscaster for ABC links the terrorist attacks on the World Trade Center and the Pentagon on September 11 to lax gun laws and reminds Americans how easy it is for terrorists to "exploit the slack enforcement and oversight of gun shows," it is obvious that journalists and editors frame political issues for the mass public. However, framing decisions do not occur only on the evening news. The great majority of political information is transmitted outside of traditional forums for political communication. As Mutz (2002, 231) aptly notes, "what citizens call news now covers dozens of channels and many programs that are not ostensibly news programs." Fundamental changes in the communications landscape broadened by the Internet and other digital delivery systems have produced new information venues like on-line chat rooms, expanded cable and twenty-four-hour satellite news shows, and digital-age Web sites. News is often delivered by customized e-mail and news flashes from Internet service providers. These news sources create a broader flow of information and require a more complex framing model, one that may disrupt the ability of the media and other elites to establish dominant frames (see Entman and Herbst 2001; Baum 2002). Thus, research that aims to examine the dynamics of framing in American politics cannot limit itself to the traditional news media—network news, daily newspapers, and magazines; it must include many other news sources that are not explicitly political.

Furthermore, since the new media environments are highly graphic and visual, the analysis must stress a broader definition of frames that includes nonverbal or "visual" framing. Research shows that visual images instruct people about political issues and strongly reinforce verbal slants and themes (see Gilliam 1998; Gilliam and Iyengar 2000; Gilens 1996; Entman 1993). Because visual representations are typically processed in a nonconscious manner, the cognitive influence of visual frames in subsequent opinion formation is potentially more powerful than an issue framed in textual form.[1] And what about the visual images from interactive graphics, animation, and still or full-motion videos on the Web? How do they influence framing effects?

There are other venues to explore as well. Today popular culture offers a unique ability to frame political issues for the mass public. For instance, NBC's prime-time television show *The West Wing* offers engaging discussions of contemporary issue debates, apparently with a distinct ideological bias—that is, liberal policy slants and anticonservative plotlines.[2] To what extent are the policy frames highlighted in this fictional White House more memorable and influential than those presented by the news media, especially for politically uninvolved citizens? It is essential to understand how popular programs like this one convey issue information to the mass public.

What about the impact of citizens' changing consumption patterns? While the major news networks often cater to large audiences and adjust their frames to dominant public opinion, less traditional news sources might use frames that appeal to a smaller target audience. Existing technologies and the Internet enable individuals to choose which news to receive, based on their political tastes and their own view of world affairs. For example, an eager NRA supporter might choose to receive her news from a specialized NRA-affiliated Web site that screens out competing frames, transmitting only the news that fits the frames she already supports. Thus, the same technological innovations that have revolutionized communication and generally help citizens acquire diverse political knowledge also have their dark side: they allow us to present biased themes, without verification or debate. Consequently, we must move away from a model that sees citizens as merely passive recipients of frames created by interest groups and politicians and reinforced by the media. The new model must account for the fact that individuals actively seek out certain frames and avoid others.[3]

Framing research can also benefit greatly from the inclusion of comparative studies, which have several conceptual and methodological advantages. In particular, comparative research can help to clarify and modify existing theories as "an essential antidote to naive universalism" (Gurevitch and Blumler 1990, 82). Studying how policy issues are framed in other countries can provide important insights into the origins of frames and the dynamic influence dominant media frames have on public opinion. Although journalists tend to have homogeneous political attitudes (Donsbach 1983, 23), there are significant cross-national differences in journalistic norms. For example, German journalists are more committed to political advocacy roles, while British and U.S. journalists desire to be more neutral or politically independent (Patterson 1998). Does role perception influence the type of frames journalists adopt? Do differences in roles also influence citizens' receptiveness to frames? If citizens view journalists as an unbiased source of information with little or no intent to persuade, they may be more susceptible to framing effects. Objective sources have been shown to be far more persuasive than sources that appear to have a vested interest in the issue (e.g., Petty and Cacioppo 1981).

What about factors in the broader political environment, such as interactions among the media, government officials, and interest groups? The U.S. news media maintain close relationships with the U.S. government and are often accused of merely representing the government's point of view because of the perceived expertise inherent in governmental sources (see Tuchman 1972; Gitlin 2003). Do the media in other countries play a more adversarial role, relying less on official sources? If so, how does that affect the media's framing decisions?

Refining Framing Theory

Future research should refine framing theory in other ways. First, although we know that different frames produce different effects—a shift in the direction of attitudes—we do not fully understand how frames work. Clearly, we have moved far beyond Klapper's famous verdict of "minimal media effects." But can we say more explicitly what these effects are? Is more involved than saliency and beliefs importance? What else might intervene? What about emotions? Do emotions mediate the impact of frames? Psychologists have long recognized that activating distinct emotions like fear and anxiety can have important behavioral consequences.[4] While emotional effects have been explored in studies of citizen response to political issues and candidates (e.g., Abelson et al. 1982; Roseman, Abelson, and Ewing 1986; Marcus 2000), they are conspicuously absent in the framing literature (for some exceptions, see Just, Crigler, and Neuman 1998; Gross and Brewer 2002; and Callaghan and Schnell, this volume). Yet the emotional underpinnings of framing effects are important to understand, as emotive-laden frames may have the greatest potential to influence politics. The interesting causal pathways to explore are those that link frames directly to citizens' emotional responses and ultimately policy support, as well as political behavior. If political mobilization follows straightforwardly from emotionally rooted frames, as Schnell and I suggest, then frames have broader implications than is often assumed.

Second, can we be more explicit about the conditions that moderate and perhaps eliminate framing effects? Whereas mediating variables reflect transformation processes internal to the individual, such as the activation of emotions, the concept of moderation implies that the relationship between a stimulus and an individual response changes as a function of some other variable (Baron and Kenny 1986, 1175). Obviously, some of these moderating effects are found within individuals, while others are external to the individual, derived from the larger political environment.

Scholars have identified several individual-level moderators that determine whether or not an individual will be influenced by frames (e.g., political expertise, racial prejudice, political group identifications, and political cynicism). However, more research is needed. I am not suggesting that we simply add more variables to this list. Rather, we need to build on earlier results that explore fundamental moderating effects and resolve existing conflicts. For example, theory and conflicting evidence have confused the relationship between political sophistication and framing effects.[5] Some studies show that sophistication weakens framing effects (e.g., Kinder and Sanders 1990; Zaller 1992; Page and Shapiro 1992). Others find that sophistication can actually strengthen framing effects or that no empirical relationship exists (e.g., Druckman and Nelson 2003; Iyengar 1991; Nelson, Clawson, and Oxley 1997; Popkin 1991; Baek 2002; Callaghan and Schnell 2000). Sophistication effects must be deciphered explicitly if we are to properly evaluate the robustness of framing effects in the real world.

Also important, we know very little about how political elites respond to frames. By elites I mean the ensemble of individuals *directly* involved in the policy-making process (e.g., elected or appointed government officials, interest-group leaders), not simply those with greater political knowledge. It seems plausible that within a particular policy arena elites are less likely to be persuaded by frames, given their strong attitudes and higher levels of knowledge about issues. While this can also be true for citizens, government officials and other political elites have motivations beyond their immediate policy preferences—which often expose them to richer information environments consisting of multiple frames. In the absence of a highly persuasive frame, do elites pay more attention to those frames they find familiar or consistent with prior beliefs? How much are elites themselves influenced by persistently used media frames? What happens when those frames are advocated by the media that attract a disproportionate elite readership such as those "inside the beltway" (e.g., the *New York Times,* the *Washington Post*) or championed by other elites who serve as positive referents? Furthermore, to what extent do elites focus on media frames that reflect public opinion? In other words, do elites use dominant media frames as a shortcut to discern public opinion? Given that the most consequential policy decisions in a democracy are made by political elites (not directly by citizens in policy referenda), it is crucial to explore whether media frames constrain the options and opinions of policy leaders. In short, we need to study "elite" samples.

Citizen susceptibility to elite framing attempts is also influenced by factors external to the individual, and framing researchers are just beginning to document these effects. Among the mechanisms considered recently are elite competition and rhetoric, exogenous events, source cues, and interpersonal communication.[6] In addition, certain "issue-specific" characteristics may affect the degree to which frames influence public attitudes and opinions, and these should be added to the literature as well. For example, issues might be classified in terms of their complexity, level of affect, and political longevity. Framing effects should be most pronounced and politically consequential for issues that are complex. Substantively complex issues include tax policy, nuclear power, telecommunication policy, international trade, and most foreign policy issues. These issues are highly technical and require "knowledge of important factual assumptions to be appreciated or understood" (Carmines and Stimson 1980, 80).[7]

Issues with multiple policy dimensions that simultaneously influence groups in several venues are also complex.[8] In this case, complexity emerges from the infusion of new information or an exogenous shock that expands the focus of an issue from a single policy dimension to multiple policy considerations. For example, traditionally the nuclear-power issue was framed as a means to provide efficient and inexpensive energy. However, nuclear catastrophes such as Three Mile Island and Chernobyl expanded the focus to environmental and economic concerns. Because complex issues like nuclear energy are less likely to be linked effectively to preestablished beliefs and attitudes, the framing effects of these issues would be quite large.[9] By the same token, issues long on the public agenda (e.g., social welfare) have a crystallized meaning for the public, one that is unlikely to be changed by alternative frames. These frames have preestablished or "built-in" reference points (historical continuity, values, and symbols) that heuristically allow citizens to comprehend the issue substance and respond to the frame.

Finally, emotive issues (e.g., abortion, school prayer, same-sex marriage, and gun control) may be quite resistant to framing effects because these issues are strongly anchored to underlying values. For example, abortion is often associated with religious beliefs or is perceived as an issue that speaks explicitly to a woman's right to choose. In either case, opinions on this issue are highly emotional and anchored in deep-seated value structures. Furthermore, the abortion issue is characterized by remarkably stable opinions over time (e.g., Converse and Markus 1979; Page and Shapiro 1992). Not surprisingly, attitudes toward abortion are resistant to framing attempts (see Schnell 1993).[10] However, attitudes toward other issues appear to be more susceptible to framing effects. For instance, racial attitudes, while generally stable (Kinder and Sanders 1990), can often be effectively paired with other issue domains and contexts to reframe opinion.

To sum up, framing effects may be stronger for nonemotive issues, new issues, and complex issues—to the extent that complex issues reach the public agenda and receive requisite media attention (see note 9). Such broad groupings of issues, not just groupings by issue domain, can be useful in identifying when framing effects are likely to occur.[11] This approach can help offset the "file-drawer" problem. Because academic journals refrain from publishing experiments with "null" findings, researchers put these studies aside and focus on positive results. Undue attention to positive findings may result in an overestimation of framing effects and their prevalence in American politics (Druckman forthcoming; Scargle 2000).

Framing research can also benefit from studies that combine multiple moderating variables to explore interaction effects. For example, political sophistication may have different levels of effect on policy support for issues framed in different ways. Furthermore, sophistication may moderate framing effects for certain types of issues. For instance, political sophistication may have little moderating impact for issues long on the public agenda, regardless of their frames. However, it may have a large impact for issues that have received little media coverage. Only sophisticates would have the ability to follow and understand public policy debates that emerge around unpublicized issues (Converse 1964). It is quite possible that the null findings of framing researchers with regard to political sophistication may be due to the fact that they focused on long-standing and highly salient issues.

For the most part, the chapters in this volume take an elite, "top-down" approach to framing. Future research should also consider whether the appropriate model is both elite and citizen based. The implicit (sometimes explicit) assumption is that elites develop the frames that are then imposed upon citizens. Although none of the chapters suggests that framing is the exclusive domain of political elites or that citizens are passive recipients of elite influence, they focus on how elites impact citizens, not on how citizens impact elites or each other. Yet citizens do impact elite frames and do influence each other in important ways, and these and other processes should be incorporated in future studies. Although some promising research places citizens in a central role in the framing process,[12] more work needs to be done.

A final area worth exploring concerns the way people process framed information. Frames can be depicted using a "net" metaphor to describe the process of human memory and information processing (McGraw and Pinney 1990). Psychological theory suggests that information in long-term memory is organized associatively in meaningful packets of conceptual knowledge (Collins and Loftus 1975). These bundled concepts are linked together in an associative network (Rumelhart and Norman 1983). Does presenting an issue with a frame blend these two concepts or "nodes" in memory and therefore enhance "online" processing? Or is it best described as a process of "memory-based" cognition? Nelson and Wiley (2001) argue that frames tend to work through "memory-based" processing in that they operate by activating information already at the recipients' disposal (stored in long-term memory). However, studies of how we process information about political candidates (Lodge, Steenbergen, and Brau 1995; Lodge, McGraw, and Stroh 1989; Hastie and Park 1986), policy issues (McGraw and Pinney 1990), and political groups (Callaghan and Schnell 2001b) suggest that people are "on-line" processors. That is, as people are exposed to political information, they immediately link each bit of framed information and its associated affect to an existing policy concept in memory and form an evaluation; they do not compute an evaluative judgment later on from memory traces (memory-based processing).[13] The information-processing model has not been evaluated in an issue-framing context. Thus, further explorations into frames and their mode of processing—whether is it is a process of on-line or memory-based cognition—are in order. We need to understand these processes, not just as a means to inform psychological theory about how frames are processed, but to enhance our understanding of political issue evaluation.

While many of the hypotheses discussed above remain untested or insufficiently tested to allow us to speak with confidence about their conclusions, they provide fruitful avenues for future research and as such can only add to the framing literature. Indeed, framing researchers have many new avenues to explore.

Frames and American Democracy

Framing, as we have seen, is pervasive in American politics. This brings us to an important question: are frames the ideal vehicle for political issue communication? In chapter 4, Kinder and Nelson argue persuasively that public opinion depends in an intelligent way on how an issue is framed: "Frames supply a common vocabulary, one that enables elites and citizens to take part in the same conversation." Thus, frames are the common denominator of mass communication. Other studies suggest that frames help prioritize values (see Nelson, Maruska, and Braman 2002; Kellstedt, this volume). Furthermore, cognition research and rational-choice approaches note that, given their processing limitations, humans seek cognitive reduction; thus, frames serve as a type of "heuristic" that shortens information-processing time (e.g., H. Simon 1985; Calvert 1985; Taylor and Crocker 1981; Tversky and Kahneman 1974, 1982; Downs 1957; Lippmann 1922). This indicates a psychological need for framing. But frames also oversimplify reality. This occurs at both the macro- and the individual level.

At the macrolevel, the issues that come to the forefront of American politics are complex. However, because the media emphasize simplification (Graber 1993), and the mass public pays limited attention to policy issues and politics in general (Converse 1964), journalists rarely try to present multiple, complex issue frames to the public. Complex issues, if they are to reach the mass public at all, must first be framed in simplistic terms. Alternatively, the issue may be fragmented into isolated, simplistic subframes that are easier for the mass media to disseminate and, in turn, for the public to digest. But this alters the nature of the policy debate.

The health care issue illustrates the problem of issue fragmentation. Elite debate about President Bill Clinton's 1993 Health Care Security Act was tremendously complex, involving a myriad of interest groups and other political players, but only a few frames trickled down to the public agenda. One evolved from the "Harry and Louise" commercials that framed the president's health care proposal in a highly negative way, playing to the public's fear about socialized medicine and the rationing of health care services. The "Socialism" frame received extensive news coverage and was constantly discussed by journalists. Thus, while issue framing is the "common denominator" between elites and the general public, simplifying a complex policy issue can hurt democratic debate.

In a similar vein, the 1996 Telecommunications Reform Act covered almost every aspect of media and communications in the United States; it was the first major overhaul of the telecommunications industry since 1934. Yet the issue debate was limited to singular, fragmented frames put forth by a few key players. The media framed the issue as a sharp dichotomous choice rather than as part of the broader debate on deregulation. Either consumers would get more television channels and a sharper picture (the "Public Services" frame), or a few companies would increasingly monopolize a crucial communication medium—that is, "the big fish who swallowed the little fish would be pursued by the hungry whale" (the "Monopolies" frame).[14]

At the individual level, the media's focus on a single, simplistic frame may prevent individuals from conducting more thorough information searches or from meaningfully integrating new issue frames (see Krosnick 1988; Bargh 1984; Devine 1989; Fazio 1986; Higgins and King 1981; Hastie 1983). By condensing a given issue debate into a handful of themes, the media create an atmosphere in which citizens believe they possess full information about the issue. In reality, they may know very little about it but may be less inclined to seek out more information. Furthermore, repeated exposure to a common frame may form permanent links in a person's memory between the issue and the predispositions the frame evokes (Petty and Caccioppo 1981). Thus, the frame becomes a chronically accessible construct that the citizen has internalized.[15]

The problem of internalization may be particularly acute for issues long on the public agenda (e.g., race policy), which are likely to receive consistent media attention and be discussed within existing paradigms. After sufficient exposure to such frames, citizens eventually internalize them, making it harder for new or unfamiliar frames to gain salience and desensitizing people to alternative frames that might question the effectiveness of a particular policy issue or program.[16] A case in point is the issue of nuclear power. According to Gamson and Modigliani (1989, 8), the "Progress" theme, which promoted nuclear power as an "example of society's commitment to technological growth, dominated news coverage for decades and was so taken for a fact that it required no defense." When policy frames skeptical of nuclear power and its potential for radiation accidents finally did emerge (e.g., the "Accountability" frame), they were disregarded.[17]

The media's tendency to pair issue frames with evocative imagery and symbols is also problematic. For example, the "Pro-Life" frame in the abortion debate is often presented with evocative images (e.g., aborted fetuses); the "Pro-Choice" frame uses a similar approach (e.g., wire hangers) (see Terkildsen and Schnell 1997). Thus, cognitive processing of the framed information will likely be dominated by heuristic cues as opposed to more thorough or systematic forms of information processing (Sears 1993; S. Miller and Fredericks 1990; Fiske and Pavelchak 1986; Fazio 1986; D. Hamilton and Trolier 1986). This form of processing can also reinforce citizens' preconceived beliefs.

Kinder and Nelson argue that framing can have positive benefits. I agree but suggest that frames as a heuristic device can also produce cognitive processing biases, a point I think the authors would agree with. In this regard, I want to draw special attention to another point: a pressing need remains to educate the American public—ordinary citizens and opinion leaders alike—on the effects of framing. In a very real sense, frames present a challenge to individuals' independent thought processes. Thus, alerting citizens to the characteristic ways elites try to influence issue opinions, specifically teaching them to recognize subtle attempts to persuade them ideologically or emotionally with frames, seems a worthwhile goal. The benefits of framing in the form of a communication "shortcut" might possibly outweigh the costs in the form of biased information processing.

Framing effects also lay bare another fundamental question about democratic debate: are they evidence of citizen incompetence? Democratic theorists extol the virtues of well-formed, reasoned, and stable opinions. Yet studies show that frames arbitrarily shift individual citizens' policy views. For example, people will favor oil drilling in Alaska when it is presented as a way to limit dependency on foreign oil but will oppose it when drilling is presented as a way to lower oil prices. Furthermore, responses to framed questions in opinion surveys often vary so widely that it is difficult to pinpoint exactly where the public stands on the issues. As Iyengar (1991, 130) has noted, findings like these provide "further confirmation of the inherently circumstantial nature of human judgment." The picture that seems to emerge is one of citizen incompetence; as Hamilton, Madison, and Jay would argue, a capricious citizenry is easily misled by the artful misrepresentations of men.

Is the picture correct? In order to reach a definitive conclusion on citizen competence, we must be clear about the extent to which frames move people to take political action that contradicts their deeply considered opinions. Yet evidence is indistinct. Some studies show that framing effects are intimately related to the content of people's predispositions, while other studies refute this position. As noted previously, in some cases, politically astute individuals are the most likely to be influenced by frames. What they know does not mitigate framing effects but in fact enhances them. Frames, especially those used by the media, have been shown to cut across other normally strong alternative cognitions such as political ideology (Terkildsen and Schnell 1997), self-interest (i.e., the perception that out-group members pose a threat to valued resources; see Bobo 1983), or women's group identity and experience with gender discrimination (see Sears and Huddy 1990; E. Klein 1984). Clearly, more research is needed on the individual-level factors that determine whether media frames will be given priority in cognitive thought processes. It is important to continue this research at least to resolve conflicting conclusions about how we view citizens in a democratic society. Despite the long history of frame analysis, dating back to Berelson's work in the 1940s, scholars are just beginning to understand when and how framing effects occur. Do they occur more or less often than expected? How large is the effect? These are necessary questions to address if we are to understand the democratic consequences of elite framing effects.

In conclusion, the range of frames citizens are exposed to will continue to be limited. Certain political players will continue to dominate the framing process. And of course, frames will continue to be a potent tool for persuasion and attitude change. For example, citizens may have found a strong show of force in Afghanistan and the "war on terrorism" acceptable because military action was justified with two provocative themes: "Infinite Justice" and "Enduring Freedom." Here we see a strong potential for elites to establish the terms of political issue debates through framing and to influence American public opinion. Furthermore, framing effects can alter public perceptions of reality. Larger or smaller in certain circumstances, frames do matter. We hope our readers find this volume useful and that the discussions here will stimulate further research on framing.

Notes

Introduction: Framing Political Issues in American Politics

1. In the 1930s Father Coughlin, a Roman Catholic priest, broadcast a weekly radio program to millions of Americans that was highly political and anti-Semitic. For instance, Coughlin blamed the Jews for engineering U.S. entry into World War II (Athans 1992). From 1928 to 1932 Governor Huey Long of Louisiana ruled in a dictatorial fashion and created a powerful propaganda machine (Oskampf 1977; A. Lee and E. Lee 1939).

2. See, e.g., Klapper 1960; Berelson, Lazarsfeld, and McPhee 1954; Lazarsfeld, Berelson, and Gaudet 1944, 1948.

3. Berelson, Lazarsfeld, and McPhee 1954. See also Hovland, Lumsdaine, and Scheffield 1949; Lazarsfeld, Berelson, and Gaudet 1944.

4. Still, some scholars are less skeptical about the minimal effects paradigm. See, e.g., Schudson 1995; McQuire 1985; and Robinson and Sheehan 1983.

5. More specifically, priming, as some political scientists use the term, refers to the greater influential weight attached to an issue once it receives media coverage. Thus, how voters' prior attitudes toward an issue are more likely to predict candidate evaluations once they have been primed by the media. For example, opinions toward U.S. support for the Nicaraguan contras became twice as important as a determinant of President Reagan's popularity after coverage of the Iran-Contra scandal than prior to coverage (Krosnick and Kinder 1990). Because the media emphasized Iran-Contra, evaluations of Reagan were more likely to be based on this issue than others.

6. For the social-cognitive aspects of framing, see Rhee 1997; Pan and Kosicki 1993; Chong 1993; Krosnick 1988; Goffman 1974; and others. For a review of this research, see Druckman 2001a.

7. See, e.g., Tversky and Kahneman 1981, 1987; Kahneman and Tversky 1984; Quattrone and Tversky 1988; Druckman 2001a; Bartels 1998; Schuman and Presser 1981.

8. See Berelson 1948, 1952, and 1971 for a review of these studies.

9. We adopt Robert Entman's (1993, 52) definition of a research paradigm as a "general theory that informs most scholarship on the operation and outcomes of any particular system of thought and action."

10. In his theory of dialectic, Hegel envisaged a worldview in which change takes place through the "struggle of opposites." According to Hegel, one concept (thesis) inevitably generates its opposite (antithesis). This conflict of opposing forces leads to a positive societal outcome: growth and development (see Berthold-Bond 1993). For an explicit discussion of the role of counter-themes in contemporary political life, see Entman 2004; Sniderman and Theriault 1999; Terkildsen, Schnell, and Ling 1998; Riker et al. 1996; Tourangeau and Rasinski 1988.

11. See also Gais, Peterson, and Walker 1984; J. Berry 1989; Schlozman and Tierney 1986. Of course, not all groups are equally powerful. As Schattschneider (1960, 34) asserted, the flaw in the "pluralist heaven" is that "the heavenly chorus sings with a strong upper class accent." More recently, Baumgartner and Leech (1999) have noted that the "pro-business" orientation

of the dominant players in American public policy debates is even greater than most previous scholars have recognized.

12. Political actors compete with one another for press coverage not only at the ideological extremes but also within comparable ideological frameworks, thereby forcing alterations in one another's and their own issue frames. For instance, government officials engage in formal and informal forms of communication with each other that may impact the type of issue frame they convey. Even interest groups that share a core set of common beliefs and frequently interact with each other differ on politically contentious issues and frames. For example, Terkildsen, Schnell, and Ling (1998) found that, due to evolving debates about women and their roles in politics and society, "profeminist" groups advocated different frames about gender equality. These included frames about gender roles, economic or political rights, and feminism. Thus, players can influence one another's issue frames within their respective circles.

13. See, e.g., Cohen 1963; O'Heffernan 1994; Bennett 1990, 2003; Bennett and Manheim 1993; Zaller and Chiu 1996; Herman and Chomsky 1988; Patterson 2002. Also see note 23.

14. In 1994, the Republican House leadership under Speaker Newt Gingrich offered the "Contract with America" as a political platform for all Republican candidates. The main purpose was to challenge the policies of President Bill Clinton.

15. Republicans were even able to counterframe "Entitlement" within the context of the debate about social welfare policy by calling their welfare reform package "The Personal Responsibility Act," which would "overhaul the American welfare system [in order] to reduce government dependency, attack illegitimacy, require welfare recipients to enter work programs, and cap total welfare spending" (Gillespie and Schellhas 1994). In doing so, Republicans successfully linked their Democratic opponents to negative welfare frames like "Corruption" and "Economic Drain."

16. For instance, *Roe v. Wade* (1973) upset the balance of power in favor of pro-choice advocates. In turn, abortion foes turned to public strategies aimed at expanding the conflict and involving the mass public. After the Supreme Court upheld a rather restrictive Missouri anti-choice law (*Webster v. Reproductive Health Services,* 1989), the balance of power shifted dramatically in favor of pro-life advocates. As a result, attempts by pro-choice forces to redress the balance by "going public" increased significantly (see Goggin 1993).

17. Within this context, political candidates are particularly advantaged because elections include fewer major actors than the policy arena and the discussion of issues during elections is seldom dependent on understanding the intricacies of public policy. Instead candidates are able to frame issues broadly via symbols and buzzwords (e.g., Willlie Horton in the 1988 presidential election) that are often intended to influence voter choices.

18. In a complex information environment like that surrounding a ballot initiative, voters also turn to credible information sources such as consumer advocate Ralph Nader for frames that might help them understand an issue (Lupia 1994). Thus, these policy leaders can effectively frame issues and affect outcomes in their respective areas of expertise simply because the media and the public see them as credible sources.

19. From this perspective, the media resemble a minefield that strategic policy actors must negotiate carefully in order to put forth their issue frames successfully. However, the relationship is also symbiotic, based on a reciprocal "give-and-take." That is, policy actors and candidates need the media to put forth an issue frame successfully; the media need policy actors to serve as spokespersons to fill news holes, meet deadlines, provide drama, and add issue balance (Hess 1984; Gans 1979; Grossman and Kumar 1981).

20. Our conclusions about framing and social policy issues are drawn from the analysis of several issues, rather than a single (and perhaps peculiar) issue, thus enhancing theoretical conclusion validity. By the same token, these issues constitute major, relatively long-standing policy debates. Thus, we cannot speculate about less salient issues. Furthermore, public and elite preferences on these issues, except abortion, coincided at the time the studies were conducted. Obviously, in situations where journalists face equally supported opposing interests

on an issue (i.e., public and elite preferences follow a bimodal distribution), the media may be less likely to pursue one side of the debate over the other. Final conclusions about media framing for other less viable or evolving issue debates (e.g., domestic terrorism, tort reform, bioethics) must remain contingent on further analyses.

21. However, the extent to which the media shape or lead public policy debates is likely fluid and varies from one issue domain to another, as well as within the context of societal and historical constraints. In foreign affairs, for example, the model appears to be different. Compounding factors include government officials who dominate the framing process, a mass public that is generally inattentive to foreign affairs, and a policy and opinion elite that typically support the "official" government view (see Bennett 1990; Zaller and Chiu 1996). Furthermore, as Entman (2004) notes, changes in international politics and media behavior after the Cold War require the reevaluation of models of media behavior specified prior to 1991.

22. See also Elizabeth Becker, "Prickly Roots of 'Homeland Security,'" *New York Times,* Aug. 31, 2002.

23. Given that values are multidimensional constructs (e.g., McClosky and Zaller 1984), frames that emphasize a particular value dimension can also be influential. For example, Tabrizi (2002) has shown that framing issues like health care reform, social welfare policy, or affirmative action in terms of "equality of opportunity" rather than "equality of results"—the two primary value dimensions of "equality"—not only elicits more support for the policy but alters the mix of considerations that underlie individuals' evaluations of these issues. Thus, individuals interpret the politics of these issues in terms of the meaning of equality that is emphasized in the frame.

24. In *The American Ethos,* McClosky and Zaller (1984, 13) define an opinion leader as "a person who exerts a disproportionate influence on public affairs" by virtue of greater political activity and knowledge. This includes public officials, party leaders, interest group activists and all others who "help to formulate opinion and decide policies."

Chapter 1: News from Somewhere

1. *Donor Briefing,* "Foundations Join Forces on 'Public Life and the Press,'" July 14, 1993.

2. *Presstime,* "Newsbeat: Power to the People," Dec. 1993.

3. A related initiative (known as "civic" rather than "public" journalism), supported by the Pew Charitable Trusts and led by former news executive Ed Fouhy, was also active and influential during this period.

4. My analysis of the debate over public journalism is based on reading over 450 articles, columns, and editorials published in the popular press, trade journals, and professional journals from December 1993 through December 1997. These do not include examples of public journalism articles (though I have read many such examples, and the articles, etc., I do include in this analysis often refer to specific examples of public journalism) but rather are limited to pieces that explain, defend, analyze, or attack the theories and practices of public journalism. Articles, etc., used in this chapter were collected through a combination of an independent LexisNexis search that I conducted and use of material made available to me by the Project on Public Life and the Press. While this approach undoubtedly missed some relevant material, I am confident that it is at minimum a representative sample of the published debate and close to the universe of published material on this debate. This chapter depends on a qualitative analysis—the summaries and quotes used are illustrative and representative of the larger body of material. My reading of these articles was supplemented by reading a number of public journalism articles; my participation in an on-line discussion group with public journalists; and having attended two meetings of public journalists at the American Press Institute in Reston, Virginia.

5. For examples of the body of research, see Iyengar and Kinder 1987; Kahneman and Tversky 1987; Iyengar 1991; Sniderman, Brody, and Tetlock 1991; and Cappella and Jamieson 1997. I do not attempt to catalog or discuss all the frames used by journalists (or others) in this chapter, focusing only on those that emerge as part of the debate over public journalism. Nor do I address in any detail the larger issues regarding the relationship of framing to other important concepts such as agenda-setting and priming. For a more extensive review of these issues and their impact on public and elite opinion, see Graber 1984; Iyengar and Kinder 1987; Iyengar 1991; Neuman, Just, and Crigler 1992; Page and Shapiro 1992; Ansolabahere, Behr, and Iyengar 1993; Cappella and Jamieson 1997; Pfetsch 1998; and Jacobs and Shapiro 2000.

6. For media campaign consultants, see Sabato 1981; Salmore and Salmore 2000; and chap. 4, this volume. For the increasing use of media strategies, see Ryan 1991; Bennett and Mannheim 2001; Jamieson 2001; and chaps. 2 and 3, this volume. For the blending of strategies by policy makers, see Linsky 1986, Hertsgaard 1988, and Cook 1998. For the growth of an institutionalized bureaucracy in government, see Maltese 1994 and Cook 1998. For the use of media strategies by foreign governments, see MacArthur 1992 and Mannheim 1994.

7. See Gans 1980, Manoff and Schudson 1986, Patterson 1993, and Cappella and Jamieson 1997.

8. Rather than resulting from the interaction of normative goals and practical constraints, it is possible that journalistic frames emerge largely out of practical concerns and that normative arguments are little more than post hoc justifications for day-to-day behavior. While determining the direction of causality in the relationship among norms, constraints, and behaviors is important, the answer to this question does not fundamentally affect the central argument of this chapter.

9. This frame also undoubtedly originates from the behavior of politicians and other elites (Jacobs and Shapiro 2000; Brewer and Sigelman 2002), though the causal link between the behavior of elites and of those who cover them is complex, interactive, and ultimately mutually reinforcing.

10. Davis Merritt, quoted in Bud Norman, "Eagle Editor to Take a Look at Journalism," *Wichita Eagle,* Dec. 26, 1993.

11. Tom Rosenstiel, "Reporters Putting Their Own Spin on News Events," *Los Angeles Times,* Nov. 25, 1993.

12. Rosenstiel, "Reporters Putting Their Own Spin on News Events."

13. Mickey Davis, feature writer for the *Dayton Daily News,* quoted in Morgan 1994, 31 (emphasis added).

14. Antonio Olivio, "Ex-Editor Advocates Civic Journalism," *Morning Call* (Allentown), Apr. 25, 1997.

15. Walter Goodman, "Inverse Relationship of Heat and Light," *New York Times,* Feb. 14, 1996.

16. Michael Kelly, "Mea Culpa," *New Yorker,* Nov. 4, 1996, 46.

17. Max Jennings, "Politicians Deserve More Respect," *Dayton Daily News,* June 9, 1996.

18. Davis Merritt, "Unconventional Wisdom," *New York Times,* Aug. 23, 1996.

19. Eric Black, *Minneapolis Star Tribune,* Jan. 28, 1996 (emphasis added).

20. Tom Fiedler, quoted in Howard Kurtz, "Florida Newspapers Team Up in Attempt at Voter-Friendly Coverage," *Washington Post,* June 5, 1994.

21. David Hawpe, "When Listening Becomes Limiting," *Courier-Journal,* Oct. 6, 1996.

22. Philip Gailey, "The Media Failed to Follow the Money," *St. Petersburg Times,* Apr. 27, 1997.

23. William E. Jackson Jr., "The Press Cops Out," *New York Times,* Oct. 7, 1996.

24. Hawpe, "When Listening Becomes Limiting."

25. Jackson, "The Press Cops Out."

26. Kelly, "Mea Culpa," 46.

27. Laurence Jarvik, "The Pitfalls of Public Journalism," *Washington Post,* Nov. 16, 1996.

28. Kelly, "Mea Culpa," 48–49.

29. Davis Merritt, quoted in M. L. Stein, "A Catalyst for Public Awareness?" *Editor and Publisher,* Oct. 15, 1994, 41.

30. Dan Schilling, "We Need to Listen to Each Other," *Phoenix Gazette,* Aug. 25, 1995.

31. Jon Shure, "Activist Journalism Can Help Diffuse Community Tensions," *New Jersey Lawyer,* Apr. 10, 1995, 3.

32. Joel Kramer, "Ask Yourself if Your Work Makes the Community a Better Place," *Minneapolis Star Tribune,* Oct. 16, 1994.

33. Cole Campbell, quoted in Tony Case, "Public Journalism Denounced," *Editor and Publisher,* Nov. 12, 1994, 15.

34. Jay Rosen, quoted in Case, "Public Journalism Denounced," 15.

35. William Glaberson, "The New Press Criticism: News as the Enemy of Hope," *New York Times,* Oct. 9, 1994 (emphasis added).

36. Schilling, "We Need to Listen to Each Other."

37. Paul Greenberg, "Public Journalism Harms Newspaper's Credibility," *Post Courier,* Nov. 18, 1996 (syndicated column).

38. Maureen Dowd, "Liberties; Bottomless and Topless," *New York Times,* June 9, 1996.

39. Jack Fuller, quoted in Max Frankel, "Get Thee to a Mental Gym," *New York Times,* May 19, 1996.

40. Jay Rosen, quoted in Morgan 1994, 31.

41. Cole Campbell, "We Must Discuss Issues to Ensure a Stronger and Less Divisive Society," *Virginia Pilot,* Apr. 9, 1995.

42. Davis Merritt, summarized in Stein, "A Catalyst for Public Awareness?" 41.

43. Dennis Royalty, "Reader Input Vital in Arts Funding Discussion," *Indianapolis Star,* July 9, 1995.

44. Frank Denton, "City's Schools Need Guidance from the People," *Wisconsin State Journal,* Aug. 27, 1995.

45. K. E. Grubbs, "Journalism Spinning Out of Control," *Orange County Register,* Aug. 20, 1996.

46. Bill Hawkins, "Endorsements Policy Helps Protect Distinction between News, Opinion," *Herald-Sun* (Durham), Nov. 3, 1996.

47. Greenberg, "Public Journalism Harms Newspaper's Credibility."

48. Frankel, "Get Thee to a Mental Gym."

49. Sheri Dill, "Writing News to Engage Citizens," *Wichita Eagle,* July 10, 1994.

50. Max Jennings, "Saving Our Children, a Community Effort," *Dayton Daily News,* Apr. 17, 1994 (emphasis added).

51. Jonathan Krim, quoted in Pete Carey, "Your Voices Count: 'Public Journalism' Project Asks Community to Address Special-Interest Influence," *San Jose Mercury News,* June 18, 1995.

52. Ed Miller, associate of the Poytner Institute for Media Studies, quoted in Carl Redman, "Critic Urges Media to Help Public Set Agenda, Issues for Elections," *Capitol City Press* (Baton Rouge), Nov. 15, 1994.

53. Davis Merritt and Jay Rosen, "Letters: In Defense of Public Journalism," *Editor and Publisher,* Dec. 31, 1994, 7.

54. David Matthews, president of the Kettering Foundation, quoted in Morgan 1994, 31.

55. Max Jennings, editor of the *Dayton Daily News,* quoted in Morgan 1994, 32.

56. Lou Ureneck, "Reader Roundtables: A Setting for Public Conversation," *Maine Sunday Telegram,* Nov. 28, 1993.

57. Dorothy Gilliam, "No More Surprises, Please," *Washington Post,* Sept. 17, 1994.

58. Max Frankel, former executive editor of the *New York Times,* summarized in Hoyt 1995, 29.

59. William Glaberson, "A New Press Role: Solving Problems," *New York Times,* Oct. 3, 1994.

60. Len Downie, executive editor of the *Washington Post,* quoted in Shephard 1994, 30.

61. Bill Heath, "How Public Should We Be," *Marshfield News-Herald,* Oct. 22, 1994.

62. Glaberson, "A New Press Role."

63. Jane Eisner, "Should Journalists Abandon Their Detachment to Solve Problems?" *Philadelphia Inquirer,* Oct. 16, 1994.

64. Robert Holland, "For News Biz, a Shift to a New Paradigm?" *Richmond Times Dispatch,* Dec. 28, 1994.

65. Richard Harwood, "The Power Ignored by the Press," *Washington Post,* Feb. 24, 1997.

66. William Glaberson, "Fairness, Bias and Judgement: Grappling with the Knotty Issue of Objectivity in Journalism," *New York Times,* Dec. 12, 1994.

67. Bill Evans, former editor of the *Dallas Morning News,* as quoted in Kim Horner, "Radio Station Launches Arlington Study," *Dallas Morning News,* Feb. 9, 1997. Not surprisingly, proponents of public journalism also drew on the consensus frame, regularly acknowledging the importance of objectivity and traditional investigative reporting, the need to guard against becoming advocates for particular groups and causes, and the failure of some experiments. Mainstream journalists assume, wrote Davis Merritt, that public journalists "must be talking about abandoning such indisputably important and useful roles as watchdog, outsider from government, independent observer, uninvolved-and-thus credible source of information. Some recent experiments under the name of public journalism, unfortunately and avoidably, have left themselves open to criticism because they have abandoned one or more of these ideals. But that need not be the case. Public journalism and those traditional ideals are neither in conflict nor mutually exclusive" (quoted in R. Davis 1996, 30).

68. Respectively: Gartner 1997, 69; Iver Peterson, *New York Times,* Feb. 3, 1997; Robert Holland, *Richmond Times Dispatch,* Jan. 22, 1997; Greg Collard, *Charleston Gazette,* Mar. 21, 1997; Laurence Jarvik, *Washington Post,* Nov. 16, 1996; Jonathan Yardley, *Washington Post,* Sept. 30, 1996; Harry Rosenfeld, *Times Union* (Albany), Oct. 1, 1995.

69. Philip Gailey, "Freedom Not Only for the Press, but for All," *St. Petersburg Times,* Jan. 12, 1997.

70. Robert Holland, "Public Journalism Pushes Elitist Agenda," *Richmond Times Dispatch,* Jan. 22, 1997.

71. Harwood, "The Power Ignored by the Press."

72. Stephen Bell, "Media Examination Falls to Shallow Fallows," *Buffalo News,* Feb. 11, 1996.

73. Greenberg, "Public Journalism Harms Newspaper's Credibility."

74. Wesley Pruden, "The Newsroom Blues: Who's Got the Tonic?" *Washington Times,* Apr. 16, 1996.

75. Robert Holland, "From Multicultural Goose to Educationist Gobbledlygook," *Richmond Times Dispatch,* Dec. 4, 1996.

76. Erik Spanberg and Becky Bull, "Newsmakers 1996: Media," *Business Journal–Charlotte,* Dec. 30, 1996.

77. Ross MacKenzie, "Maybe the Lopsided Polls Are Saying Something about Credibility," *Richmond Times Dispatch,* June 15, 1997.

78. G. Woodson Howe, "Change Needed, but Retain Fundamentals," *Omaha World Herald,* Dec. 25, 1994.

79. Hiley Ward, "Book Reviews: Arthur Charity's *Doing Public Journalism,*" *Editor and Publisher Magazine,* Apr. 1996, 23.

80. Tony Snow, "It's Muckrakers versus Buckrakers," *Cincinnati Enquirer,* Sept. 18, 1996.

81. Jerry Finch, "Should Press Take on the Role of Referee on Public Issues," *Richmond Times Dispatch,* Dec. 11, 1994.

82. Shephard 1994, 29–34.

83. Bill Steigerwald, "Top Reporter Tallies Sins of Journalism," *Commercial Appeal* (Memphis), Feb. 18, 1996.

84. Holland, "For News Biz, A Shift to a New Paradigm?"

85. Greenberg, "Public Journalism Harms Newspaper's Credibility."

86. T. Koch 1994, 19.

87. Terry Golway, "The Inkless Wonder and 'Civic' Journalism," *New York Observer,* Feb. 19, 1996. While less common, public journalists also slipped into conflict frames. For example, one article by Davis Merritt was entitled "Missing the Point," while an article by Jay Rosen was entitled "Journalists to Citizens: Drop Dead." Similarly, public journalists were not above simplifying traditional journalistic routines or attacking individual journalists—Maureen Dowd, Howard Kurtz, and Leonard Downie, among others, were all subject to sometimes scathing attacks in various articles.

88. Although I have focused largely on the print media, the central argument of this chapter—that the norms and constraints of journalism combine to produce frames that inevitably lead to "biased" presentations of the world—is or more applicable to the new media environment emerging as a result of cable and satellite television, the Internet, the growth in new genres such as "soft news programs," the more general blurring of news and entertainment, and the like. These developments, coupled with economic changes in the media that have increased the pressure for profitability in the news, have exacerbated the influence of the practical constraints discussed in this chapter, weakened the role of traditional journalists as the primary gatekeepers for politically relevant information, and implicitly challenged the normative underpinnings of the social responsibility theory of the press. As these changes create new frames—for example, what Baum (2002, 94) calls "cheap" frames "emphasizing dramatic and sensational human-interest stories, intended primarily to appeal to an entertainment-seeking audience"—and new framers—for example, talk-show hosts and comedians—it is all the more vital to make explicit the public interest obligations of the media in their myriad forms and their appropriate relationship to citizens in a democracy. For a fuller discussion of these issues, see B. Williams and Delli Carpini (in progress).

Chapter 2: Campaign Frames

The names of the authors appear in alphabetical order and imply that this paper is in every way a collaborative enterprise. The data were supported by a grant from the National Science Foundation (SBR-9308421).

1. In particular, we look at 97 of the 104 races between 1988 and 1992. Four races in 1990 were removed because an incumbent was uncontested: Arkansas, Georgia, Mississippi, and Virginia. We also decided to remove the two races in Louisiana because of the state's unique electoral laws. In Louisiana, all candidates enter one race. If one candidate does not capture a majority of the votes, then a runoff is held. Since Louisiana is the only state with this system, we decided to hold these elections aside. Finally, we did not examine a special election held in North Dakota on December 4, 1992; this was the only special election held on a unique date during the 1988–92 election cycle.

2. In addition to information concerning the content of the candidates' messages, we obtained Federal Election Commission (FEC) data to assess the spending patterns of candidates. Campaign spending is an excellent measure of the candidate's level of campaign activity (Westlye 1991; Jacobson 1980). Thus, spending provides us with some sense of how often candidates were able to dispense their messages to the voters.

3. Three coders were sent to the archive in Oklahoma to content analyze the political advertisements. Each coder was trained at Arizona State University on a sample of ads. All coders worked separately at the archive. Twenty-five percent of the ads (i.e., 148 ads) were

coded by all three to assess reliability. Intercoder reliability among the three coders across the ads averaged 80 percent. The codesheet used by coders when examining each ad can be located in Kahn and Kenney 1999 (appendix B).

4. The economy was the most popular issue discussed during this time period (Kahn and Kenney 1999), and these four economic frames (i.e., jobs, budget, taxes, general discussion) are the most common ones.

5. We were tutored about the folkways of smaller newspapers "picking up" stories by Mike Connolly, the editor of the largest-circulating newspaper in St. Paul. We are grateful for his assistance.

6. The coding of the articles was a labor-intensive enterprise. Coders were trained to copy articles from microfilm, while another set of coders was taught how to content analyze the articles. In all, twenty coders were trained and participated in the media project. Intercoder reliability was assessed repeatedly during the coding process. On average, there was 92 percent agreement across the content codes. The codesheet used by coders when examining each article can be located in Kahn and Kenney 1999 (appendix D).

7. The goal of this chapter is to examine whether candidates are able to influence how the media frames the coverage of campaigns. We assume that the media reacts to the candidates' strategies, and not vice versa. The "reactive" nature of press coverage has been documented elsewhere (Fenno 1996; Cook 1989; Clarke and Evans 1983; Goldenberg and Traugott 1984).

Nevertheless, it is possible, of course, that candidates monitor press coverage of their campaign and adjust their messages accordingly. We were sensitive to this problem and conducted several tests to determine the likelihood that candidates react to press coverage when producing their advertisements. Although we do not know the exact date when commercials were aired, we do know that most senatorial candidates save their advertising blitz for the month of October. The spending patterns of candidates (FEC reports indicate that 60 percent of spending occurs after October 1), an examination of case studies of senatorial campaigns (Westlye 1991), data from field research (Fenno 1996), and a recent analysis of Senate election advertising (Krasno and Seltz 2000) all indicate that candidates put forth a heavy advertising blitz late in the campaign.

Assuming, then, that most commercials were presented in October, we measured press coverage from the month of September. We are certain of the timing of the media's stories because they were dated when analyzed. With time order established, we examined whether media coverage in September influenced the content of candidates' ads. Specifically, we conducted four tests using Ordinary Least Squares (OLS) regression. First, we examined whether press coverage of issues in September influenced the likelihood that candidates took issue positions in their ads. Second, we looked to see whether press coverage of issues before October 1 influenced when candidates claimed credit for policy outcomes in their ads. Third, we documented whether the amount of economic coverage in September influenced whether candidates mentioned the economy in their ads. In this analysis, we also controlled for the predominance of economic issues by examining media coverage about the economy as early as February of the election year. Finally, we examined whether criticisms reported in September influenced the likelihood that candidates produced negative ads. In each of these equations, we controlled for other forces known to influence candidate strategies (e.g., competition, spending, perceptions of opponents' strategies). In every test, candidates developed messages in their ads independent of press reports in September. The coefficients measuring the influence of press coverage never reached statistical significance.

8. We log spending to base 10 since outliers are created because of heavy spending in some small states (e.g., Wyoming, Maine, Vermont, Idaho), even controlling for the size of the state. This is typical in Senate elections, and logging is the solution used by previous scholars (e.g., Abramowitz 1988; Green and Krasno 1990). This allows us to keep all of the cases for analysis, instead of discarding the outliers (Tufte 1975).

9. We examine news coverage between October 1 and election day. We restrict our analysis to this time period in order to ensure that poll standings and candidate spending occur before newspaper coverage. It is necessary to use measures of spending and poll standings that occur before campaign coverage, given the potential reciprocal relationship among coverage, money, and poll standings (Kahn and Kenney 1999). In the case of poll standings, we look at polls published between September 16 and September 30. With regard to candidate spending, we look at expenditures between late August and late September. All analyses rely on OLS regression.

10. We examine two categories of candidates: (1) incumbents and open winners and (2) challengers and open losers. In this chapter we will refer to the incumbent/open-winner category as the incumbent category and the challenger/open-loser category as the challenger category. In each analysis, we initially included an open-race variable to see whether coverage patterns differed for candidates running in open races versus candidates running in incumbent races. The open variable reaches statistical significance in only one of the analyses in this chapter. In this one case, the open variable is included in the model presented in table 2.2. We also included several additional control variables in preliminary analyses (i.e., challenger quality, seniority of senator, whether candidates were involved in scandals, and the economic climate of the state as assessed by the *Congressional Quarterly* in February of the election year). None of these variables reached statistical significance, and they are not included in the models presented in this chapter, with the exception of economic climate in table 2.3.

11. The dependent variable is the total number of paragraphs discussing issues for the candidate. We look at paragraphs as opposed to articles because articles vary greatly in length, especially across different newspapers. In contrast, paragraphs are virtually the same length, regardless of the newspaper. In this analysis, we are looking at whether the "positional" frame creates more press attention for issues in general. "Positional" frame is a binary measure where 1 = candidate takes a position on an issue, 0 = otherwise.

12. The dependent variable is the total number of paragraphs discussing the candidates' issue positions.

13. All remaining variables in the model are set to their means (see Lewis-Beck 1980).

14. The dependent variable is the number of paragraphs published in the newspaper giving the candidate credit for favorable policy outcomes.

15. Credit claiming is a binary measure where 1 = candidates claim credit for favorable policy outcomes in their ads, 0 = otherwise.

16. Virtually none of the candidates emphasized inflation during the 1988–92 period, with good reason: inflation rates were very low, as the nation suffered through a recession.

17. The dependent variable is the number of paragraphs printed about the economy. The candidates' frames were coded as binary variables measuring whether a candidate used a specific frame or not. For example, 1 = candidates who framed their economic messages in terms of the general economy, 0 = otherwise.

18. The number of economic frames is an interval variable ranging from 0 (none of the economic frames was used) to 4 (four economic frames were employed).

19. The candidates' negative frames were coded as binary variables measuring whether a candidate used a specific negative frame or not.

20. The endorsement variable is coded 1 if the incumbent/open winner is endorsed, 0 if neither candidate is endorsed, −1 if the challenger/open loser is endorsed.

21. The number of negative frames is an interval variable ranging from 0 (none of the negative frames was used) to 3 (three negative frames were employed).

22. All remaining variables in the model are set to their means (see Lewis-Beck 1980).

Chapter 3: Obstacles and Opportunities

I would like to thank Senator Elizabeth Dole and her staff for providing a sample of her campaign speeches. I would also like to thank Stuart Hill for his comments on an earlier draft of this essay and David F. Damore, Alisa Gaunder, and the editors for their more recent suggestions and assistance.

1. While interest groups, presidential appointees, civil servants, congressional staff members, researchers, and academics are important players in issue framing, these individuals are neither as visible nor as powerful in this realm as are elected officials. They are less likely to receive recognition for the construction of frames and, in some cases, have faced insufficient incentives to create frames of reference. The Supreme Court is also key in the construction of issue frames, but the dynamics of the Court, its role, and its relationships with other actors greatly distinguish it from elected officials, thus making those factors that constrain the Court significantly different from those constraining elected officials.

2. See Fenno 1977 and Mayhew 1974. Additional incentives for advancing an issue frame may include drawing public attention to one's area of legislative expertise, building a reputation, and advancing positions to create a platform for a campaign for higher office.

3. The decision-making process is not the focus of this chapter. My primary focus is on the factors that constrain the frames available to elected officials at a given time and on a particular issue. Because I emphasize constraints, my analysis does not capture the full context in which elected officials act. Future research must also examine how elected officials' interactions with one another and other elites constrain their framing options (Damore 2002; A. Simon 2002; but also Kahn and Kenney 1999). In the electoral context, not only candidates but also parties and interest groups take part in the shaping of public opinion through issue framing in political advertisements.

4. The literature on the agenda-setting process can be characterized as attending to two primary arenas of action. The first predominantly studies the interplay of political elites in structuring choice situations and manipulating the ordering of items on the decision agenda for goal maximization, while the second examines the interactions among political elites, linkage institutions, and the public in determining the most important issues of the day for focused government attention and public deliberation. I make this distinction in order to avoid confusion, since the term *agenda-setting,* implied by the notion of an issue gaining national attention, also refers to the study of the political decision agenda strictly confined to legislative bodies (Arrow 1951; Black 1958; Krehbiel 1986; Riker 1980; Shepsle 1979; Shepsle and Weingast 1987).

5. Several other significant constraints are mentioned in this volume—and in the literature at large—including election results or the partisan composition of the national government, the credibility and organizational resources of the elected official, and the independent power of the mass media in the framing process. The mass media are a crucial component of the agenda-setting process, but the limited scope of this chapter cannot address the intricacies of the press—more detailed examinations of the role of the mass media can be found elsewhere and in other chapters of this volume (Bartels 1993; Iyengar and Kinder 1987; Iyengar 1991; Jamieson and Waldman 2003; Mucciaroni 1994; R. Smith 1993; Zaller 1996; chaps. 1, 2, and 6, this volume).

6. This research has moved in several directions, including examinations of the intersections of partisan politics and political theory (Portis, Gunderson, and Shively 2000); descriptive accounts of the parties' ideologies (Banning 1978; Foner 1970; Gerring 1998; Kohl 1989; Meyers 1957; Silbey 1991; Watson 1990); and analyses of the role of ideology in structuring legislative and judicial decision making (Poole and Rosenthal 1997; Segal and Spaeth 2002).

7. See Converse 1964; Lupia 1994; Popkin 1991; Sniderman, Brody, and Tetlock 1991; and Zaller 1992.

8. My interest in these two related factors stems from Orren and Skowronek's (1994) in-

sight into the intersections of institution and history as keys to understanding American political development.

9. The mass media have the power to influence the agenda of the attentive public (Iyengar and Kinder 1987), and political elites have the strength to set the agenda (Kingdon 1984).

10. At the same time, when the public mood is at odds with the ideological leanings of an elected official and his or her goals, insider strategies may prove more effective. Note that the public mood is only one of the four constraints I outline here. A conservative public mood does not present the opportunity for all issues to be framed in a conservative manner. The issue-specific constraints, soon to be addressed, will in part determine the success of a conservative appeal on a particular issue, depending upon the values that underpin that issue. More generally, in contrast to a strongly ideological mood, a moderate public mood offers more flexibility to all elected officials and increases the possibility of more genuine and deliberative public debate. It is not that ideological debate is not genuine, but rather that the opportunity for political gain is too great to encourage compromise when the public mood shifts to one or another ideological extreme. The increased leverage of either conservatives or liberals will in turn reduce the shared issue space available for compromise and bipartisan efforts.

11. Quoted in Jann S. Wenner, "Bill Clinton: The *Rolling Stone* Interview," *Rolling Stone* 858–59 (2001): 91.

12. "Contract with America" (1994), retrieved June 17, 2003, available at http://www.house.gov/house/Contract/CONTRACT.html.

13. David Van Biema, "The Storm over Orphanages," *Time*, Dec. 12, 1994, 58.

14. Quoted in Bill Sammon, "Cheney Will Be Running Mate," *Washington Times,* Nov. 8, 2002.

15. Quoted in Dana Milbank and Mike Allen, "White House Claims Election Is Broad Mandate," *Washington Post,* Nov. 7, 2002.

16. In addition to the ideological composition of an elected official's constituency, other factors such as religion, race, and the primary industries within the district may also constrain the official on particular issues. While these types of constituencies are important, my emphasis is broader, so I do not examine in depth the power of these constituencies in constraining the frames available to elected officials.

17. MacKuen 1984; Kinder and Sanders 1990. Political sophisticates are also more likely to bias information that they have previously evaluated and endorsed (McGraw and Hubbard 1996; Sniderman, Brody, and Tetlock 1991; Zaller 1992). The term *political sophisticates* has been a rather slippery one. For some it is a measure of general knowledge, while for others the term indicates an ability to understand politics in ideological terms. For my purposes, I follow Chong (1996) and Jacoby (2000), who find that ideological strength and coherence dampen framing effects.

18. Research on interest-group contributions to elected officials shows that interest groups are most likely to contribute to incumbents and friends and that these contributions have little effect on roll-call votes (Grenzke 1989). However, few researchers have explored the relationships between interest-group contributions and the framing of political issues. Scholars argue that interest groups contribute to incumbents in order to thwart the efforts of the opposition or level the playing field (Austen-Smith and Wright 1994), that contributions lead to lobbying access but lobbying has an independent effect on elected officials' behavior (Wright 1990), and that lobbying efforts may produce positive actions by elected officials when directed at appropriate officials (Hall and Wayman 1990). More recent work argues that we must examine interest groups' goals along with their tactics and the targets of those actions in order to more fully understand interest-group behavior (Hojnacki and Kimball 1999). Interest-group actions may both constrain elected officials from adhering to specific positions and encourage officials to advance particular positions, but the evidence is not yet conclusive.

19. Charles Lane, "On Second Thought . . . ," *Washington Post,* Apr. 11, 2003.

20. In a string of recent Supreme Court rulings, the Court has limited the scope of the

Americans with Disabilities Act by framing it in terms of federalism and state immunity rather than civil rights. For information regarding the Supreme Court's rulings on the ADA and evidence of the civil rights frame in regards to disability issues, see the Disability Rights Education and Defense Fund at http://www.dredf.org.

21. For evidence of the link between district ties and interest groups' direct lobbying, see Austen-Smith and Wright 1994, Hojnacki and Kimball 1998, and Rothenberg 1989.

22. R. Douglas Arnold (1990) focuses on this particular calculus and offers a persuasive account of the factors members of Congress weigh when determining the likelihood of arousing the attention of the attentive public.

23. Following the logic on issue positions, it is more likely that the official will avoid public support of either frame exclusively until forced into a committed position by constituency demands, electoral opposition, or an imminent legislative decision of consequence (Page 1978).

24. The broader array of categorized information from which politically sophisticated individuals may draw in decision-making processes allows for the construction of alternative frames. Thus, elected officials have a broader array of information they can attend to when considering political issues than is available to most individuals in the mass public, and elected officials (and other political elites) are less likely to be constrained by the values embedded in an issue frame than are members of the mass public (Klyza 1994). Given that the values associated with issue frames endure particularly long with the attentive public, fewer frames are available to elected officials who attempt to redefine an issue (A. Simon 2002). They are more likely to succeed by moving on the margins or working within the previously established value context of the issue than if they attempt to focus attention on other values previously not considered in regards to that particular issue. Thus, the official must expend more resources and time to alter a previous consensus formed when the issue was salient to the attentive public.

25. For an excellent example of how frames became institutionalized in different areas of public land policy, see Klyza 1994.

26. Madison, "Federalist Paper Number Forty-Nine," in A. Hamilton and Jay 1987, 313.

27. Clearly, not all institutionalized issues will be equal in the extent to which they lend themselves to reframings by the opposition. The power of those interests that have invested in a particular institutionalized issue frame must be considered. Corporate interests will be much more formidable than will consumer interests, and the scale of the policy will also determine to an extent the strength of institutionalization. For example, rethinking nuclear power is inherently different from rethinking grazing-land policy.

28. Because political conflict is most often exhibited as a contest in which there are winners and losers (a frame frequently used by the media, as shown in chap. 1, this volume), and the partisan and ideological dimensions guiding conflict are the most enduring, the power of partisanship and ideology frequently overwhelms other considerations.

29. For examples of these frames and a history of the issue, see the policy information for Congress at the American Association for the Advancement of Science Web site at http://www.aaas.org/spp/cstc/briefs/stemcells/index.shtml.

30. The notion of partisan realignment on a broad, national scale has become suspect in recent years, yet researchers have provided evidence that specific issues (though they are rare) can have a realigning effect on partisanship (Carmines and Stimson 1989; Stimson 2002) and that realignments may occur regionally rather than nationally (Nardulli 1995). Despite the decline of partisanship in the electorate, the two major parties are still powerful vehicles for defining conflict for elected officials (Aldrich 1995; Crotty and Jacobson 1980; Gibson et al. 1983).

31. On these issues, movement is most likely when there is a strong leaning in the direction of the public mood that is accurately identifiable to elected officials. When the public mood approaches the extremes, elected officials are more likely to be emboldened by their

perception of a strong ideological climate and are therefore more likely to take action on issues that adhere to this type of conflict. Without such strong encouragement, little incentive exists for elected officials to attempt to bring to the fore such rigidly cast issues.

32. The literature on this frame and the policy implications that stem from it are too voluminous to cite for this general example.

33. The organization's aims can be found at http://www.drugpolicy.org/about/. The quotation was taken from http://www.drugpolicy.org/drugwar/. Other interesting examples are Dean Schabner, "Higher Immorality? For Some Religious Groups Drug Laws Do More Harm than Drugs Themselves," June 20, 2002, available at http://abcnews.go.com/sections/us/DailyNews/christians_drugs020620.html; and the views of the Cato Institute, which can be found at http://www.cato.org/current/drug-war/.

34. With these major frames other important factors are also highlighted, such as race and federalism. Race plays a role in many of these frames, but it has been most pronounced in social justice frames, which have been used by a variety of actors and organizations to attack the differential sentences for crack and cocaine possession—differences created by a law-and-order approach to drug policy. The federal dimension of drug policy has come to the fore with the passage of medical-marijuana initiatives in various states and localities that clearly conflict with national drug laws and enforcement policies. For a recent example, see "Judge Says Jurors Can't Retry Convicted Marijuana Grower," *San Francisco Chronicle*, May 17, 2003, available at http://sfgate.com/cgi-bin/article.cgi?f=/c/a/2003/05/17/BA29569.DTL.

35. It must also be noted that the framing of issues is not the only means of interpretation people use to understand political issues. Gamson (1992) argues persuasively that to make sense of political issues individuals use daily experience and conventional wisdom in addition to the framing of issues in the mass media. Frames of reference may also fall outside the realm of acceptable public opinion for reasons outside of ideology, such as highlighting an evaluative dimension that does not resonate with widely accepted cultural values (Hilgartner and Bosk 1988). Analogous to the distinction made between a rigid information environment (where framing options are severely constrained) and a more fluid one (where more framing opportunities exist) is the distinction between the partisan environments of elected officials and the mass public. As stated earlier, partisanship and ideology act as the primary dimensions shaping political conflict for elected officials. However, in an electorate in which partisan affiliation is declining, partisan appeals may be less persuasive and the environment open to a variety of frames that would resonate less clearly in a strongly partisan electorate. As in the example of public mood, which allows an ideologically moderate citizenry to respond to a greater variety of frames, when the electorate is not strongly anchored to party ties, officials have a greater diversity of frames available to them if they can perceive these opportunities. Thus, elected officials are constrained by the manner in which conflict is mapped onto the enduring dimensions of ideology and partisanship.

36. Jeffrey M. Jones, "Bush Approval Rating Stabilizes at 63%," *Gallup Poll News Service*, June 20, 2003, available at http://www.gallup.com/content/login.aspx?ci=8671.

37. "Congress Vows Unity, Reprisals for Attacks," Sept. 11, 2001, available at http://web.archive.org/web/20010912112319/www.cnn.com/2001/US/09/11/congress.terrorism/.

38. Sarah Binder and Bill Frenzel, "Policy Dialogue: The Business of Congress after September 11: A Look Back and at What's Ahead for 2002," Policy Dialogue 1, the Brookings Institution, Jan. 2002, available at http://www.brook.edu/dybdocroot/comm/policybriefs/pd01.pdf.

39. This information is available at http://thomas.loc.gov.

40. Anthony Romero, "ACLU Joins with Broad New Coalition in Defense of Freedom: 'America Must Not Cede Democracy to Terrorism,'" press release, Sept. 20, 2001, available at http://archive.aclu.org/news/2001/n092001a.html.

A similar concern was expressed by Morton Halperin, a senior fellow of the Council on Foreign Relations: "Civil libertarians recognize along with everyone else that the government may well need additional powers to deal with international terrorists determined to kill Americans at home and abroad. But they also realize that a careful and deliberative process must be followed when the government moves aggressively to expand its powers at the expense of individual freedoms. What is troubling in this case is that in the drafting and passage of this bill, no such process was followed. The administration refused to identify what emergency authorities it might need to prevent additional attacks while a careful examination was conducted of what exactly went wrong and how, or even if, existing powers proved inadequate. It refused to limit the new powers to investigations of terrorists who threaten Americans, and it refused to meet with outside experts to discuss how to narrow the provisions so that civil liberties are not violated. The administration simply dusted off every proposal it had on the shelf, many of which had been defeated previously. It wrapped the old proposals into a new bill and sent the bill up to Congress without new interagency review, demanding that it be passed immediately. When the House Judiciary Committee unanimously reported a bill with some safeguards, the administration successfully pressured the House leadership to abandon the bill and adopt most of the far worse Senate measures. The final text was drafted in a secret and closed informal conference. No conference report or committee reports exist to support the bill's passage. This is a dangerous way to legislate the delicate balance between national security and civil liberties." See Morton Halperin, "Protecting Civil Liberties at a Time of Crisis," Oct. 25, 2001, available at http://www.cdt.org/security/011025halperin.shtml.

41. Richard S. Dunham and Amy Borrus, "Got a Bill to Push? Wrap It in the Flag," *Business Week* 3752 (2001): 46. To this list we might also add gun control; see chap. 5, this volume.

42. I have treated these two goals separately, and they are analytically distinct. The congressional leadership certainly aims to coordinate the legislative and electoral agendas using strategies for partisan gain. But that goal is often frustrated by candidate-centered campaigns.

Throughout this essay, I assume that elected officials consider the partisan advantages of publicly framing and reframing issues. Below, I assert that candidates "used" and "referenced" the September 11 attacks and the war on terror for partisan gain. Such language may sound callous or unreasonably Machiavellian, which is not my intention. The terrorist attacks of September 11 have become a part of our political life; candidates would be remiss if they did not speak of the tragic events of that day, of how these events have altered our political landscape, and of how they interpret those events and their implications for Americans' most cherished political beliefs. In other words, we should expect political candidates to interpret the terrorist attacks and their implications in ideological terms.

43. It may be that in the electoral setting issue framing also has the power to mobilize supporters, but few researchers have addressed this question.

44. Understanding the role of the media and effectively constructing campaign messages in order to attain media attention is another means by which candidates can reach voters; see chap. 5, this volume.

45. Pew Research Center, "House Voting Intentions Knotted, National Trend Not Apparent," Nov. 3, 2002, 1.

46. Lydia Saad, "Have Americans Changed? Effects of Sept. 11 Have Largely Faded," Sept. 11, 2002, available at http://www.gallup.com/content/login.aspx?ci=6790; Lydia Saad, "Americans Troubled by Issues, Upbeat about Leaders This Election Day," Nov. 5, 2002, available at http://www.gallup.com/content/login.aspx?ci=7159; Lydia Saad, "National Issues May Play Bigger-than-Usual Role in Congressional Elections," Oct. 31, 2002, available at http://www.gallup.com/content/login.aspx?ci=7114.

47. Jones, "Bush Approval Rating Stabilizes at 63%."

48. David W. Moore, "Focus on Iraq Could Help Republicans in November Elections," Sept. 19, 2002, available at http://www.gallup.com/content/login.aspx?ci=6835; Saad, "National Issues May Play Bigger-than-Usual Role"; Pew Research Center, "House Voting Intentions Knotted."

49. Saad, "Have Americans Changed?"; Saad, "Americans Troubled by Issues"; Saad, "National Issues May Play Bigger-than-Usual Role."

50. This example is designed to be illustrative. I chose these candidates based upon the above criteria and the absence of local circumstances that might override these criteria such as the very sad and untimely death of Senator Paul Wellstone in the tight Minnesota race or the late withdrawal of Robert Torricelli and his replacement by Frank Lautenberg in New Jersey. Each of the chosen candidates was a competitor in a "race to watch" as identified by veteran political commentator Charlie Cook. However, the list is not exhaustive; other candidates might also have been included. In addition, I have focused upon Republican candidates, but several Democratic candidates, including Jim Talent's opponent, Senator Jean Carnahan, sought to frame issues in light of the terrorist attacks of 2001.

51. Jim Talent, quoted in Josh Flory, "Candidate Talent Aligns Himself with President, Republicans Hold Lincoln Day," *Columbia Daily Tribune,* Feb. 2, 2002; Elizabeth Dole, "Remarks Announcing Her Candidacy," Campaign Kick-Off Rally, Salisbury, NC, Feb. 23, 2002. All Dole speeches provided courtesy of Senator Elizabeth Dole's senatorial office.

52. Ad context taken from Jo Mannies, "Talent's Ads Stress Experience and His Support for Military," *St. Louis Post-Dispatch,* July 25, 2002; ad copy taken from Meg Kinnard, "Talent Talks Up Reform, Security," NationalJournal.com © National Journal Group Inc., Aug. 14, 2002.

53. Dole, "Remarks Announcing Her Candidacy."

54. Ad copy taken from Meg Kinnard, "Chambliss Ad Features Saddam, Bin Laden," NationalJournal.com © National Journal Group Inc., Oct. 15, 2002; Saxby Chambliss statement taken from Burrelle's Information Services on LexisNexis, CBS News Transcripts, *The Early Show,* Nov. 6, 2002.

55. Jim Talent, from the Talent/Carnahan debate, quoted by Brit Hume and Carl Cameron, Fox News Network, *Special Report with Brit Hume,* Oct. 22, 2002.

56. As Paul Glastris explained: "Even if Democrats believed that worker protections were more important to the country than the flexibility the president requested . . . it was devastatingly shortsighted of them not to give into the president's demands in order to pass the homeland security bill. To have done so would have enabled them to legitimately claim leadership on an important national security matter." See *Washington Monthly,* Dec. 2002, 11.

57. Jim Talent, quoted in Jo Mannies, "Candidates Tell How They Differ; Quick Responses Mark Only Event Featuring All Four Who Are Running," *St. Louis Post-Dispatch,* Oct. 25, 2002; Saxby Chambliss, quoted in Cathy Wilfong, "U.S. Senate Candidates Square Off on Issues," *Chattanooga Times Free Press,* Oct. 27, 2002.

58. Dole, "Remarks Announcing Her Candidacy."

59. Talent, quoted in Flory, "Candidate Talent Aligns Himself with President"; Elizabeth Dole, "God and Country," speech delivered in New Bern, NC, date unavailable.

60. Jim Talent, quoted in Associated Press, "Former GOP Representative Jim Talent Defeats Democratic Senator Jean Carnahan," Nov. 6, 2002, available at http://www.kmov.com/news/Election/cmov_election_021106_talentwins.2172b153.html; Saxby Chambliss quote is from CNN, *CNN Live Event/Special,* Nov. 6, 2002, transcript #110624CN.V54, accessed through LexisNexis, June 17, 2003; Dole, "Remarks Announcing Her Candidacy," and "Remarks for the NAACP North Carolina Convention," Wilmington, NC, Oct. 12, 2002.

61. Milbank and Allen, "White House Claims Election Is Broad Mandate"; Carl Cannon and Richard Cohen, "The Politics of Promise: How Bush and the GOP Pursue Their Agenda Will Be as Important as the Policies Themselves," *National Journal,* Nov. 16, 2002, 3385.

62. "National Overview for December 2002," *Cook Political Report,* Dec. 20, 2002, available at http://www.cookpolitical.com/overview/2002/december02.php.

Chapter 4: Democratic Debate and Real Opinions

1. We express our thanks to Judith Admire and Julie Weatherbee for assistance in preparing the original version of the manuscript; to the Rackham School of Graduate Studies at Michigan, which provided support in the form of a Research Partnership Grant; and to Stanley Feldman, Steven Rosenstone, Douglas Rivers, and John Zaller for their helpful advice. The data reported here were originally collected by the Center for Political Studies of the Institute for Social Research for the National Election Studies (NES). Neither CPS nor NES bears any responsibility for the analysis or interpretation we present here.

1. For more details on sampling design and interview content, see the 1989 NES Pilot Study Codebook, available from the Center for Political Studies at the University of Michigan.

2. For a book-length argument on behalf of experimentation as a mode of political inquiry, see Kinder and Palfrey 1993.

3. We did not expect that the distinction between framed and stripped presentations would have anything to do with persuading citizens to adopt a particular position. After all, we had attempted to identify the frames prevailing in public discourse on both sides of each of the three issues. Such frames had already passed various tests of credibility and persuasiveness. Therefore, if we had identified them properly and evoked them reasonably adeptly in our survey questions, then we should not see differences in the balance of opinion as a function of their (joint) presence; the rival frames are, or should be, roughly equally effective.

Analysis confirms this expectation: the central tendency of opinion on each of the three issues is essentially unaffected by whether the issue was presented in framed or stripped fashion. On the question of abortion, public opinion generally favored the pro-choice position, and this was so regardless of whether or not the issue was presented embedded in the arguments and vocabulary of the opposing camps. Likewise, public opinion on U.S. relations with the Soviet Union was tilted toward those who emphasized cooperation against those who pressed for a tougher stance, but again, quite independently of whether or not the issue was framed. Finally, public opinion was a bit stronger against government assistance to blacks under the framed condition—when the issue was presented in the context of the opposing arguments—than under the stripped presentation, but the difference does not reach statistical significance ($\chi^2 = 5.55$, $p < .24$). As anticipated, framing the issue does not seem to shift the balance of opinion in one direction or another.

4. The story is a bit more complicated than we suggest in the text. For reasons that need not concern us here, the 1989 NES survey was actually divided into four forms of roughly equal numbers. Some of our analyses compare Forms A and B versus C and D; others compare A and C versus B and D (see the 1989 American National Election Pilot Study Codebook for details). As a general matter, respondents assigned to the four forms were indeed comparable: we found no differences in age, gender, education, race, income, turnout in 1988, ideological identification, or political information (all these variables came from the 1988 NES interview). One clear difference did emerge, however. By chance, Form C includes too many Democrats. Combining strong, weak, and leaning identifiers, the Form C group was 56 percent Democratic; in the other three groups, the comparable percentage was 37 percent (A), 46 percent (B), and 48 percent (D). This difference is annoying not only because it is statistically and substantively significant but because partisanship is central to other key political variables. Sure enough, Form C respondents were also more critical of President Ronald Reagan's performance ($p < .01$); sure enough, had the 1988 presidential election been confined to Form C respondents, Dukakis would have won in a landslide (57 percent of Form C respondents reported voting for Dukakis, compared to roughly 45 percent in the other three groups). The importance of this difference for our analysis is mitigated by the fact that none of our comparisons rests on Form C respondents alone: as noted above, all our comparisons combine the four conditions into two. This diminishes the importance of Form C respondents' unusual affinity for Democrats, but we must keep the difference in mind. Where appropriate, our analysis will include partisanship as a control variable.

5. Notice that of the three issue questions, only the abortion item does not include a filter asking respondents whether or not they had thought about the issue.

6. We coded responses to each issue as "extreme" when either endpoint of the opinion scale was chosen and "moderate" when they fell at some point in between. (For the purpose of this analysis, "don't know" responses were excluded.) We performed a contingency table analysis, where extremity was crossed with frame, for each of the three issues. The results reveal no consistent effect of frame on extremity. Stripped opinions are slightly more extreme in the case of abortion (49.0 versus 44.7 percent) and the Soviet Union (27.1 versus 23.1 percent) and somewhat less extreme in the case of government assistance to blacks (39.9 versus 47.1 percent). Of the three comparisons, only the last approaches statistical significance ($\chi^2 = 1.97$, $p < .16$).

7. Technically, the interaction between the expression of an opinion on a comparable issue in the 1988 NES survey and the presence of a frame in the 1989 survey was nonsignificant, for all three issues, by logistic regression. The comparable issues are variables 734 (abortion), 707 (relations with Russia), and 631 and 639 (aid to blacks) from the 1988 NES Codebook.

8. That is, the interaction between political knowledge and framing is insignificant, again by logistic regression, again for all three issues. To measure political knowledge, we relied on variable 7011, an index developed by Zaller (1986), which summarizes answers to a series of questions concerning basic facts about the contemporary American political situation. In the 1988 NES, survey participants were asked to name the candidates for the House of Representatives from their district in the 1988 election; to identify (i.e., name the job or position held by) Ted Kennedy, George Schultz, William Rehnquist, Mikhail Gorbachev, Margaret Thatcher, Yasser Arafat, and Jim Wright; to identify the majority party in the House and Senate; to identify the relative positions of the Republican and Democratic parties on the issues of defense spending, social services spending, health insurance, government guarantees of a job and a good standard of living, and women's roles; and to properly label Ronald Reagan and the Republicans as conservative and the Democrats as liberal. The index also includes an interviewer estimate of the survey participant's political knowledge. Please see the 1989 Pilot Study Codebook for further details.

9. For corroborating results from a similar set of experiments, see Zaller 1990.

10. Zaller does see such evidence, however. Working independently, Zaller (1990) worked out a set of five experiments, similar to our own, also embedded in the 1989 NES, again comparing the quality of opinion elicited by framed versus stripped questions. Zaller's experimental tests focused on public opinion toward federal spending on the B2 bomber, oil drilling in Alaska, aid to the Contras, the death penalty for convicted murderers, and drug testing. In general, the results from these experiments replicate the findings presented here, with the proviso that Zaller finds, as we do not, that framing produces more stable opinions.

11. We include these demographic and political variables in the equations, but we do not report their effects in the table, primarily for aesthetic reasons.

12. For attitudes toward blacks, $t = 2.30$, p (one-tailed) $< .01$.

13. Only the latter difference reaches statistical significance: $t = 1.50$, p (one-tailed) $< .10$.

14. For anti-Communism, $t = 1.00$, p (one-tailed) $< .15$. For Gorbachev. $t = .94$, p (one-tailed) $< .20$.

15. $t = .71$, p (one-tailed) $< .25$.

16. $t = .74$, p (one-tailed) $< .25$.

17. Converse makes a congenial point in his discussion of the diffusion of ideological systems through mass society. "The shaping of belief systems of any range into apparently logical wholes that are credible to large numbers of people," Converse wrote, "is an act of creative synthesis characteristic of only a minuscule proportion of any population. . . . To the extent that multiple idea-elements of a belief system tend to be diffused from such creative sources, they tend to be diffused in 'packages,' which consumers come to see as 'natural' wholes, for they are presented in such terms" (1964, 211).

Chapter 5: Terrorism, Media Frames, and Framing Effects

The following individuals and their organizations provided comments, suggestions, resources, or other assistance for this project: Joanna Weiss, the *Boston Globe;* Ana Marie Arumi, NBC; and Rita Peters, Jillian DiSpiro, and Marie DiNatoli, Department of Political Science, University of Massachusetts, Boston. Research assistance was provided by Jennifer Callaghan. The research reported in this chapter was part of the program on Terrorism, Media and Public Life at the Shorenstein Center for Press, Politics, and Policy, the John F. Kennedy School of Government, Harvard University, and the 2003 meeting of the American Political Science Association, Philadelphia, Pennsylvania. This study was funded by a grant from the American Political Science Association.

1. Vercellotti 2002; Pew Research Center for the People and the Press, Dec. 6, 2001.

2. For example, one year after 9/11 nearly three-quarters of Americans believed the country was still "at war" (Patrick May, "Sept. 11 Still Spawns Fears," *Boston Globe,* Sept. 1, 2002). Two years after 9/11 nearly three-quarters of Americans still expected terrorist acts in the United States (Pew Center for the People and the Press, Sept. 4, 2003).

3. For instance, the Web page of Iowa Representative Greg Ganske (R) notes that Senator Tom Harkin (D) opposed a 1995 constitutional amendment to ban flag burning. In this context the Web page also criticizes Harkin for not sharing America's patriotism and appreciation for the flag ("War on Terror Colors the Battle for Congress," *Washington Post,* July 5, 2002).

4. On the stability of gun attitudes, see Weisberg, Krosnick, and Bowen 1996. On the intensity of opinions, see Schuman and Presser 1996.

5. But see Callaghan and Schnell 2001a; Terkildsen, Schnell, and Ling 1998; Schudson 1990; and Gans 1980 for a discussion of journalistic objectivity and its limitations.

6. The Second Amendment was the dominant theme, although other rights were discussed, such as the Fourth Amendment right to be secure in persons and property, the Tenth Amendment delegation of power to the states, and the Fifth Amendment right of due process (Glendeon 1991). In the latter case, gun rights groups argued that banning a weapon like the Colt AR-15 without banning other companies' rifles with identical functions (caliber, rate of fire, etc.) violates the due process clause, which guarantees equal treatment to all.

7. The notable exception is the National Firearms Act of 1934, the first major crime-control law in this country. For a brief period of time, the historical focus on "pro-gun" themes shifted toward an "anti-gun" emphasis on crime and violence. In 1933 there was an assassination attempt on President Franklin D. Roosevelt in Miami. Of course, in 1929, the most spectacular mob hit in gangland history—the St. Valentine's Day Massacre—occurred in Chicago. Mobsters from the infamous Al Capone gang machine-gunned to death rival gang members, though the target of the plan, "Bugs" Moran, was not among the men executed. No one was arrested for this crime or for several other mob-related crimes that occurred during this era. A sudden change in the public debate occurred. Gun control was now framed as a problem of "Mob Violence." However, this new theme was largely symbolic: it superficially denounced firearms without intent to inconvenience American firearms companies or their customers in any way (see Patterson and Eakins 1998, 49).

8. This analysis was based on an examination of all evening newscasts (N = 403) involving the Brady Bill and the Assault Weapons Ban that were aired by the three major broadcast networks, ABC, NBC, and CBS, from 1988 to 1996. Videotapes were supplied by the Vanderbilt Television News Archives.

9. For example, 14 percent of broadcasts framed the issue in terms of a "Political Contest" and emphasized the conflict surrounding the issue.

10. These figures exclude unrelated press releases such as political endorsements and general announcements.

11. *ABC Evening News,* Feb. 28, 2002.

12. We excluded NBC from this analysis because transcripts were not easily accessed on-

line. Previous research, however, found no significant differences in coverage of the gun control issue across networks (Callaghan and Schnell 2001a).

13. Even two and a half years after the massacre at Columbine High School in Littleton, Colorado, the event continued to have an effect on media coverage. Eleven broadcasts dealt directly or indirectly with the mass shootings in Columbine.

14. Newspaper coverage of the issue was very similar. We assessed *New York Times (NYT)* stories on gun control by examining how often the words *terrorism* and *guns* appeared within ten words of each other. In the six-month period following the attacks, the *NYT* contained thirty-two relevant articles. For instance, on October 7, 2001, it reported that American-made .50 caliber rifles were probably still available to Al Qaida members for attacks against American troops in Afghanistan (James Dao, "A Nation Challenged: The Weapons; In '80s Afghan Militias Used U.S. Rifles"). On October 21, the *NYT* described how gun ownership had increased among Westchester, New York, residents: "Gripping the heavy pistol, it was the first time she has felt powerful since then. She decided to buy a gun, she said, 'because I had to do something to protect myself'" (Jessica Kovler, "Gun Sales Increase as Residents Seek Protection"). In contrast, the same search for the six-month period preceding 9/11 produced only two results. One article dealt with U.S. attempts to quiet fighting in Macedonia. The second article, a film review, was unrelated.

15. See also Baumgartner, Jones, and MacLeod 2000.

16. Although we employ a nonrandom sample of students for our experiment, there is no reason to expect differences between college students and adults in their basic cognitive processes (Sears 1986). Further, research shows that framing effects do not differ between student and nonstudent samples (e.g., Kuhberger 1998; J. Miller and Krosnick 2000). However, better-educated individuals may be more likely to view Muslims as victims of discrimination triggered by 9/11, which would transfer to more *positive* affect toward Muslims (Sniderman and Hagen [1985] draw this conclusion in an analogous domain—race). However, this would bias against finding a negative impact of the terrorism frames on the group's evaluations, as we hypothesize.

17. Subjects who listed their religious affiliation as Muslim were also excluded from the analysis of questions bearing directly on that affiliation.

18. The gun control issue resembles many other salient, long-standing issues that were influenced by the attacks on 9/11 (e.g., civil liberties, national security, defense spending, immigration policy). Thus, we expect our research findings to generalize across other issue domains.

19. In order to test the validity of our experimental materials, we asked subjects whether they thought the passages were interesting and easy to read. We found no difference in subjects' assessment of the level of interest ($F = .329$, $p < .85$) or the complexity of the framed passages ($F = .944$, $p < .44$). These results reassure us that the passages were essentially equal in structure.

20. Since our analysis compares each issue frame with the typical opinion in the "no-frame" condition (i.e., the control group), we oversampled subjects in the control group to gain greater confidence in our statistical tests. Furthermore, we conducted a series of tests on key subject characteristics (partisanship, ideology, prior gun experience, media usage, and gender) by framing conditions to see if our random-assignment procedure worked. None of the *F*-values for the one-way ANOVAs was significant.

21. The significance of pairing an emotive issue like terrorism with gun control is that it may decrease the likelihood of individuals counterarguing the message. That is, individuals will be less likely to see the flaws in the argument and thus will be more susceptible to framing effects (see Petty and Caccioppo 1981).

22. However, the framing effect in the "Dual Frame" condition is significantly larger than the control group, indicating that this frame caused subjects to express more positive affect toward Muslims. Compared to the other terrorism frames, these results are counterintuitive

and suggest that the complexity of counterframe information needs to be addressed in future research.

23. After Columbine, gun control activists seized the opportunity to rally support for new legislation. Furthermore, the media paid more attention to the "Crime and Violence" theme than they had previously (see Callaghan and Schnell 2001a). In the gun control debate, the NRA often stood as the accused. For instance, the group's reluctance to move its annual convention from Denver, Colorado, two weeks after the Columbine shootings generated a public outcry and a good deal of negative media attention.

24. This measure is a modified version of Rokeach's (1973) value survey. We used a ranking approach to measure values because, unlike value ratings (usually measured on a 1–7 scale), the ranking technique assumes that values are comparative and competitive (see Alwin and Krosnick 1985; Rankin and Grube 1980). This kind of operationalization comes closer to the theoretical conceptualization of values as "enduring beliefs that a specific mode of conduct or end state of existence is personally or socially preferable to an opposite or converse mode of conduct or end state of existence" (Rokeach 1973, 5).

25. This procedure gave a value of 5 to the first issue item, 4 to the second item, and so on, until the last issue item was valued as 1 (for a similar procedure see Lau 1986). The weighted counts of the number of issues falling into each issue category were divided by a weighted count of the total number of issues mentioned by the subject. For example, suppose a subject named the "war on terrorism" as the most important issue, followed by "corporate accountability" and "welfare reform." This subject would have a base count of 12 (5 for the first issue, 4 for the second issue, and 3 for the third issue). The first issue falls into the issue category of national security, thus resulting in a score of .417 (from [5 + 0 + 0] / 12). If none of the issues was related to national security and defense, the subject's score for this issue category would be 0 (0 / 12). Conversely, if all three issues mentioned were defense-related, the subject's score would be 1.0 (from [5 + 4 + 3] / 12. This procedure controls for the total number of issues mentioned in each issue category, as well as the verbosity of the individual subject. Every subject received a score ranging from 0 to 1.0 for each of the three issue dimensions. Subjects who did not name any issues at all were given a score of 0 on each dimension.

26. However, the "Dual Frame" increased subjects' interest in becoming informed about gun control. Perhaps the nature of two-sided arguments in the Dual Frame enhances the desire to learn more about a subject to determine which side is right.

27. Do emotional responses hold a key to the political significance of terrorism frames, explaining, for example, higher levels of interest in supporting gun rights groups through political activism? A correlational analysis is suggestive. The average person's correlation (Pearson's r) between the levels of anxiety evoked by the "Guns Stop Terrorism" frame and a composite measure of behavioral intention was moderately large and close to statistical significance ($r = .32, p = .12$).

28. At times, the "Constitutional Rights" frame was also successful (see especially table 5.4). One reason for the success of this frame might be that it is not really part of the old framing debate. The federal courts have recently confirmed what some historians and constitutional scholars have consistently argued: that the Second Amendment of the U.S. Constitution, like other rights amendments, guarantees an individual right of the people. The courts' rejection of the "collective rights" theory as the sole interpretation of constitutional law has revived the debate. Alternatively, as Harding (quoted in Glendeon 1991, 36) has pointed out, "rights talk" is, and will likely remain, crucial to Americans.

29. U.S. Department of Justice, National Instant Criminal Background Check System (NICS) Operations Report for 2001. This report by the FBI's Criminal Justice Information Services Division reviews firearms records as mandated by the Brady Handgun Violence Protection Act of 1993.

30. Note that NICS background checks measure only retail firearm sales. Private transactions are not included in this report. Nor are the arms-related expenditures that may have oc-

curred during this time period, such as the purchase of sighting devices, gun clips, and ammunition. These are also important indicators of gun-related activity.

31. In this study, we did not consider the correlates of overall opinion. For example, how much do specific beliefs and emotions contribute to the total variance in policy preferences? Do emotions contribute uniquely to judgments about political issues that are framed in terms of 9/11, or are beliefs more important than emotions? Further, to what extent do factors such as partisanship transform the emotions in the frame into distinct emotional responses (Roseman, Abelson, and Ewing 1986)? While these questions are important, presenting such analyses is beyond the scope of this chapter.

32. Empirical research on framing and gun control suggests that the media and other political players (e.g., gun control groups and politicians) often chastise the NRA for its lobbying tactics, advertisements, and issue message; it has been vilified as the enemy of responsible gun laws (see Callaghan and Schnell 2001a).

Chapter 6: Super-Predators or Victims of Societal Neglect?

1. The effect of these stereotypes on the formation of opinions about crime is similar to the influence of a particular speaker's message or agenda on public tolerance of the right to free expression (e.g., Sullivan, Pierson, and Marcus 1993; McCloskey and Brill 1983; Sniderman 1996; Gibson and Gouws 1997) or to the effect of the "deservingness" of a particular welfare recipient on expressed support for welfare spending (e.g., Gilens 1999; Iyengar 1991; T. Smith 1987).

2. Our decision to collapse these categories—white and Asian—is explained in the "Results" section.

3. These stories focused on (in order) firefighters' efforts to put out a series of wildfires, the passage of a local ordinance requiring property owners in Los Angeles to retrofit their buildings in compliance with new seismic safety guidelines, beach closures due to seepage of sewage, testing of missiles by the Chinese government, and an electrical fire in a downtown office building.

4. Using Los Angeles as the baseline, our sample overrepresents African Americans, underrepresents Latinos, and matches exactly the proportion of whites.

5. The zero-order correlation between the two questions was .26 ($p < .01$), and Cronbach's alpha was .51. The index mean was .53.

6. The zero-order correlation between the two counts was .25 ($p < .01$), and Cronbach's alpha was .49. The index can range from 0 to –4 and has a mean of 1.01. That is, on average, the open-ended responses included one reference to punitive factors.

7. The stereotype index was based on five trait ratings: "Now, here are some different questions about these same groups (Asian Americans, Hispanic Americans, African Americans, white Americans). We want you to rate these groups in terms of particular attributes that may or may not characterize them. Please consider the group named at the top of each list of attributes or behaviors and rate how well each attribute applies to that group in general. A score of 1 would mean that you think the attribute applies very well to that group, while a score of 4 would mean that you think the attribute does not apply to the group at all. If you have no opinion at all about how well an attribute applies to a particular group, you may choose 9." The African American stereotype index was constructed using the traits of "law-abiding," "sexually responsible," "violent," "lazy," and "use drugs." The items were scored so that negative characterizations were scored as 1 and others as 0. The stereotype score was defined as the average of the five ratings (Cronbach's alpha was .62).

8. We also included several other antecedents of crime attitudes, including victimization in the last twelve months, family income, home ownership, political knowledge, and age. Since their coefficients proved nonsignificant, they were dropped from the final analysis.

9. Full results are available upon request.

Chapter 7: Media Frames, Core Values, and the Dynamics of Racial Policy Preferences

1. There is one exception in American politics to this reality: those that are endlessly interested in the machinations of the U.S. Congress can watch nearly endless hearings, debates, and deliberations on C-SPAN and, if that doesn't fill the need, even turn to C-SPAN2.

2. See Zaller and Feldman 1992; Zaller 1992.

3. See Tocqueville 1945; for more recent evidence, see Bellah et al. 1985.

4. See especially McCloskey and Zaller 1984; Kinder and Sanders 1996, tables 6.1 and 6.2.

5. Certainly, it is reasonable to consider other possible themes in media coverage about race that might be causally related to racial policy preferences. Coverage that emphasizes black poverty or black crime certainly comes to mind, among other kinds of coverage. I have examined many of these themes in media coverage, and many of them are meaningful politically. However, they turn out *not* to be meaningful (statistically) for racial policy preferences as I measure them. As a result, to preserve space, I omit them from my discussion here.

6. In the content analyses that follow, I use InfoTrend 1.0 (InfoTrend, Inc., 2115 Dudley Ave., St. Paul, MN 55108). This technology allows for the translation of words (and specified combinations of words) into user-defined ideas (e.g., individualism and egalitarianism). The analyst provides a dictionary of key words and how they combine to form ideas.

7. For a full discussion of the pros and cons of choosing *Newsweek,* see Kellstedt 2003, chap. 2.

8. The figure of 2,087 stories for the latter period comes from a Boolean search in Nexis for at least two mentions of the words *negro, black,* or *African-American* from 1975 through 1994. This search produced 3,243 "hits," many of which were clearly irrelevant. Those that were not about blacks in the United States were deleted, leaving 2,087. The remaining stories were used in their entirety.

9. It is natural to wonder whether *Newsweek* is representative of the mainstream press more broadly. In other work, I have described validation exercises that compare the *Newsweek* series with those from a shorter series derived from *New York Times* stories. The results are quite encouraging and indicate that *Newsweek* is not unique or idiosyncratic. See Kellstedt 2003, chap. 2.

10. There is one difference between Durr's measure of expectations and mine. Durr purges his measure of economic expectations of the influence of political events (such as presidential approval and honeymoon periods), whereas I do not. This difference should have minimal effects, if any, because Durr's aggregation interval is quarters, whereas mine is years.

11. The universe of items used in my measure of Policy Mood is slightly different from Stimson's. He includes questions about race in his measure of Policy Mood; I recompute his index excluding the items that have racial content, for the obvious reason that including the same indicators of racial policy preferences in two separate measures would artificially produce some association between them.

12. It could be argued that this series should start in 1964, when the Civil Rights Act was passed. None of the subsequent results are at all affected by using different measures of generational replacement.

13. A word about causal ordering: the theory outlined above predicts that egalitarian and individualistic media framing will drive racial policy preferences through time, rather than either reverse or reciprocal causal scenarios. And the possibility of reverse causality—that is, the possibility that mass policy preferences on race drive media coverage on the topic—is both sensible and very real. A time-series technique designed to test precisely these types of hypotheses, Granger causality tests, has been performed and discussed in other contexts (see Kellstedt 2000, table 1). The results support the theory I am herein proposing and indicate that temporal ordering flows from media to public opinion, not the reverse.

14. See Woolley 2000 for an extended discussion.

15. See McAdam 1982.

Conclusion: Controversies and New Directions in Framing Research

1. Verbal frames may be especially persuasive when they include symbolic visual images (e.g., flags, balloons, guns). For instance, NBC's "Moment of the Week" presented scenes of Senator Alfonse D'Amato displaying a pig on the floor of Congress while singing "Old McDonald Had a Farm" to further enhance his framing of President Bill Clinton's health care bill as "pork barrel" legislation (Aug. 27, 1994). A simple visual enhancement of a political issue frame like this can be very evocative.

2. See the Media Research Center's Web site's CyberAlert at http:www.mrc.org/cyberalerts/2002/cyb20020306.asp.

3. Of course, citizens have always been able to turn to alternative sources of news, each in its own little ideological niche. However, today's expanded news markets provide instant, almost effortless access to news frames from more specialized sources with the click of a mouse button or TV remote or simple voice command. This new technology makes it easier for citizens to more actively seek out supporting information so as to bolster or protect their prior attitudes and beliefs. Prior attitudes are often resistant to change, especially when they are constantly being reinforced.

4. As early as 1920 scholars noted that an active organism intervenes between a psychological stimulus (S) and response (R). The "S-R" model that dominated psychological research throughout the first half of the twentieth century was respecified as an "S-O-R" model (i.e., "stimulus-organism-response") when researchers began to look inside the "black box" of the mind to understand human behavior (see, e.g., Baron and Kenny 1986; McGraw and Lodge 1995). An interest in "mediating" variables burgeoned.

5. The story on political sophistication is more complicated than that. On one hand, political sophisticates, with their higher levels of ideological reasoning (Hamill, Lodge, and Blake 1985; Converse 1964), would be expected to counterargue dominant media messages. For well-publicized issues, political sophisticates may be less susceptible to framing effects than those who are less sophisticated (holding constant other factors like individual levels of affect or perceived salience of an issue). Nonsophisticates, on the other hand, may be less likely to see the flaws or biases in the media's portrayal of an issue and thus be more susceptible to these messages (Iyengar 1991; Iyengar and Kinder 1987). However, since nonsophisticates are the least likely to attend to media frames, media messages are most likely to influence the attitudes of those with moderate levels of political awareness (Goidel, Schields, and Peffley 1997).

6. See Druckman 2003; Druckman and Nelson 2003; Sniderman and Theriault 1999; Haider-Markel and Joslyn 2001; Callaghan and Schnell 2004. Druckman (2003), for example, has recently explored the moderating effects of interpersonal communication.

7. According to Carmines and Stimson (1980), issues can be thought of as "easy" or "hard." Hard issues focus on technical debates that are concerned with policy means or implementation. Easy issues have long been on the public agenda; they focus on nontechnical debates, and they are emotive and most concerned with policy outcomes. The significance of this distinction concerns the level of information and cognition citizens require to evaluate specific issues. While hard issues require higher levels of cognition and greater levels of information to form an opinion, easy issues are readily interpreted by virtue of their association to individual values and the emotions such links elicit.

8. For example, traditionally the tobacco issue was strictly an economic issue focusing on government subsidies for tobacco farmers. Then overwhelming medical research began to suggest a link between health problems and smoking. In light of this new information, the debate regarding tobacco took on a second policy dimension: health care concerns (Baumgartner and Jones 1993; Fritschler and Hoeffler 1996).

9. Given the nature of media coverage, complex frames are unlikely to penetrate the public agenda. And due to sparse media coverage, public exposure to complex issues and their frames is likely to be low. In this regard, studies that examine the influence of substantively complex issue frames on ordinary citizens would seem to be impractical, unless the issue had

already been fragmented or isolated into simplistic subcomponents of the larger complex issue and thus could be more easily digested by the mass public. Alternatively, one could reasonably explore the framing effects of substantively complex issues on political elites.

10. Evocative issues are very likely to be polarized because activists on either side of the issue are unlikely to find common ground over the policy ends or the means associated with the issue. Consider the abortion issue. It entails conflict between fundamental and mutually incompatible values and is one of the most entrenched issues in American politics. Similarly, the debate about same-sex marriage and the Defense of Marriage Act is constrained by religious, moral, and "family values" on one side and egalitarian beliefs on the other side—other less evocative frames, such as the economic implications of granting marriage benefits to gay couples, are peripheral.

11. In addition to influencing the degree to which framing can influence individual opinions, issue-specific characteristics can determine how influential frames will be at the macrolevel. By exploring the influence these issue characteristics have on elites' ability to frame issues—and examining elites' framing attempts for these issues—future research can address the question of what kind of issues are likely to be "framed."

12. For example, using an experimental study, Druckman and Nelson (2003) demonstrated that citizen conversations can eliminate framing effects. As the authors aptly note, interpersonal discussions permeate the world; thus, failure to consider their impact can lead to a misunderstanding about the influence of frames. In another context, T. Lee (2002) has shown that grassroots organizations and the political protests of ordinary citizens can push policy demands into the consciousness of the mass public, which in turn influences the policy agendas of political elites. Thus, Lee's work challenges the conventional view that public opinion is shaped by elites (also see Walsh 2001).

13. Although we did not test this hypothesis directly, our experimental study of group labeling and the women's movement suggests an on-line process (Callaghan and Schnell 2001b). An information-processing-accuracy and free-recall test showed that the cognitive components of group labels related to the women's movement (e.g., "feminists," "women's libbers") were disconnected from the evaluations citizens made about the broader social movement they represented, even for self-identified feminists and other individuals with strong alternative cognitions. These results suggest that when group labels are used to define a group's political domain, they lock group-related beliefs into a narrow, fixed space that represents a mere caricature of the movement itself, rather than its full range of ideas—seemingly in a process of "on-line" cognition.

14. The "Monopolies" frame argued that expanded media ownership would allow big companies like Time Warner to purchase almost as many television and radio stations as they could afford. See Ron Weiskind and Adrian McCoy, "Increasing Frequency: Since the Telecommunications Act, Players and Stations in the Pittsburgh Market Seem to Turn Over Faster Than You Can Stab Your Seek Button, *Pittsburgh Post-Gazette,* Nov. 17, 1996.

15. Even cognitive awareness of presented frames is not enough to prevent citizens from being seduced by them. Skepticism about an issue frame and the media's balanced treatment of a policy issue can exist simultaneously with unconscious persuasion. In other words, one can be critical of the news and still be persuaded by framed messages.

16. Studies show that while no single news story in and of itself has a huge impact on individual citizens, the cumulative effect of many stories over time may be great (Iyengar 1991). Thus, one might expect repetitive frames to have a similar effect.

17. My argument, that the media shy away from complex themes and thus citizens are not exposed to them, raises another important question. If more complex frames were available, would the public pay attention to this information? Perhaps not. Recent research on media framing and the news coverage of election campaigns finds that despite access to a wide variety of information, voters prefer news reports that include the simple "Horse Race" and "Political Strategy" frames over more complex campaign information (Iyengar and Norpoth 2004).

References

Abelson, Robert P., Donald R. Kinder, M. D. Peters, and Susan T. Fiske. 1982. Affective and semantic components in political person perception. *Journal of Personality and Social Psychology* 42:619–30.

Abramowitz, Alan I. 1988. Explaining Senate election outcomes. *American Political Science Review* 82:385–403.

Abramson, Jeffrey B., F. Christopher Arterton, and Gary R. Orren. 1988. *The electronic commonwealth: The impact of new media technologies on democratic politics.* New York: Basic Books.

Albers, Rebecca Ross. 1994. Going public: Public journalism unites some publishers and newsrooms in a controversial mission. *Presstime* (September): 28–30.

Alderman, J. 1994. Leading the public: The media's focus on crime shaped sentiment. *Public Perspective* 5:26–27.

Aldrich, John H. 1980. *Before the convention.* Chicago: University of Chicago Press.

———. 1995. *Why parties? The origin and transformation of political parties in America.* Chicago: University of Chicago Press.

Aldrich, John H., and David W. Rhode. 1996. The Republican revolution and the House Appropriations Committee. Paper 96-08, Political Institutions and Public Choice, Michigan State University.

Altheide, D. 1987. Format and symbol in television coverage of terrorism in the U.S. and Great Britain. *International Studies Quarterly* 31:161–76.

Alwin, D. F., and Jon A. Krosnick. 1985. The measurement of values in surveys: A comparison of ratings and rankings. *Public Opinion Quarterly* 49:535–52.

Amundson, D. R., L. S. Lichter, and S. R. Lichter. 2000. What's the matter with kids today? Television coverage of adolescents in America. In *Reframing Youth Issues,* ed. S. Bales. Washington, DC: Working Papers, Frame Works Institute and Center for Communications and Community, UCLA.

Ansolabahere, Stephen, Roy Behr, and Shanto Iyengar. 1993. *The media game: American politics in the television age.* New York: Macmillan Publishing Company.

Ansolabahere, Stephen, and Shanto Iyengar. 1994. Riding the wave and claiming ownership over issues: The joint effects of advertising and news coverage in campaigns. *Public Opinion Quarterly* 58:335–57.

Arnold, R. Douglas. 1990. *The logic of congressional action.* New Haven: Yale University Press.

Arrow, Kenneth. 1951. *Social choice and individual values.* New York: Wiley.

Athans, Mary Christine. 1992. *Coughlin-Fahey connection: Father Denis Fahey, C.S.SP., and religious anti-Semitism in the United States, 1938–1954.* New York: Peter Lang.

Austen-Smith, David, and John Wright. 1994. Counteractive lobbying. *American Journal of Political Science* 38:25–44.

Baek, Mijeong. 2002. Framing effects and political sophistication. Paper presented at the annual meeting of the American Political Science Association, Boston.

Bagdikian, Ben. 1992. *The media monopoly.* Boston: Beacon Press.

Bales, S., and Frank Gilliam Jr. 2003. Framed: How media frames affect public perceptions of youth. Unpublished manuscript.

Banning, Lance. 1978. *The Jeffersonian persuasion: Evolution of a party ideology.* Ithaca: Cornell University Press.

Bargh, John A. 1984. Automatic and conscious processing of social information. In *The handbook of social cognition,* ed. Robert S. Wyer and Thomas K. Srull. Hillsdale, NJ: Lawrence Erlbaum.

Baron, Reuben M., and David A. Kenny. 1986. The moderator-mediator variable distinction in social psychological research: Conceptual, strategic and statistical considerations. *Journal of Personality and Social Psychology* 51:1173–82.

Bartels, Larry. 1988. *Presidential primaries and the dynamics of public choice.* Princeton: Princeton University Press.

———. 1993. Messages received: The political impact of media exposure. *American Political Science Review* 87:267–85.

———. 2003. Democracy with attitudes. In *Electoral democracy,* ed. Michael B. MacKuen and George Rabinowitz. Ann Arbor: University of Michigan Press.

Basil, Michael, Caroline Schooler, and Byron Reeves. 1991. Positive and negative political advertising: Effectiveness of ads and perceptions of candidates. In *Television and political advertising,* vol. 1, *Psychological processes,* ed. Frank Biocca. Hillsdale, NJ: Lawrence Erlbaum.

Baum, Matthew. 2002. Sex, lies, and war: How soft news brings foreign policy to the inattentive public. *American Political Science Review* 96:91–109.

Baumgartner, Frank, and Bryan Jones. 1993. *Agendas and instability in American politics.* Chicago: University of Chicago Press.

Baumgartner, Frank, Bryan Jones, and Beth Leech. 1997. Media attention and congressional agendas. In *Implications for candidate evaluation: Do the media govern? Politicians, voters, and reporters in America,* ed. Shanto Iyengar and Richard Reeves. Thousand Oaks, CA: Sage Publications.

Baumgartner, Frank, Bryan Jones, and Michael MacLeod. 2000. The evolution of legislative jurisdictions. *Journal of Politics* 61:321–49.

Baumgartner, Frank, and Beth L. Leech. 1999. Basic interests: The importance of groups in politics and political science. *Public Opinion Quarterly* 63:151–53.

Bellah, Robert N., Richard Madsen, William M. Sullivan, Ann Swindler, and Steven M. Tipton. 1985. *Habits of the heart: Individualism and commitment in American life.* Berkeley: University of California Press.

Bennett , W. Lance. 1990. Toward a theory of press-state relations in the U.S. *Journal of Communication* 40:103–25.

_____. 1996. An introduction to journalism norms and representations of politics. *Political Communication* 13:373–84.

_____. 2003. *News: The politics of illusion.* 5th ed. New York: Longman.

Bennett, W. Lance, and Robert M. Entman, eds. 2001. *Mediated politics: Communication in the future of democracy.* New York: Cambridge University Press.

Bennett, W. Lance, J. J. DiIulio Jr., and J. P. Walters. 1996. *Body count: Moral poverty . . . and how to win America's war against crime and drugs.* New York: Simon and Schuster.

Bennett, W. Lance, and Jarol Manheim. 1993. Taking the public by storm: Information, cuing, and the democratic process in the Gulf Conflict. *Political Communication* 10:331–52.

_____. 2001. The big spin: Strategic communication and the transformation of pluralist democracy. In Bennett and Entman 2001.

Berelson, Bernard. 1948. Communications and public opinion. In *Communications in modern society,* ed. William Schramm. Urbana: University of Illinois Press.

_____. 1952. Content analysis for the social sciences and humanities. Reading, MA: Addison-Wesley.

_____. [1952] 1971. *Content analysis in communication research.* New York: Hafner.

Berelson, Bernard R., and Paul F. Lazarsfeld. 1948. *The analysis of communication content.* Mimeograph.

Berelson, Bernard R., Paul F. Lazarsfeld, and William McPhee. 1954. *Voting: A study of public opinion formation in a presidential campaign.* Chicago: University of Chicago Press.

Berkman, H. 1995. A gunshot in Boston sends tremors nationwide. *National Law Journal* 18 (October 9, 1995).

Berry, Jeffrey. 1989. *The interest group society.* New York: Longman.

Berry, V., and C. Manning-Miller. 1996. *Mediated messages and African-American culture.* Thousand Oaks, CA: Sage Publications.

Berthold-Bond, Daniel. 1993. *Hegel's grand synthesis: A study of being, thought and history.* New York: Harper.

Birkland, Thomas A. 1997. *After disaster: Agenda setting, public policy, and focusing events.* Washington, DC: Georgetown University Press.

Black, Duncan. 1958. *The theory of committees and elections.* Cambridge: Cambridge University Press.

Bobo, Lawrence. 1983. Whites' opposition to busing: Symbolic racism or realistic group conflict? *Journal of Personality and Social Psychology* 45:1196–1210.

Bobo, Lawrence, and J. Kluegel. 1993. Opposition to race targeting: Self-interest, stratification ideology, or racial attitudes? *American Sociological Review* 58:443–64.

Bobo, Lawrence, C. Zubrinsky, J. Johnson Jr., and M. Oliver. 1994. Public opinion before and after a spring of discontent. In *The Los Angeles riots: Lessons for the urban future,* ed. M. Baldessare. Boulder: Westview Press.

Brewer, Paul, and Lee Sigelman. 2002. Political scientists as color commentators: Framing and expert commentary in media campaign coverage. *Harvard International Journal of Press/Politics* 7 (1): 23–35.

Brody, Richard A. 1991. *Assessing the president: The media, elite opinion, and public support.* Stanford: Stanford University Press.

Brown, David. 1994. Public journalism: Rebuilding communities through media. *Philanthropy Journal of North Carolina* (July–August): 11.

Brown, William P. 1990. Organized interests and their issue niches: A search for pluralism in a policy domain. *Journal of Politics* 52:477–509.

Browne, W., J. Skees, L. Swanson, P. Thompson, and L. Unnevehr. 1992. *Sacred cows and hot potatoes: Agrarian myths in agricultural policy.* Boulder: Westview Press.

Bruce, John M., and Clyde Wilcox. 1998. Introduction. In *The changing politics of gun control,* ed. John M. Bruce and Clyde Wilcox. New York: Rowman and Littlefield Publishers.

Buckner, Jennie. 1997. Public journalism: Giving voters a voice. *Media Studies Journal* (Winter): 65–68.

Budzilowicz, Lisa. 2002. *Framing responsibility and local television news.* A Report of the Local TV News Media Project, the Center for Communication Research and Service and the Graduate School of Urban Affairs and Public Policy, University of Delaware.

Bureau of Justice Statistics. 1997. *Sourcebook of criminal justice statistics.* Washington, DC: Government Printing Office.

Butler, Lisa, Cheryl Koopman, and Phil Zombardo. 1995. The psychological impact of viewing the film *JFK:* Emotions, beliefs, and political behavioral intentions. *Political Psychology* 16 (2): 237–58.

California Commission on the Status of African-American Males. 1996. *African-American males: A struggle for equality.* Sacramento: Government Printing Office.

Callaghan, Karen, and Frauke Schnell. 2000. Media frames, public attitudes and elite response: An analysis of the gun control issue. *Public Integrity* 1 (4): 47–74.

_____. 2001a. Assessing the democratic debate: How the news media frame elite policy discourse. *Political Communication* 18:193–212.

_____. 2001b. Understanding the consequences of group labeling for the women's movement: An experimental investigation. *Women and Politics* 23 (4): 31–60.

_____. 2005. The role of source cues in media framing: An experimental investigation. Unpublished manuscript.

Calvert, Randall. 1985. The value of biased information: A rational choice model of political advice. *Journal of Politics* 47:530–55.

Cappella, Joseph N., and Kathleen Hall Jamieson. 1997. *The spiral of cynicism: The press and the public good.* New York: Oxford University Press.

Carey, James. 1988. *Communication as culture: Essays on media and society.* London: Unwin Hyman.

_____. 1989. Commentary: Communication and the progressives. *Critical Studies and Mass Communication* 6:264–82.

Carmines, Edward, and James Kuklinski. 1990. Incentives, opportunities, and the logic of public opinion in American political representation. In Ferejohn and Kuklinski 1990.

Carmines, Edward, and James A. Stimson. 1980. The two faces of issue voting. *American Political Science Review* 74:78–91.

_____. 1986. On the structure and sequence of issue evolution. *American Political Science Review* 80:901–20.

_____. 1989. *Issue evolution: Race and the transformation of American politics.* Princeton: Princeton University Press.

Carroll, J., ed. 1956. *Selected writings of Benjamin Lee Whorf.* Cambridge: MIT Press.

Chong, Dennis. 1993. How people think, reason and feel about rights and liberties. *American Journal of Political Science* 37:867–99.

_____. 1996. Creating common frames of reference on political issues. In Mutz, Sniderman, and Brody 1996.

Clarke, Peter, and Susan Evans. 1983. *Covering campaigns: Journalism in congressional elections.* Stanford: Stanford University Press.

Clarke, Peter, and Eric Fredin. 1978. Newspapers, television, and political reasoning. *Public Opinion Quarterly* 42:143–60.

Cobb, Roger, and Charles Elder. 1976. Issue creation and agenda-building. In *Cases in public policy-making,* ed. James Anderson. New York: Praeger Publishers.

_____. 1983. *Participation in American politics: The dynamics of agenda-building.* 2d ed. Baltimore: Johns Hopkins University Press.

Cohen, Bernard. 1963. *The press and foreign policy.* Princeton: Princeton University Press.

_____. 1995. Presidential rhetoric and the public agenda. *American Journal of Political Science* 39:87–108.

Collins, A. M., and E. F. Loftus. 1975. A spreading-activation theory of semantic processing. *Psychological Review* 82:407–28.

Congressional Quarterly. 1992. Preelection outlook. Washington, DC: Congressional Quarterly Press.

Converse, Philip E. 1964. The nature of belief systems in mass publics. In *Ideology and discontent,* ed. David E. Apter. New York: Free Press.

_____. 1970. Attitudes and non-attitudes: Continuation of dialogue. In *The quantitative analysis of social problems,* ed. Edward R. Tufte. Reading, MA: Addison-Wesley.

_____. 1987. Changing conceptions of public opinion in the political process. *Public Opinion Quarterly* 51:312–24.

Converse, Philip E., and Gregory Markus. 1979. Plus ca change . . . : The new CPS election study panel. *American Political Science Review* 73:32–49.

Cook, Timothy E. 1989. *Making laws and making news: Media strategies in the U.S. House of Representatives.* Washington, DC: Brookings Institution.

_____. 1996. Afterword: Political values and production values. *Political Communication* 13:469–82.

_____. 1998. *Governing with the news: The news media as a political institution.* Chicago: University of Chicago Press.

Cook, Thomas, and Donald T. Campbell. 1979. *Quasi-experimentation*. Chicago: Rand McNally.

Cox, Gary W., and Matthew D. McCubbins. 1993. *Legislative leviathan: Party government in the House*. Berkeley: University of California Press.

Crotty, William, and Gary C. Jacobson. 1980. *American parties in decline*. Boston: Little, Brown.

Curry, G. D., and I. A. Spergel. 1992. Gang involvement and delinquency among Hispanic and African-American adolescent males. *Journal of Research in Crime and Delinquency* 29:273–92.

Dahl, Robert A. 1989. *Democracy and its critics*. New Haven: Yale University Press.

Damore, David F. 2002. Candidate strategy and the decision to go negative. *Political Research Quarterly* 55:669–86.

Davis, Darren W. 1997. Donning the black mask. *American Journal of Political Science* 41:309–22.

Davis, Richard. 1996. *The press and American politics: The new mediator*. Upper Saddle River, NJ: Prentice Hall.

Devine, Patricia. 1989. Stereotypes and prejudice: Their automatic and controlled components. *Journal of Personality and Social Psychology* 56:5–18.

Dewey, John. [1927] 1954. *The public and its problems*. Athens, OH: Swallow Press.

DiIulio, J. J., Jr. 1995. The coming of the super-predators. *Weekly Standard* (November 27): 23.

Donahue, William A., Deborah A. Cai, and Monique M. Mitchell. 2001. *Communicating and connecting: Functions of human communication*. Dubuque: Kendall Hunt Publishers.

Donsbach, W. 1983. Journalists' conceptions of their audience: Comparative indicators for the way British and German journalists define their relations to the public. *Gazette* 32:19–36.

Dorfman, L., K. Woodruff, V. Chavez, and L. Wallack. 1995. Youth and violence on local television news. Unpublished report, Berkeley Media Studies Group.

———. 1997. Youth and violence on local television news in California. 1997. *American Journal of Public Health* 87 (8): 1311–16.

Downs, Anthony. 1957. *An economic theory of democracy*. New York: Harper and Row.

Druckman, James N. 2001a. The implications of framing effects for citizen competence. *Political Behavior* 23:225–56.

———. 2001b. Using credible advice to overcome framing effects. *Journal of Law, Economics and Organization* 17 (1): 62–82.

———. 2003. Political preference formation: Competition, deliberation, and the (ir)relevance of framing effects. Paper presented at the summer Political Methodology Meeting, University of Minnesota, July 17–19.

———. Forthcoming. Political preference formation: Competition, deliberation, and the (ir)relevance of framing effects. *American Political Science Review*.

Druckman, James N., and Kjersten R. Nelson. 2003. Framing and deliberation: How citizens' conversations limit elite influence. *American Journal of Political Science* 47:728–44.

Durr, Robert H. 1993. What moves policy sentiment? *American Political Science Review* 87:158–70.

Einhorn, Hillel J., and Robin M. Hogarth. 1987. *Rational choice: The contrast between economics and psychology.* Chicago: University of Chicago Press.

Emery, Michael, and Edwin Emery. 1988. *The press and America: An interpretive history of the mass media.* Englewood Cliffs, NJ: Prentice Hall.

Entman, Robert M. 1989. *Democracy without citizens: Media and the decay of American politics.* New York: Oxford University Press.

_____. 1992. Blacks in the news: Television, modern racism, and cultural change. *Journalism Quarterly* 69:341–62.

_____. 1993. Framing toward clarification of a fractured paradigm. *Journal of Communication* 43 (4): 51–58.

_____. 2004. *Projections of power: Framing news, public opinion, and U.S. foreign policy.* Chicago: University of Chicago Press.

Entman, Robert M., and Susan Herbst. 2001. Reforming public opinion as we have known it. In Bennett and Entman 2001.

Entman, Robert M., B. H. Langford, D. Burns-Melican, I. Munoz, S. Boayue, C. Groce, A. Raman, B. Kenner, and C. Merritt. 1998. *Mass media reconciliation.* Cambridge, MA: John F. Kennedy School of Government.

Epstein, Edward Jay. 1973. *News from nowhere.* New York: Vintage Books.

Erikson, Robert S., Michael B. MacKuen, and James A. Stimson. 2002. *The macro polity.* New York: Cambridge University Press.

Escort, Paul D. 1979. *Slavery remembered: A record of twentieth-century slave narratives.* Chapel Hill: University of North Carolina Press.

Fazio, Russell. 1986. How do attitudes guide behavior? In Sorrentino and Higgins 1986.

Feldman, Stanley, and John Zaller. 1992. The political culture of ambivalence: Ideological responses to the welfare state. *American Journal of Political Science* 36:268–307.

Fenno, Richard. 1977. *Homestyles: House members in their districts.* Boston: Little, Brown.

_____. 1996. *Senators on the campaign trail.* Norman: University of Oklahoma Press.

Ferejohn, John, and James Kuklinski, eds. 1990. *Information and democratic processes.* Urbana: University of Illinois Press.

Fine, Terri Susan. 1992. The impact of issue framing on public opinion: Toward affirmative action programs. *Social Science Journal* 29 (3): 323–34.

Fiske, Susan T., and Mark Pavelchak. 1986. Category-based versus piece-meal affective responses. In Sorrentino and Higgins 1986.

Fiske, Susan T., and Shelley E. Taylor. 1984. *Social cognition.* New York: Random House.

_____. 1991. *Social cognition.* 2d ed. New York: McGraw-Hill.

Foner, Eric. 1970. *Free soil, free labor, free men: The ideology of the Republican party before the Civil War.* Oxford: Oxford University Press.

Franklin, Charles H. 1991. Eschewing obfuscation? Campaigns and the perceptions of U.S. Senate incumbents. *American Political Science Review* 85:1193–214.

Freedman, Paul. 2003a. Framing the abortion debate. Paper presented at the annual meeting of the American Political Science Association, Chicago.

————. 2003b. Partial victory: The power of an unenforced abortion ban. *Slate* (December 9). Available at http://slate.msn.com/id/2092192.

Fritschler, A. Lee, and James M. Hoeffler. 1996. *Smoking and politics: Policy making and the federal bureaucracy.* 5th ed. Upper Saddle River, NJ: Prentice Hall.

Gais, T. L., M. A. Peterson, and J. L. Walker. 1984. Interest groups, iron triangles and representative institutions in American national government. *British Journal of Political Science* 14:161–85.

Gamson, William A. 1992. *Talking politics.* New York: Cambridge University Press.

Gamson, William A., and K. E. Lasch. 1983. The political culture of social welfare policy. In *Evaluating the welfare state,* ed. S. E. Spiro and E. Yuchtman-Yaar. New York: Academic Press.

Gamson, William A., and Andre Modigliani. 1987. The changing culture of affirmative action. *Research in Political Sociology* 3:137–77.

————. 1989. Media discourse and public opinion on nuclear power: A constructionist approach. *American Journal of Sociology* 95 (1): 1–37.

Gans, Herbert. 1979. *Deciding what's news. A study of* CBS Evening News, NBC Nightly News, Newsweek, *and* Time. Evanston, IL: Northwestern University Press.

————. 1980. 2d ed. *Deciding what's news: A study of* CBS Evening News, NBC Nightly News, Newsweek, *and* Time. New York: Random House.

Garramone, Gina. 1984. Voter response to negative political ads: Clarifying sponsor effects. *Journalism Quarterly* 61:250–59.

Garrett, L. 1995. Murder by teens has soared. *New York Newsday* (February 17).

Gartner, Michael. 1997. Public journalism: Seeing through the gimmicks. *Media Studies Journal* (Winter): 69–73.

Gerring, John. 1997. Ideology: A definitional analysis. *Political Research Quarterly* 50: 957–94.

————. 1998. *Party ideologies in America, 1828–1996.* Cambridge: Cambridge University Press.

Gibson, James, Cornelius P. Cotter, John F. Bibby, and Robert Huckshorn. 1983. Assessing party organizational strength. *American Journal of Political Science* 27:193–201.

Gibson, James, and A. Gouws. 1997. *Political intolerance in South Africa.* Unpublished manuscript, University of Houston.

Gilens, Martin. 1996. "Race coding" and white opposition to welfare. *American Political Science Review* 90:596–604.

————. 1999. Race and poverty in America: Public misperceptions and the American news media. *Public Opinion Quarterly* 60:515–41.

Gillespie, Ed, and Bob Schellhas, eds. 1994. *Contract with America: The bold plan by*

Rep. Newt Gingrich, Rep. Dick Armey, and the House Republicans to change the nation. New York: Random House.

Gilliam, Frank, Jr. 1998. *Reframing childcare: The impact of local television news.* Washington, DC: Charles S. Benton Foundation.

———. 1999. The "welfare queen" experiment. *Nieman Reports* 53 (2): 112–19.

Gilliam, Frank, Jr., and Shanto Iyengar. 1997. Prime suspects: Script-based reasoning about race and crime. Unpublished manuscript, UCLA.

———. 2000. Prime suspects: The impact of local television news on attitudes about crime and race. *American Journal of Political Science* 44:560–73.

Gilliam, Frank, Jr., Shanto Iyengar, Adam F. Simon, and Oliver Wright. 1996. Crime in black and white: The violent, scary world of local television news. *Harvard International Journal of Press/Politics* 1 (3): 6–23.

Gilliam, Frank, Jr., Patti Miller, Macrae Parker, and Kevin Donegan. 2001. *The local television news media's picture of children.* Oakland: Children Now.

Gitlin, Todd. 1980. *The whole world is watching: Mass media in the making and unmaking of the New Left.* Berkeley: University of California Press.

———. 2003. *The whole world is watching: Mass media in the making and unmaking of the New Left.* 2d ed. Berkeley: University of California Press.

Glendeon, Mary Ann. 1991. *Rights talk: The impoverishment of political discourse.* New York: Free Press.

Goffman, Erving. 1974. *Frame analysis: An essay on the organization of experience.* New York: Harper and Row.

Goggin, Malcolm L., ed. 1993. *Understanding the new politics of abortion.* Newbury Park, CA: Sage Publications.

Goidel, Robert K., Todd G. Schields, and Mark Peffley. 1997. Priming theory and RAS models: Toward an integrated perspective of media influence. *American Politics Quarterly* 25:287–301.

Goldenberg, Edie N. 1975. *Making the papers: The access of resource-poor groups to the metropolitan press.* Lexington, MA: Lexington Books.

Goldenberg, Edie N., and Michael W. Traugott. 1984. *Campaigning for Congress.* Washington, DC: Congressional Quarterly Press.

Graber, Doris. 1984. *Processing the news: How people tame the information tide.* New York: Longman.

———. 1988. *Processing the news: How people tame the information tide.* 2d ed. New York: Longman.

———. 1993. *Mass media and American politics.* Washington, DC: Congressional Quarterly Press.

———. 1997. *Mass media and American politics.* 5th ed. Washington, DC: Congressional Quarterly Press.

———. 2002. *Mass media and American politics.* 6th ed. Washington, DC: Congressional Quarterly Press.

Graber, Doris, Denis McQuail, and Pippa Norris, eds. 1998. *The politics of news: The news of politics.* Washington, DC: Congressional Quarterly Press.

Gray, Virginia, and David Lowery. 1996. *The population ecology of interest representation: Lobbying communities in the American states.* Ann Arbor: University of Michigan Press.

Green, Donald Philip, and Jonathon S. Krasno. 1990. Rebuttal to Jacobson's new evidence for old arguments. *American Journal of Political Science* 34:363–72.

Gremillion, Jeff. 1997. Time traveling: *Time Magazine* visits America's small towns for news. *Mediaweek* (June 2): 24–27.

Grenzke, Janet M. 1989. PACs and the congressional supermarket: The currency is complex. *American Journal of Political Science* 33:1–24.

Gross, Kimberly, and Paul Brewer. 2002. Thinking about frames: News framing effects on opinion and emotion. Paper presented at the annual meeting of the American Political Science Association, Boston.

Grossman, Michael B., and Martha J. Kumar. 1981. *Portraying the president: The White House and the news media.* Baltimore: University of Maryland Press.

Gurevitch, Michael, and Jay G. Blumler. 1990. Political communication systems and democratic values. In *Democracy and the mass media,* ed. Judith Lichtenberg. New York: Cambridge University Press.

Gurevitch, Michael, and Mark Levy. 1985. Introduction. In *Mass communication review yearbook,* ed. Michael Gurevitch and Mark Levy. Newbury Park, CA: Sage Publications.

Habermas, Jürgen. 1982. A reply to my critics. In *Habermas: Critical debates,* ed. John B. Thompson and David Held. Cambridge: MIT Press.

Hagedorn, J. M. 1991. Gangs, neighborhoods, and public policy. *Social Problems* 38:529–45.

Haider-Markel, Donald P., and Mark R. Joslyn. 2001. Gun policy opinion, tragedy, and blame attribution. *Journal of Politics* 63:520–43.

Hall, Richard, and Frank Wayman. 1990. Moneyed interests and the mobilization of bias in congressional committees. *American Political Science Review* 84:797–820.

Hallin, Daniel. 1991. *The presidency, the press and the people.* Oakland: University of California Regents.

————. 1992. Sound bite news: Television coverage of elections, 1968–1988. *Journal of Communication* 42:5–24.

Hamill, Ruth, Milton Lodge, and Frederick Blake. 1985. The breadth, depth, and unity of partisan, class, and ideological schemas. *American Journal of Political Science* 29:850–70.

Hamilton, Alexander, and John Jay. [1787–89] 1987. *Federalist papers.* Ed. Isaac Kramnick. New York: Penguin Books.

Hamilton, David L., and T. K. Trolier. 1986. Stereotypes and stereotyping: An overview of the cognitive approach. In *Prejudice, discrimination, and racism,* ed. John F. Dovidio and Samuel L. Gartner. New York: Academic Press.

Hastie, Reid. 1983. Social inference. *Annual Review of Psychology* 34:511–42.

Hastie, Reid, and Bernadette Park. 1986. The relationship between memory and judgment depends on whether the task is memory-based or on-line. *Psychological Review* 93:258–68.

Herman, Edward S., and Noam Chomsky. 1988. *Manufacturing consent: The political economy of the mass media.* New York: Pantheon Books.

Herrnson, Paul S. 1995. *Congressional elections: Campaigning at home and in Washington.* Washington, DC: Congressional Quarterly Press.

Hertsgaard, Mark. 1988. *On bended knee: The press and the Reagan presidency.* New York: Farrar Straus Giroux.

Hess, Stephen. 1984. *The government/press connection.* Washington, DC: Brookings Institution.

Higgins, E. Tory, and Gillian King. 1981. Category accessibility and information processing: Consequences of individual and contextual variability. In *Personality, cognition, and social interaction,* ed. Nancy Cantor and John Kihlstrom. Hillsdale, NJ: Lawrence Erlbaum.

Hilgartner, Stephen, and Charles Bosk. 1988. The rise and fall of social problems: A public arenas model. *American Journal of Sociology* 94 (1): 53–78.

Hochschild, Jennifer L. 1981. *What's fair? American beliefs about distributive justice.* Cambridge: Harvard University Press.

Hojnacki, Marie, and David C. Kimball. 1998. Organized interests and the decision of whom to lobby in Congress. *American Political Science Review* 92:775–90.

———. 1999. The who and how of organizations' lobbying strategies in committee. *Journal of Politics* 61:999–1024.

Hovland, Carl I. 1959. Reconciling conflicting results derived from experimental and survey studies of attitude change. *American Psychologist* 14 (January): 8–17.

Hovland, Carl I., A. A. Lumsdaine, and F. D. Sheffield. 1949. *Experiments on mass communication.* Princeton: Princeton University Press.

Hoyt, Mike. 1995. Are you now, or will you ever be a civic journalist? *Columbia Journalism Review* (September): 29.

Hume, Ellen. 1995. *Tabloids, talk radio, and the future of news: Technology's impact on journalism.* Washington, DC: Annenberg Washington Program in Communications Policy Studies of Northwestern University.

Inglehart, Ronald. 1984. Post materialism in an environment of insecurity. In *Controversies in voting behavior,* 2d ed., ed. Richard Niemi and Herbert R. Weisberg. Washington, DC: Congressional Quarterly Press.

Iyengar, Shanto. 1990. Shortcuts to political knowledge: Selective attention and the accessibility bias. In Ferejohn and Kuklinski 1990.

———. 1991. *Is anyone responsible? How television frames political issues.* Chicago: University of Chicago Press.

Iyengar, Shanto, and Donald R. Kinder. 1987. *News that matters.* Chicago: University of Chicago Press.

Iyengar, Shanto, Donald Kinder, Mark D. Peters, and Jon A. Krosnick. 1984. The evening news and presidential evaluations. *Journal of Personality and Social Psychology* 46:778–87.

Iyengar, Shanto, and William McGuire, eds. 1993. *Explorations in political psychology.* Durham: Duke University Press.

Iyengar, Shanto, Helmut Norpoth, and K. S. Hahn. 2004. Consumer demand for election news: The horserace sells. *Journal of Politics* 66:157–75.

Jacobius, A. 1996. Going gangbusters: Prosecutors fight gangs with injunctions banning conduct such as using beepers and applying graffiti. *American Bar Association Journal* 82:24–26.

Jacobs, Lawrence, and Robert Shapiro. 2000. *Politicians don't pander.* Chicago: University of Chicago Press.

Jacobson, Gary C. 1980. *Money in congressional elections.* New Haven: Yale University Press.

Jacoby, William G. 2000. Issue framing and public opinion on government spending. *American Journal of Political Science* 44:750–67.

James, William. [1890] 1981. *The principles of psychology.* Cambridge: Harvard University Press.

Jamieson, Kathleen Hall. 2001. Issue advocacy in a changing discourse environment. In Bennett and Entman 2001.

Jamieson, Kathleen Hall, and Karlyn Kohrs Campbell. 2000. *The interplay of influence.* Belmont, CA: Wadsworth Press.

Jamieson, Kathleen Hall, and J. N. Cappella. 1998. The role of the press in the health care reform debate of 1993–1994. In Graber, McQuail, and Norris 1998.

Jamieson, Kathleen Hall, and Paul Waldman. 2003. *The press effect: Politicians, journalists, and the stories that shape the political world.* Oxford: Oxford University Press.

Janis, Irving L. 1968. Group identification under conditions of external danger. In *Group dynamics,* ed. D. Cartwright and A. Zander. New York: Free Press.

Janis, Irving L., and S. Feshbach. 1953. Effects of fear-arousing communications. *Journal of Abnormal and Social Psychology* 48:78–92

Joslyn, Richard. 1984. *Mass media and elections.* Boston: Addison-Wesley.

Just, Marion R., Ann N. Crigler, and W. Russell Neuman. 1998. Cognitive and affective dimensions of political conceptualization. In *The psychology of political communication,* ed. Ann N. Crigler. Ann Arbor: University of Michigan Press.

Kahn, Kim Fridkin. 1991. Senate elections in the news: An examination of the characteristics and determinants of campaign coverage. *Legislative Studies Quarterly* 16:349–74.

Kahn, Kim Fridkin, and John G. Geer. 1994. Creating impressions: An experimental investigation of the effectiveness of television advertising. *Political Behavior* 16:93–115.

Kahn, Kim Fridkin, and Patrick J. Kenney. 1999. *The spectacle of U.S. Senate campaigns.* Princeton: Princeton University Press.

_____. 2002. The slant of the news: How editorial endorsements influence campaign coverage and citizens' views of candidates. *American Political Science Review* 96:381–94.

Kahneman, Daniel, Paul Slovic, and Amos Tversky, eds. 1982. *Judgment under uncertainty: Heuristics and biases.* New York: Cambridge University Press.

Kahneman, Daniel, and Amos Tversky. 1984. Choice, values, and frames. *American Psychology* 39:341–50.

_____. 1987. Rational choice and the framing of decisions. In Einhorn and Hogarth 1987.

Kellstedt, Paul M. 2000. Media framing and the dynamics of racial policy preferences. *American Journal of Political Science* 44:245–60.

_____. 2003. *The mass media and the dynamics of American racial attitudes.* New York: Cambridge University Press.

Kernell, Samuel. 1993. *Going public: New strategies of presidential leadership.* 2d ed. Washington, DC: Congressional Quarterly Press.

Killian, Linda. 1998. *The freshmen: What happened to the Republican revolution?* Boulder: Westview Press.

Kinder, Donald R. 1998. Communication and opinion. *Annual Review of Political Science* 1:167–97.

Kinder, Donald R., and Thomas R. Palfrey, eds. 1993. *Experimental foundations of political science.* Ann Arbor: University of Michigan Press.

Kinder, Donald R., and Lynn M. Sanders. 1990. Mimicking political debate with survey questions: The case of white opinion on affirmative action for blacks. *Social Cognition* 8:83–103.

_____. 1990. Reenacting political debate with survey questions: The case of public opinion on affirmative action. *Social Cognition* 8:73–103.

_____. 1996. *Divided by color: Racial politics and democratic ideals.* Chicago: University of Chicago Press.

Kingdon, John. 1984. *Agendas, alternatives, and public policies.* Boston: Little, Brown.

Klapper, Joseph. 1960. *The effects of mass communication.* New York: Free Press.

Klein, Ethel. 1984. *Gender politics.* Cambridge: Harvard University Press.

Klein, M. 1995. *The American street gang: Its nature, prevalence, and control.* New York: Oxford University Press.

Klite, P., R. Bardwell, and J. Salzman. 1997. Local television news: Getting away with murder. *Harvard International Journal of Press/Politics* 3 (2): 102–12.

Klyza, Christopher. 1994. Ideas, institutions, and policy patterns: Hardrock mining, forestry, and grazing policy on the United States public lands, 1870–1985. *Studies in American Political Development* 8:341–74.

Koch, Adrian, and William Peden. 1944. *The life and selected writings of Thomas Jefferson.* New York: Modern Library.

Koch, Tom. 1994. Computers versus community. *Quill* (May): 18–19.

Kohl, Lawrence Frederick. 1989. *The politics of individualism: Parties and the American character in the Jacksonian era.* New York: Oxford University Press.

Krasno, Jonathan S., and Daniel E. Seltz. 2000. *Buying time: Television advertising in the 1998 congressional elections.* New York: Brennan Center for Justice at New York University School of Law.

Krehbiel, Keith. 1986. Unanimous consent agreements: Going along in the Senate. *Journal of Politics* 48:541–64.

Krosnick, Jon A. 1988. The role of attitude importance in social evaluation: A study of policy preferences, presidential candidate evaluations, and voting behavior. *Journal of Personality and Social Psychology* 55:297–308.

Krosnick, Jon A., and Laura Brannon. 1993. The impact of the Gulf War on the ingredients of presidential evaluations: Multidimensional effects of political involvement. *American Political Science Review* 87:963–75.

Krosnick, Jon A., and Donald R. Kinder. 1990. Altering the foundations of support for the president through priming. *American Political Science Review* 84:497–512.

Kuhberger, Anton. 1998. The influence of framing on risky decisions: A meta-analysis. *Organizational Behavior and Human Decision Processes* 75:23–55.

Lakoff, G. 1987. *Women, fire and dangerous things.* Chicago: University of Chicago Press.

Lane, Robert E. 1962. *Political ideology.* New York: Free Press.

Lasswell, Harold D. 1941. *Democracy through public opinion.* New York: George Banta.

Lasswell, Harold D., Daniel Lerner, and I. De Sola Pool. 1952. *The comparative study of symbols.* Stanford: Stanford University Press.

Lau, Richard R. 1986. Political schemata, candidate evaluations, and voting behavior. In Lau and Sears 1986.

Lau, Richard R., and David Sears, eds. 1986. *Political cognition.* Hillsdale, NJ: Lawrence Erlbaum.

Lazarsfeld, Paul F., Bernard R. Berelson, and Hazel Guadet. 1944. *The people's choice: How the voter makes up his mind in a presidential campaign.* New York: Duell, Sloan, and Pearce.

———. 1948. *The people's choice.* New York: Columbia University Press.

Leary, Mary Ellen. 1977. *Phantom politics: Campaigning in California.* Washington, DC: Public Affairs Press.

Lee, A. McC., and E. B. Lee. 1939. *The fine art of propaganda: A study of Father Coughlin's speeches.* New York: Harcourt, Brace.

Lee, Takeu. 2002. *Mobilizing public opinion: Black insurgency and racial attitudes in the civil rights era.* Chicago: University of Chicago Press.

Levanthal, H., J. C. Watts, and F. Pagano. 1967. Effects of fear and instructions on how to cope with danger. *Journal of Personality and Social Psychology* 6:313–21.

Levin, Irwin P., Richard D. Johnson, and Marja L. Davis. 1987. How information frame influences risky decisions: Between-subjects and within-subject comparisons. *Journal of Economic Psychology* 8:43–54.

Lewis-Beck, Michael. 1980. *Applied regression.* Quantitative Applications in the Social Sciences. Newbury Park, CA: Sage Publications.

Linsky, Martin. 1986. *Impact: How the press affects federal policymaking.* New York: W. W. Norton and Company.

Lippmann, Walter. 1922. *Public opinion.* New York: Free Press.

———. 1925. *The phantom public.* New York: Harcourt and Brace.

Lodge, Milton, Kathleen McGraw, and Patrick Stroh. 1989. An impression driven model of candidate evaluation. *American Political Science Review* 83:399–420.

Lodge, Milton, Marco Steenbergen, and Shawn Brau. 1995. The responsive voter: Campaign information and the dynamics of candidate evaluation. *American Political Science Review* 89:309–26.

Luker, Kristin. 1984. *Abortion and the politics of motherhood.* Berkeley: University of California Press.

Lupia, Arthur. 1994. Shortcuts versus encyclopedias: Information and voting behavior in California insurance reform elections. *American Political Science Review* 88:63–76.

MacArthur, John R. 1992. *Second front: Censorship and propaganda in the Gulf War.* New York: Hill and Wang.

Mackie, Christopher J. 2001. Affective interpolation: Estimating emotional content in text. Paper presented at the annual meeting of the American Political Science Association, San Francisco.

MacKuen, Michael B. 1981. Social communication and the mass policy agenda. In *More than news: Media power in public affairs,* ed. Michael B. MacKuen and S. L. Coombs. Thousand Oaks, CA: Sage Publications.

———. 1984. Exposure to information, belief integration, and individual responsiveness to agenda change. *American Political Science Review* 78:372–91.

Males, M. 1996. *The scapegoat generation: America's war on adolescents.* Monroe, ME: Common Courage Press.

Maltese, John. 1994. *Spin control: The White House Office of Communications and the management of presidential news.* Chapel Hill: University of North Carolina Press.

Manheim, Jarol. 1994. *Strategic public diplomacy and American foreign policy: The evolution of influence.* New York: Oxford University Press.

Manoff, Robert Karl, and Michael Schudson, eds. 1986. *Reading the news.* New York: Pantheon Books.

Marcus, George E. 2000. Emotions in politics. *Annual Review of Political Science* 3:221–50.

Marcus, George E., W. Russell Neuman, and Michael B. MacKuen. 2000. *Affective intelligence and political judgment.* Chicago: University of Chicago Press.

Mauer, M. 1990. *Young black men and the criminal justice system: A growing national problem.* Sentencing Project Report, Washington, DC.

Mayer, William G. 1993. Trends: Trends in media usage. *Public Opinion Quarterly* 57:593–611.

Mayhew, David. 1974. *Congress: The electoral connection.* New Haven: Yale University Press.

McAdam, Doug. 1982. *Political processes and the development of black insurgency, 1930–1970.* Chicago: University of Chicago Press.

McCloskey, Herbert, and A. Brill. 1983. *Dimensions of tolerance: What Americans believe about civil liberties.* New York: Russell Sage.

McCloskey, Herbert, and John Zaller. 1984. *The American ethos: Public attitudes toward capitalism and democracy.* Cambridge: Harvard University Press.

McCombs, Maxwell. 1981. The agenda-setting approach. In *Handbook of political communication,* ed. D. Nimmo and K. Sanders. Beverly Hills: Sage Publications.

McCombs, Maxwell, and Donald E. Shaw. 1972. The agenda setting function of mass media. *Public Opinion Quarterly* 36:176–87.

McGraw, Kathleen, and Clark Hubbard. 1996. Some of the people some of the time: Individual differences in acceptance of political accounts. In Mutz, Sniderman, and Brody 1996.

McGraw, Kathleen, and Milton Lodge. 1995. Introduction. In *Political judgment: Structure and process.* Ann Arbor: University of Michigan Press.

McGraw, Kathleen, and Neil Pinney. 1990. The effects of general and domain-specific expertise on political memory. *Social Cognition* 8:9–30.

McGuire, William J. 1985. Attitudes and attitude change. In *Handbook of social cognition,* 3d ed., ed. G. Lindzey and E. Aronson. New York: Random House.

Merritt, Davis. 1995. *Public journalism and public life.* Hillsdale, NJ: Lawrence Erlbaum.

_____. 1996. Missing the point. *American Journalism Review* (July–August): 29–31.

_____. 1998. *Public journalism and public life: Why telling the news is not enough.* New York: Lawrence Erlbaum.

Meyers, Marvin. 1957. *The Jacksonian persuasion.* Stanford: Stanford University Press.

Mill, John Stuart. 1975. Considerations on representative government. In *Three essays,* ed. Richard Wollheim. Oxford: Oxford University Press.

_____. 1982. *On liberty.* Harmondsworth: Penguin Books.

_____. 1992. *On liberty.* New York: Alfred A. Knopf.

Miller, Joanne M., and Jon A. Krosnick. 2000. News media impact on the ingredients of presidential evaluations. *American Journal of Political Science* 44:295–309.

Miller, Steven I., and Marcel Fredricks. 1990. Perceptions of the crisis in American education: The relationship of metaphors to ideology. *Metaphor and Symbolic Activity* 5:67–81.

Milton, John. [1644] 1951. *Areopagitica.* New York: Appleton-Century-Crofts.

Mitchell, Jeffrey, George S. Everly, and George S. Everly Jr. 2001. *Critical incident stress debriefing: An operations manual for CISD, defusing and other group crisis intervention services.* Ellicott City, MD: Chevron Publishing.

Morgan, Hugh. 1994. Doing it in Dayton. *Quill* (May): 30–32.

Moskowitz, David. 1998. Framing responsibility for political issues: The case of public assistance. Unpublished manuscript.

Mucciaroni, Gary. 1994. Problem definition and special interest politics in tax policy and agriculture. In Rochefort and Cobb 1994a.

Mutz, Diana. 2002. Cross-cutting social networks. *American Political Science Review* 96:111–26.

Mutz, Diana, Paul Sniderman, and Richard A. Brody, eds. 1996. *Political persuasion and attitude change.* Ann Arbor: University of Michigan Press.

Nardulli, Peter. 1995. The concept of a critical realignment, electoral behavior, and political change. *American Political Science Review* 89:10–22.

Nelson, Thomas E., Rosalee A. Clawson, and Zoe M. Oxley. 1997. Media framing in a civil liberties conflict and its effect on tolerance. *American Political Science Review* 91:567–83.

Nelson, Thomas E., and Donald R. Kinder. 1996. Issue frames and group centrism in American public opinion. *Journal of Politics* 58:1055–78.

Nelson, Thomas E., Stephanie Maruska, and Eileen Braman. 2002. What is the issue? Legal and media constructions and political attitudes. Paper presented at the annual meeting of the American Political Science Association, Boston.

Nelson, Thomas E., and Zoe M. Oxley. 1999. Issue framing effects on belief importance and opinion. *Journal of Politics* 61:1040–67.

Nelson, Thomas E., and Elaine A. Wiley. 2001. Issue frames that strike of value balance: A political psychology perspective. In *Framing public life: Perspectives on media and our understanding of the social world.* Mahwah, NJ: Lawrence Erlbaum.

Neuman, W. Russell, Marion R. Just, and Ann N. Crigler. 1992. *Common knowledge: News and the construction of political meaning.* Chicago: University of Chicago Press.

Office of Juvenile Justice and Delinquency Prevention. 2001. Law enforcement and juvenile crime. Bulletin. Available at http://www.ojjdp.ncjrs.org/.

O'Heffernan, Patrick. 1994. A mutual exploitation model of media influence in U.S. foreign policy. In *Taken by storm: The media, public opinion, and U.S. foreign policy in the Gulf War,* ed. W. Lance Bennett and Steven Paletz. Chicago: University of Chicago Press.

Orren, Karen, and Stephen Skowronek. 1994. Beyond the iconography of order: Notes for a "new institutionalism." In *The dynamics of American politics: Approaches and interpretations,* ed. Lawrence Dodd and Calvin Jillson. Boulder: Westview Press.

Oskampf, Stuart. 1977. *Attitudes and opinions.* Englewood Cliffs, NJ: Prentice Hall.

Page, Benjamin. 1978. *Choices and echoes in presidential elections: Rational man and electoral democracy.* Chicago: University of Chicago Press.

Page, Benjamin, and Robert Shapiro. 1992. *The rational public: Fifty years of trends in American's racial policy preferences.* Chicago: University of Chicago Press.

Pan, Z., and G. M. Kosicki. 1993. Framing analysis: An approach to news discourse. *Political Communication* 10:55–76.

Patrick, Brian A. 2002. *The NRA and the media: The motivating force of negative coverage.* New York: Peter Lang.

Patterson, Samuel C., and Keith R. Eakins. 1998. Congress and gun control. In *The changing politics of gun control,* ed. John M. Bruce and Clyde Wilcox. New York: Rowman and Littlefield Publishers.

Patterson, Thomas. 1980. *The mass media election.* New York: Praeger Publishers.

———. 1993. *Out of order.* New York: Alfred Knopf.

———. 1998. Political roles of the journalist. In Graber, McQuail, and Norris 1998.

———. 2002. *The vanishing voter: Public involvement in an age of uncertainty.* New York: Alfred A. Knopf.

Peffley, Mark, and Jon M. Hurwitz. 1999. Introduction. In *Perception and prejudice: Race and politics in the United States,* ed. Mark Peffley and Jon M. Hurwitz. San Diego: Academic Press.

Peffley, Mark, T. Shields, and Bruce Williams. 1996. The intersection of race and crime in television news stories: An experimental study. *Political Communication* 13:309–28.

Perry, Joseph, and M. D. Pugh. 1978. *Collective behavior: Response to social stress*. St. Paul, MN: West Publishing.

Peters, John Durham. 1995. Historical tensions in the concept of public opinion. In *Public opinion and the communication of consent,* ed. Theodore L. Glasser and Charles T. Salmon. New York: Guilford Press.

Petrocik, John. 1996. Issue ownership in presidential elections, with a 1980 case study. *American Journal of Political Science* 40:825–50.

Petty, Richard, and John Caccioppo. 1981. *Attitudes and persuasion*. Dubuque, IA: Wm. C. Brown Co.

Pfetsch, Barbara. 1998. Government news management. In Graber, McQuail, and Norris 1998.

Poole, Keith, and Howard Rosenthal. 1997. *Congress: A political-economic history of roll call voting*. New York: Oxford University Press.

Popkin, Samuel. 1991. *The reasoning voter: Communication and persuasion in presidential campaigns*. Chicago: University of Chicago Press.

———. 1993. Decision-making in presidential primaries. In Iyengar and McGuire 1993.

Portis, Edward, Adolf Gundersen, and Ruth Shively, eds. 2000. *Political theory and partisan politics*. Albany: State University of New York Press.

Postman, Neil. 1985. *Amusing ourselves to death*. New York: Viking.

Price, Vincent, and Eun-Kyung Na. 2000. Citizen deliberation and resistance to framing effects. Paper presented at the annual meeting of the American Association for Public Opinion Research, Portland, OR.

Quattrone, George, and Amos Tversky. 1988. Contrasting rational and psychological analyses of political choice. *American Political Science Review* 82:719–36.

Rankin, W. L., and J. W. Grube. 1980. A comparison of ranking and rating procedures for value system measurement. *European Journal of Social Psychology* 10:233–46.

Rhee, June Woong. 1997. Strategy and issue frames in election campaign coverage: A social-cognitive account of framing effects. *Journal of Communication* 49 (3): 26–48.

Riker, William H. 1980. Political theory and the art of heresthetics. In *The state of the discipline,* ed. Ada Finifter. Washington, DC: American Political Science Association.

———. 1986. *The art of political manipulation*. New Haven: Yale University Press.

Riker, William H., Randall L. Calvert, John Mueller, and Rick K. Wilson. 1996. *The strategy of rhetoric: Campaigning for the American Constitution*. New Haven: Yale University Press.

Robinson, Michael J., and Margaret Sheehan. 1983. *Over the wire and on TV: CBS and UPI in Campaign '80*. New York: Russell Sage.

Rochefort, David A., and Roger Cobb, eds. 1994a. *The politics of problem definition*. Lawrence: University Press of Kansas.

———. 1994b. Problem definition: An emerging perspective. In Rochefort and Cobb 1994a.

Rokeach, Milton. 1973. *The nature of human values*. New York: Free Press.

Romano, Carlin. 1986. What? The grizzly truth about bare facts. In Manoff and Schudson 1986.

Roper Starch Worldwide. 1994. *Roper Reports* 93:22–23.

Rosch, E. 1973. On the internal structure of perceptual and semantic categories. In *Cognitive development and the acquisition of language,* ed. T. E. Moore. New York: Academic Press.

Roseman, Ira, Robert P. Abelson, and Michael Ewing. 1986. Emotion and political cognition: Emotional appeals in political communication. In Lau and Sears 1986.

Rosen, Jay. 1999. *What journalists are for.* New Haven: Yale University Press.

Rothenberg, Lawrence S. 1989. Do interest groups make a difference? Lobbying, constituency influence, and public policy. Paper presented at the annual meeting of the Midwest Political Science Association, Chicago.

Rudolph, T., A. Gangl, and D. Stevens. 2000. The effects of efficacy and emotions on campaign involvement. *Journal of Politics* 62:1189–97.

Rumelhart, D. E., and D. A. Norman. 1983. *Representation in memory*. CHIP Technical Report 116. San Diego: Center for Human Information Processing, University of California.

Ryan, Charlotte. 1991. *Prime time activism: Media strategies for grassroots organizing.* Boston: South End Press.

Sabato, Larry. 1981. *The rise of political consultants*. New York: Basic Books.

Sahr, Robert. 1993. Credentialing the experts: The climate of opinion and journalist selection of sources in foreign and domestic policy. In *The media and foreign policy,* ed. Robert Spitzer. New York: Praeger Publishers.

Salmore, Stephen, and Barbara Salmore. 2000. *Candidates, parties and campaigns.* Washington, DC: Congressional Quarterly Press.

Sanford, Anthony J. 1987. *The mind of man: Models of human understanding.* Brighton: Harvester Press.

Scargle, Jeffrey D. 2000. Publication bias: The file-drawer problem in scientific inference. *Journal of Scientific Exploration* 14 (1): 91–106.

Schattschneider, E. E. 1960. *The semi-sovereign people: A realist's view of democracy in America*. New York: Holt, Rinehart, and Winston.

Scheufele, Dietram A. 2000. Agenda-setting, priming, and framing revisited: Another look at the cognitive effects of political communication. *Mass Communication and Society* 3:297–316.

Schlozman, Kay Lehman, and John Tierney. 1986. *Organized interests and American democracy.* New York: Harper and Row.

Schnell, Frauke. 1993. The foundations of abortion attitudes: The role of values and value conflict. In *Understanding the new politics of abortion,* ed. Malcolm Goggin. New York: Sage Publications.

Schnell, Frauke, and Karen Callaghan. 2004. *Reading between the lines: Media literacy, the news and politics*. Armonk, NY: M. E. Sharpe.

Schnell, Frauke, Nayda Terkildsen, and Karen Callaghan. 2000. Symbolism and social movements: How U.S. debates are shaped and citizens' attitudes influenced by symbolic communiques. In *Beyond public speech and symbols: Explorations in the rhetoric of politicians and the media,* ed. C. DeLandtsheer and O. Feldman. New York: Praeger Publishers.

Schudson, Michael. 1990. Origins of the ideal of objectivity in the professions. In *Studies in the history of American journalism and American law, 1830–1940.* New York: Garland Publishing.

_____. 1995. *The power of news.* Cambridge: Harvard University Press.

Schuman, Howard, and Stanley Presser. 1981. *Questions and answers in survey attitudes: Experiments in question form, wording and context.* New York: Academic Press.

_____. 1996. *Questions and answers in attitude surveys.* Thousand Oaks, CA: Sage Publications.

Schuman, Howard, Charlotte Steeh, Lawrence Bobo, and Maria Krysan. 1997. *Racial attitudes in America: Trends and interpretations.* Rev. ed. Cambridge: Harvard University Press.

Sears, David. 1986. College sophomores in the laboratory: Influence of a narrow data base on psychology's view of human nature. *Journal of Personality and Social Psychology* 51:515–30.

_____. 1993. Symbolic politics: A socio-political theory. In Iyengar and McGuire 1993.

Sears, David, and Leonie Huddy. 1990. On the origins of the political disunity of women. In *Women, politics and change,* ed. Patricia Gurin and Louise Tilly. New York: Russell Sage.

Segal, Jeffrey, and Harold Spaeth. 2002. *The Supreme Court and the attitudinal model revisited.* Cambridge: Cambridge University Press.

Seidel, G. 1975. Ambiguity in political discourse. In *Political language and oratory in traditional society,* ed. W. Bloch. New York: Academic Press.

Shephard, Alicia. 1994. The gospel of public journalism. *American Journalism Review* (September): 30.

Shepsle, Kenneth. 1979. Institutional arrangements and equilibrium in multidimensional voting models. *American Journal of Political Science* 23:27–59.

Shepsle, Kenneth, and Barry Weingast. 1987. The institutional foundations of committee power. *American Political Science Review* 81:85–104.

Sherif, Carolyn W., Muzafer Sherif, and Roger E. Nebergall. 1965. *Attitude and attitude change: The social judgment-involvement approach.* Philadelphia: Saunders.

Sidanius, Jim, and Felicia Pratto. 1999. *Social dominance: An intergroup theory of social hierarchy and oppression.* Cambridge: Cambridge University Press.

Siebert, Fred, Theodore Peterson, and Wilbur Schramm. [1956] 1974. *Four theories of the press.* Urbana: University of Illinois Press.

Sigal, Leon V. 1973. *Reporters and officials: The organization and politics of newsmaking.* Lexington, MA: D. C. Heath Company.

Silbey, Joel. 1991. *The American political nation, 1838–1893.* Stanford: Stanford University Press.

Simon, Adam F. 2002. *The winning message: Candidate behavior, campaign discourse, and democracy.* Cambridge: Cambridge University Press.

Simon, Adam F., and Michael Xenos. 2000. Media framing and effective public deliberation. Paper presented at the Communication Civic Engagement Conference, Seattle.

Simon, Herbert. 1985. Human nature in politics: The dialogue of psychology with political science. *American Political Science Review* 79:293–304.

Smith, Richard. 1993. Agreement, defection, and interest-group influence in the U.S. Congress. In *Agenda formation*, ed. William H. Riker. Ann Arbor: University of Michigan Press.

Smith, T. 1987. That which we call welfare by any other name would smell sweeter: An analysis of the impact of question wording on response patterns. *Public Opinion Quarterly* 51:75–83.

Sniderman, Paul. 1996. *Clash of rights*. New Haven: Yale University Press.

Sniderman, Paul, Richard A. Brody, and Philip Tetlock. 1991. *Reasoning and choice: Explorations in political psychology*. New York: Cambridge University Press.

Sniderman, Paul, and Michael Hagen. 1985. *Race and inequality: A study in American values*. Chatham, NJ: Chatham House Publishers.

Sniderman, Paul, and Thomas Piazza. 1993. *The scar of race*. Cambridge: Harvard University Press.

Sniderman, Paul, and Sean Theriault. 1999. The dynamics of political argument and the logic of issue framing. Paper presented at the annual meeting of the Midwest Political Science Association, Chicago.

Snyder, H. 2002. *Juvenile arrests 2000*. Washington, DC: Office of Juvenile Justice and Delinquency Prevention.

Sorrentino, Richard, and E. Tory Higgins, eds. 1986. *The handbook of motivation and cognition: Foundations of social behavior*. New York: Guilford Press.

Staeheli, Lynn A., Janet E. Kodras, and Colin Flint. 1997. *State restructuring in America: Implications for a diverse society*. Thousand Oaks, CA: Sage Publications.

Steffans, Brian. 1993. Must a watchdog always bite—Are we killing our future? *Quill* (September): 3.

Stimson, James A. 1991. *Public opinion in America: Moods, cycles and swings*. Boulder: Westview Press.

———. 2002. The dimensionality of issues in two-party politics. Paper presented at the Conference on Elections, Columbia University, October 18–19, New York.

Stimson, James A., Michael B. MacKuen, and Robert S. Erikson. 1994. Opinion and policy: A global view. *PS: Political Science and Politics* 27:29–35.

Stoker, Laura. 1994. *The moral basis of political choice*. Unpublished manuscript, Department of Political Science, University of California at Berkeley.

Stouffer, Samuel A. 1955. *Communism, conformity and civil liberties*. New York: Doubleday.

Sullivan, John L., James E. Pierson, and Gregory E. Marcus. 1993. Content controlled measure of political tolerance. In *Experimental foundations of political science*, ed. Donald R. Kinder and Thomas Palfrey. Ann Arbor: University of Michigan Press.

Tabrizi, Susan. 2002. Equality and public policy: Framing the issue. Paper presented at the annual meeting of the American Political Science Association, Boston.

Tang, B. 1994. INS/VGTF and the NYPD. *Police Chief* 61:33–36.

Taylor, Shelley E., and Jennifer Crocker. 1981. Schematic bases of social information processing. In *Social cognition: The Ontario Symposium*, ed. E. Tory Higgins, C. Peter Herman, and Mark Zanna. Hillsdale, NJ: Lawrence Erlbaum.

Terkildsen, Nayda, and Frauke Schnell. 1997. Issue frames, the media, and public opinion: An analysis of the women's movement. *Political Research Quarterly* 50:877–99.

Terkildsen, Nayda, Frauke Schnell, and Christina Ling. 1998. Interest groups, the media, and policy debate formation: An analysis of message structure, rhetoric, and source cues. *Political Communication* 15:45–61.

Thompson, Dennis F. 1970. *The democratic citizen*. Cambridge: Cambridge University Press.

Thrall, A. Trevor. 1997. Elite interest group dominance of the news. Paper presented at the annual meeting of the American Political Science Association, Washington, DC.

Tocqueville, Alexis de. [1835, 1840] 1945. *Democracy in America*. New York: Vintage Books.

Tourangeau, Roger, and Kenneth A. Rasinski. 1988. Cognitive processes underlying context effects in attitude measurement. *Psychological Bulletin* 103:299–314.

Tuchman, G. 1972. Objectivity as strategic ritual: An examination of newsman's notions of objectivity. *American Sociological Review* 77:660–79.

———. 1978. *Making news: A study in the construction of reality*. New York: Free Press.

Tufte, Edward R. 1975. Determinants of the outcomes of midterm congressional elections. *American Political Science Review* 69:812–26.

Tulis, Jeffrey. 1987. *The rhetorical presidency*. Princeton: Princeton University Press.

Tversky, Amos, and Daniel Kahneman. 1974. Judgment under heuristics: Uncertainty and biases. *Science* 185:1124–31.

———. 1981. The framing of decisions and the psychology of choice. *Science* 211:453–58.

———. 1982. The framing of decisions and the psychology of choice. In *Question framing and response consistency*, ed. Robin Hogarth. San Francisco: Jossey Bass.

———. 1987. Rational choice and the framing of decisions. In Einhorn and Hogarth 1987.

Vercellotti, Timothy. 2002. Loyalist or libertarian: The tension between patriotism and civil liberties after September 11. *Political Psychologist* 7 (2): 12–18.

Vigil, James Diego. 2002. *A rainbow of gangs: Street cultures in the mega-city*. Austin: University of Texas Press.

Walinsky, A. 1995. The crisis of public order. *Atlantic* (July): 39–54.

Walsh, Katherine Cramer. 2001. The social bases of political perspectives. Unpublished manuscript, University of Wisconsin.

———. 2003. *Talking about politics: Informal groups and social identity in American life*. Chicago: University of Chicago Press.

Watson, Harry. 1990. *Liberty and power: The politics of Jacksonian America*. New York: Hill and Wang.

Weisberg, Herbert R., Jon A. Krosnick, and Bruce Bowen. 1996. *An introduction to survey research, polling, and data analysis*. Newbury Park, CA: Sage Publications.

West, C. 1993. *Race matters*. Boston: Beacon Press.

Westlye, Mark C. 1991. *Senate elections and campaign intensity*. Baltimore: Johns Hopkins University Press.

Williams, Bruce, and Michael X. Delli Carpini. In progress. And the walls came tumbling down: The blurring of news and entertainment. Unpublished manuscript.

Williams, J. Allen, Jr. 1968. Interviewer role performance: A further note on bias in the information interview. *Public Opinion Quarterly* 32:287–94.

Witters, Jim. 1994. Propaganda journalism? *American Journalism Review* (December): 5.

Wlezien, Christopher. 1995. The public as thermostat: Dynamics of preferences for spending. *American Journal of Political Science* 39:981–1000.

Woolley, John T. 2000. Using media-based data in the study of politics. *American Journal of Political Science* 44:156–73.

Wolsfeld, Gadi. 1997. Political waves and democratic discourse: Terrorism waves during the Oslo Peace Process. In Bennett and Entman 2001.

_____. 2003. The role of the news media in unequal political conflicts: From the 1987 *Infitada* to the 1991 Gulf War and back again. Cambridge, MA: Joan Shorenstein Center.

Wright, John. 1990. Contributions, lobbying, and committee voting in the U.S. House of Representatives. *American Political Science Review* 84:417–38.

Yanich, Danilo. 1998. *Crime coverage and local TV news: Covering crime in Philadelphia and Baltimore*. A Report of the Center for Community Development and Family Policy and Center on Crime, Communities and Culture, University of Delaware.

Zaller, John. 1986. *Measuring political information on NES surveys*. Technical Report to the National Election Studies Board. Center for Political Studies, University of Michigan.

_____. 1990. *Experimental tests of the question-answering model of the mass survey response*. Technical Report to the National Election Studies Board. Center for Political Studies, University of Michigan.

_____. 1992. *The nature and origins of mass opinion*. New York: Cambridge University Press.

_____. 1996. The myth of massive media impact revived: New support for a discredited idea. In Mutz, Sniderman, and Brody 1996.

_____. 2001. Monica Lewinsky and the mainsprings of American politics. In Bennett and Entman 2001.

Zaller, John, and Dennis Chiu. 1996. Government's little helper: U.S. press coverage of foreign policy crises, 1945–1991. *Political Communication* 13:385–406.

Zaller, John, and Stanley Feldman. 1992. A simple theory of the survey response: Answering questions versus revealing preferences. *American Journal of Political Science* 36:579–616.

Contributors

Karen Callaghan is an assistant professor in the political science department at Vanderbilt University. She has been a fellow at Rice University and the Center for the Study of the Presidency and was a professor of political science at the University of Massachusetts, Boston, where she served as the Director of Quantitative Methods in the public policy Ph.D. program. Her research has been published in the *Journal of Politics, Women and Politics, Political Communication, Research in Micropolitics, Beyond Public Speech and Symbols,* and elsewhere. She received a 1999 Goldsmith Research Award from Harvard University's Shorenstein Center for the Press, Politics, and Public Policy.

Michael X. Delli Carpini is dean of the Annenberg School for Communication. He received his M.A. and Ph.D. from the University of Minnesota. He has been the director of the public policy program at the Pew Charitable Trusts and chair of the political science department at Barnard College, Columbia University. He is the author of *Stability and Change in American Politics: The Coming of Age of the Generation of the 1960s* (New York University Press, 1986) and *What Americans Know about Politics and Why It Matters* (Yale University Press, 1996), as well as numerous articles, essays, and edited volumes on political communication, public opinion, and political socialization.

Teena Gabrielson is an assistant professor of political science at Southwestern University. She holds a Ph.D. from the University of California at Davis. Her research focuses on American political thought and development. She has published her research in coauthored articles in *Polity* and elsewhere.

Franklin D. Gilliam Jr. is the founding director of the Center for Communications and Community at the University of California at Los Angeles and supervises its research about the influence of television news coverage and campaign advertising on people's understanding of race, crime, and politics. He has published widely on minority politics, including articles in the *American Journal of Political*

Science; his 2001 book *Farther to Go: Readings and Cases in African American Politics* (Harcourt Brace); and a forthcoming book with Shanto Iyengar on race, television news, and American politics (Princeton University Press). He makes frequent public appearances on the *NBC Nightly News,* the *ABC Nightly News,* CNN, and C-SPAN.

Shanto Iyengar is the Harry Norman Chandler Professor of Communication and a professor of political science at Stanford University. He has published several books, including *Is Anyone Responsible? How Television Frames Political Issues* (University of Chicago Press, 1991); *News That Matters* (University of Chicago Press, 1987); *Explorations in Political Psychology* (Duke University Press, 1993); and, with Stephen Ansolabehere, *Going Negative: How Political Advertisements Shrink and Polarize the Electorate* (Free Press, 1995). His research has appeared in several journals, including the *American Political Science Review, Communication Research,* the *Journal of Personality and Social Psychology,* and the *Public Opinion Quarterly.*

Kim L. Fridkin is a professor of political science at Arizona State University. She received her B.A., M.A., and Ph.D. from the University of Michigan. She has contributed articles to the *American Political Science Review,* the *American Journal of Politics,* and the *Journal of Politics.* She is the coauthor of *No Holds Barred: Negative Campaigning in U.S. Senate Campaigns* (Prentice Hall, 2003) and *The Spectacle of U.S. Senate Campaigns* (Princeton University Press, 1999). She is the author of *The Political Consequences of Being a Woman* (Columbia University Press, 1996).

Paul M. Kellstedt is an assistant professor of political science at Texas A&M University. He previously taught at Brown University and has been a fellow in Harvard University's Shorenstein Center for the Press, Politics, and Public Policy. His recent book, entitled *The Mass Media and the Dynamics of American Racial Attitudes,* was published by Cambridge University Press. His articles have appeared in the *American Journal of Political Science* and *Political Analysis.* Kellstedt's latest work explores the media's role in shaping consumer confidence.

Patrick J. Kenney is chair and professor of political science at Arizona State University. He received his B.A, M.A.P.A., and Ph.D. from the University of Iowa. He has authored and coauthored articles in the *American Political Science Review,* the *American Politics Quarterly,* the *Public Opinion Quarterly,* the *American Journal of Political Science, Political Behavior,* the *Journal of Politics,* and the *Social Science Quarterly.* He is the coauthor of *No Holds Barred:*

Negative Campaigning in U.S. Senate Campaigns (Prentice Hall, 2003) and *The Spectacle of U.S. Senate Campaigns* (Princeton University Press, 1999).

Donald R. Kinder is the Philip Converse Collegiate Professor at the University of Michigan. He received his Ph.D. from UCLA. He is the author, with Shanto Iyengar, of *News That Matters* (University of Chicago Press, 1987) and, with Lynn M. Sanders, of *Divided by Color* (University of Chicago Press, 1996). Kinder is completing a book (*Myrdal's Prediction*) on racial politics in the United States. He has been a Guggenheim fellow and a fellow at the Center for Advanced Study in the Behavioral Sciences and is a member of the American Academy of Arts and Sciences.

Thomas E. Nelson is a professor of political science at the Ohio State University. He received a Ph.D. from the University of Michigan. Besides framing, his current research interests include racial politics and the role of values in public opinion. He has served as codirector of the Summer Institute in Political Psychology at Ohio State. He is the 2002 winner of the Erik Erikson Award for early career achievement from the International Society for Political Psychology. He has coauthored articles in the *American Political Science Review*, the *Journal of Politics*, the *Journal of Personality and Social Psychology*, the *Journal of Experimental and Social Psychology*, and *Political Behavior*.

Frauke Schnell is a professor of political science at West Chester State University. She holds a Ph.D. from the State University of New York at Stony Brook. She has written several articles and chapters on issue framing and American politics. Her research appears in the *Journal of Social Behavior and Personality*, *Political Communication*, the *Political Research Quarterly*, *Women and Politics*, *Psychology: A Journal of Human Behavior*, *Media Power in Politics*, and elsewhere.

Index